Dedicated to his Eminence

Cardinal Walter Kasper

President Emeritus of the Pontifical Council for Promoting Christian Unity and President of the Commission for Religious Relations with the Jews,
my former professor

PRAISE FOR *THE REAL LUTHER:*

This work is a masterpiece of a subtle, thorough, and deep reaching presentation of well known sources. Many points have been explored, even more have been brought to light by just following an incorruptibly thorough method of historical analysis. The book is a very welcome contribution to the newly arisen discussion about Luther's reformation breakthrough, his reception of patristic and medieval thought, and finally a wonderful survey of recent dialogues about Luther's posting of the theses to the door of the Palace Church in Wittenberg. Franz Posset analyzes the sources meticulously while never loosing contact with the most recent research. Students and researchers should read this book as a model for how to do Reformation History.

—Markus Wriedt, Dr. theol. habil.
Professor of Historical Theology/Church History
Goethe University Frankfurt/Main and Marquette University

The Real Luther provides enriching insights and a provocative perspective on established "facts" surrounding Luther's life by going back to the sources. Posset draws together the unique interrelationship of Luther, Melanchthon, and Bernard in a wonderfully compelling manner. Particularly noteworthy is Posset's iteration of the influence Bernard of Clairvaux had on Luther and, indeed, on Melanchthon. Part II offers a Bernardine theme and focus with a concentration on Luther's Erfurt experiences as well as his composition of the "propositions" (not theses). Posset's translation of the *Preface* to the Second Volume of Luther's Works (1546) from Melanchthon's *Memoirs,* as well as its utilization in Part I, provides a beneficial resource for further Luther studies.

—Timothy Maschke, DMin, PhD
Professor of Theology
Concordia University Wisconsin

It feels like a new discovery when one reads Melanchthon's Preface to the second volume of Luther's collected works of 1546. Melanchthon guides the reader through the early phase of Luther's theological development. In a comprehensive interpretation, Franz Posset utilizes this text for the biography of the early Luther. As a result, we have a fascinating history which leads the reader to the historical Luther: not a Reformer who had suddenly fallen from heaven, but a reformist theologian concerned with pastoral care (*Seelsorge*); it was not an assault of theses in 1517, but a discussion amongst scholars; not a new theology, but a renewal of monastic theology in the tradition of Bernard of Clairvaux. Luther is both a Catholic and a Reformer at the same time.

—Wolfgang Thönissen, Dr. theol. habil.
Professor of Ecumenical Theology,
Faculty of Theology, Paderborn
Managing Director of the Johann-Adam-Möhler-Institute
for Ecumenics, Paderborn
Counselor to the Pontifical Council for
Promoting Christian Unity
Consultant to the International Commission for
Lutheran/Catholic Dialogue
Member of the Ecumenical Working Group of
Evangelical and Catholic Theologians

Reading through Dr. Franz Posset's research into the Luther of history behind the Luther of legend, I was constantly fascinated and sometimes even thrilled by his insights into Dr. Martin's continuity with medieval theology, especially that of Saint Bernard of Clairvaux. I heartily recommend *The Real Luther* to anyone seriously exploring the historical context and origins for Luther's sixteenth century efforts toward ecclesial reformation and renewal.

—Bishop Richard J. Sklba
Vicar General/Auxiliary Bishop of Milwaukee
Co-chair of the National Lutheran/Catholic Dialogue

THE REAL LUTHER

THE REAL LUTHER

A FRIAR AT ERFURT AND WITTENBERG

EXPLORING LUTHER'S LIFE
WITH MELANCHTHON AS GUIDE

FRANZ POSSET

Peer Reviewed

CONCORDIA PUBLISHING HOUSE • SAINT LOUIS

Peer Reviewed

Published by Concordia Publishing House
3558 S. Jefferson Ave., St. Louis, MO 63118–3968
1-800-325-3040 · www.cph.org

Cover images courtesy of the Digital Image Archive, Pitts Theology Library, Candler School of Theology, Emory University. The left image was taken from "Acta et res gestae D. Martini Lutheri, in comitijs principum Vuormaciae," published in 1521. The right image was taken from "Von der Babylonischen gefengknuss der Kirchen / Doctor Martin Luthers," published in 1520.

Manufactured in the United States of America

Library of Congress Cataloging-in-Publication Data

Posset, Franz.
The real Luther : a friar at Erfurt and Wittenberg : exploring Luther's life with Melanchthon as guide / Franz Posset.
p. cm.
Includes bibliographical references and index.
ISBN 978-0-7586-2685-1
1. Luther, Martin, 1483–1546. 2. Melanchthon, Philipp, 1497–1560. 3. Bernard, of Clairvaux, Saint, 1090 or 91–1153. I. Title.

BR333.3.P67 2011
284.1092—dc22
[B] 2010049890

This material is being released for study and discussion purposes, and the author is solely responsible for its contents. It has not been submitted to the process for doctrinal review stipulated in the Bylaws of The Lutheran Church—Missouri Synod and does not necessarily reflect the theology of the Lutheran Confessions or the doctrinal position of The Lutheran Church—Missouri Synod.

7 8 9 10 11 28 27 26 25 24 23

CONTENTS

LIST OF ILLUSTRATIONS

PREFACE

Literary images of Luther are as varied as anyone's imagination allows. In the global village one may find people with views of Luther that might be diametrally opposed, ranging from "The Heresiarch that Burns in Hell," "Luther, a vomit from hell" or more tamely, the "Raven from Germany" in Latin America[1] to the hero of confessional Lutheranism in North America. The first one hundred years of Lutheranism in general produced mainly three images of Luther: Prophet, Teacher, and Hero.[2]

One's Luther image may largely depend upon one's up-bringing and education. A professor of German literature and a college graduate from a denominational college may see Luther quite differently. An east-German Marxist before the fall of the Berlin Wall probably did not see the same Luther that a Catholic saw who came of age after the Second Vatican Council. Somebody with the frame of mind of the modern "Counter-Reformation" that is influenced by the image offered by the early Jesuits likely has a view of Luther similar to the traditional Hispanic one mentioned above and would see Luther quite different than an anti-Roman Protestant. The Luther-image of a liberal Jew in nineteenth century Chicago[3] looked different from an ecumenical-minded Catholic in Munich neighboring the former concentration camp at Dachau in the later twentieth century, or from a feminist, a psychiatrist, or a Muslim. The latter's Luther image is likely that of a restorer of pure monotheism, and if Luther had lived

---

[1] See Alicia Mayer, "'The Heresiarch that Burns in Hell': The Image of Martin Luther in New Spain"; Peer Schmidt, "'Der Rabe aus Deutschland'. Luther, Mexiko, und die Entstehung Lateinamerikas (c. 1808–c.1860) " in *Luther zwischen den Kulturen. Zeitgenossenschaft—Weltwirkung*, eds. Hans Medick and Peer Schmidt (Göttingen: Vandenhoeck & Ruprecht, 2004), 119–140 and 141–163.

[2] See Robert Kolb, *Martin Luther as Prophet, Teacher, and Hero. Images of the Reformer*, 1520–1620 (Grand Rapids: Baker Books; Paternoster Press, 1999).

[3] See Christian Wiese, "'Auch uns sei sein Andenken heilig!' Idealisierung, Symbolisierung und Kritik in der jüdischen Lutherdeutung von der Aufklärung bis zur Schoa" in *Luther zwischen den Kulturen,* 215–259.

long enough he eventually would have rejected the Trinity.[4] The Luther image may depend also upon one's preferences for certain interpreters of Luther's life and work and Lutheranism.[5] The Luther-image of a Roman Catholic who welcomed the *Joint Declaration on the Doctrine of Justification* signed on Reformation Day 1999 by the Vatican and the Lutheran World Federation is probably different from that of a Lutheran whose denominational synod rejected the *Joint Declaration*.

Being confronted with the innumerable images of Luther through the centuries and continents, the universal question must arise: Who is the authentic Luther? And the call must he heard: Will the historical Luther please stand up! As different as each person's Luther image might be, one may surmise that there is one issue that remains the same for all: *The Search for* the real Luther. The out-come of that search might be as diverse as each author's background and research goals. Actually, each generation may be challenged having to rewrite their understanding of Luther. "Search for the real Luther is most lively and interesting in quarters where a serious attempt is being made to look again at a historical context."[6]

Biographies of Luther were shaped early in the twentieth century by Catholic scholars such as Hartmann Grisar SJ (1845–1932) and Heinrich Denifle OP (1844–1905) to whom Lutheran scholars reacted. Since the end of the Second World War Lutheran Luther researchers felt and still feel the need to defend the Reformer against an all too close affinity to the National-Socialist ideology and soon entered a golden age of ecumenical approaches to Luther. Catholic Luther research in the twentieth century developed in five major phases with some dominant features between Luther the corrupter of the faith and Luther the father in the faith:

---

[4] See Jan Slomp, "Christianity and Lutheranism from the Perspective of Modern Islam" in *Luther zwischen den Kulturen,* 277–296.

[5] On the views in the Anglo-Saxon world and in Germany in the first half of the twentieth century, see Thomas Kaufmann, "Luther zwischen den Wissenschaftskulturen: Ernst Troeltschs Lutherdeutung in der englischsprachigen Welt und in Deutschland" in *Luther zwischen den Kulturen,* 455–481, in agreement with Carter Lindberg's assessment that American interpretation of Luther depended almost exclusively upon Troeltsch.

[6] Gordon L. Isaac, "The Changing Image of Luther as Biblical Expositor" in *Ad fontes Lutheri: Toward the Recovery of the Real Luther. Essays in Honor of Kenneth Hagen's Sixty-Fifth Birthday*, eds. Timothy Maschke, Franz Posset, and Joan Skocir (Milwaukee: Marquette University Press, 2001), 67–85, here 84.

1. Luther was a corrupter of the faith, evil and mentally unstable, as portrayed by Catholic polemicists from 1900–1915. Catholic polemicists instigated decisively the "Luther Renaissance."

2. Luther was a religious person, with a new Catholic view taking shape between 1915–1930.

3. Luther was a prophet to the Church: an ecumenical Luther image was coming to light between 1930–1960.

4. The golden age of Catholic Luther research, 1960–1980s, brought forth two "schools," one around Joseph Lortz (1887–1975), the other around Heinrich Fries (1911–1998).

5. Luther as a reader of Saint Bernard of Clairvaux (1090–1153) and his monastic theology, was researched in particular since the 1980s, as part of a search for new paradigms.[7]

A review of Luther studies that were published around the year 1983 with its celebrations of Luther's 500th birthday shows that more than thirty Luther biographies were offered on the international book market. Most of them represented one of the then three major camps in Luther research: Roman Catholic, Lutheran, and Marxist.[8] I also should mention, at least briefly, that it was on Reformation Day (31 October) 1984 that I defended my doctoral thesis on *Luther's Catholic Christology According to His Johannine Lectures of 1527* at the Jesuit institution of higher learning, Marquette University.[9] The issue of a fair interpretation of the life, work, and theology of Martin Luther was on my research agenda then, still is, and always will be. Perhaps, my dissertation was so convincing that Northwestern Publishing House of the *Wisconsin Evangelical Lutheran Synod* in Milwaukee published it in 1988, virtually unaltered (now out of print). A Lutheran friend of mine commented on this unusual event (that a dissertation at a Jesuit university could have been published by a conservative Lutheran church press): "This is an ecumenical coup!"

---

[7] The number of researchers is too large to list them all (both Protestant and Catholic); see Franz Posset, "From the Corrupter of the Faith to the Father in the Faith: 100 Years of Catholic Luther Research," *Luther Study* 14 (Korea, 2000): 79–141; LD 12 (2004): 188–193. An earlier overview of the history of Catholic and Protestant Luther research is, for example: Gottfried Maron, *Das katholische Lutherbild der Gegenwart. Anmerkungen und Anfragen*, *Bensheimer Hefte* 58 (1982).

[8] See Franz Posset, "Martin Luther Biographies," *Biography: An Interdisciplinary Quarterly* 8 (1985): 356–365.

[9] Dissertation Director Kenneth Hagen; Doctoral Committee: Patrick Carey, Daniel Maguire, Paul Misner, and Oliver Olson.

The present book is the result of much of the research from the fourth and fifth phase of Catholic Luther research (see above), and it may (or may not?) represent Catholic Luther research of my generation. In particlular, this book is the concrete outgrowth of my guest lecture "In Search of the Historical Luther by a Catholic" for the Study Program of "Luther in Catholic Context" at Marquette University in Milwaukee on 9 March 2010. It is meant as a contribution to the upcoming "Luther Year 2017," when the 500th anniversary of what went down in history as the beginning of the German Reformation is to be commemorated.

It behooves us to recall, at least briefly, that a symposium celebrating the 500th anniversary of Luther's birth took place at Marquette University, on 29 and 30 October 1983. In the same year, in Milwaukee, the results of the U.S. Lutheran-Catholic Dialogue on "Justification by Faith" were promulgated. Kenneth Hagen (1936–) of Marquette University was involved in it and so was Auxiliary Bishop Richard Sklba (1935–) of Milwaukee, who served as co-chair of the national Lutheran-Catholic Dialogue.

On Reformation Day 1999, the *Joint Declaration on the Doctrine of Justification* was signed in Augsburg by the Pontifical Council for Promoting Christian Unity and the Lutheran World Federation,[10] i.e., in the city in southern Germany that lends its name to the Christians of the *Augsburg Confession*. The World Methodist Council also accepted the *Joint Declaration* in 2006. The agreement expressed that justification (salvation) is the work of the triune God. The Father sent His Son into the world to save sinners. The foundation and presupposition of justification is the incarnation, death, and resurrection of Christ. Justification thus means that Christ Himself is our righteousness, in which we share through the Holy Spirit in accord with the will of the Father. Together the Christians confess: By grace alone, in faith in Christ's saving work and not because of any merit on our part, we are accepted by God and receive the Holy Spirit, who renews our hearts while equipping and calling us to good works (*Joint Declaration on the Doctrine of Justification*).

It is against this ecumenical backdrop that I would like the reader to understand my quest for the authentic Luther, although the golden

[10] *Justification and the Future of the Ecumenical Movement. The Joint Declaration on the Doctrine of Justification*, ed. William G. Rusch (Collegeville: Liturgical Press, 2003).

age of Catholic Luther research is over. It seems that the notion "Catholic Luther Research" no longer covers any one certain unified content. One may no longer reckon with one specific "Catholic Luther Research."[11] In principle, present-day Catholic scholarship on Luther does not function differently from Protestant scholarship, as researchers are loyal to the "republic of scholars" and the ethos of argumentation. Nevertheless, one may detect a tendency on the Protestant side no longer to acknowledge the results of Catholic scholarship.[12] Catholic scholars seem to be left off-side and their recent research results, specifically on "Bernard and Luther," are often ignored. So far their results have not entered mainstream Luther research. There may still be room for Catholic contributions to Luther research. However, one may wonder whether the years leading up to 2017 will yield as many Catholic contributions, if any, to Luther scholarship as the years did that led to the birthday celebrations of Luther in 1983.[13]

On 9 March 2010 I was speaking as an alumnus of the Study Program "Luther in a Catholic Context" at Marquette University. Since the year 2010 was a Melanchthon Year, the commemoration of the 450th anniversary of Melanchthon's death in 1560 was in order. I took Philip Melanchthon as my guide to investigating the real Luther. For this purpose I produced my own fresh translation of Melanchthon's Latin biographical sketch (*Preface*) in *Corpus Reformatorum.*[14]

---

[11] See Joseph E. Vercruysse, "Luther in der römisch-katholischen Theologie und Kirche," LuJ 63 (1996): 103–128.

[12] See Otto Hermann Pesch, "Wo steht die katholische Lutherforschung?" LB 13 (2004): 85–106; English digest in LD 15 (2007) 119–120.

[13] See Gottfried Maron, *Das katholische Lutherbild der Gegenwart. Anmerkungen und Anfragen*, *Bensheimer Hefte* 58 (1982): 61.

[14] CR 6 (Halis Saxonum; Brunsvigae, 1839) columns 155–170 (no. 3478); website accessed in February 2010. I used an English and several German translations: (1) Melanchthon, Philipp / Ritter, Mathias: *Beschreibung des Lebens und Handlungen des Ehrwürdigen Herrn D. Martini Lutheri* (Frankfurt a. M.: 1554) [VD16 M 3426]. MDZ (accessed in May 2010); (2) Friedrich Theophil Zimmermann, *Philipp Melanchthon*'s *Erzählung vom Leben D. Martin Luthers (1813);* website: *books.google.com/books?id=9A86AAAAcAAJ*... (accessed in March 2010); (3) Johann Georg Walch, *Dr. Martin Luthers Sämmtliche Schriften*, vol. 14 (St. Louis, MO: Concordia, 1898) 456–473; (4) Gerhard Weng, "Das Leben Martin Luthers. Historia Lutheri, 1546" in *Melanchthon deutsch*, vol. 2, eds. Michael Beyer, Stefan Rhein, and Günther Wartenberg (Leipzig: Evangelische Verlagsanstalt, 1997) 169–188; (5) Harald Weinacht, *Melanchthon und Luther. Merkmale einer Kirchenreform.*

Initially, it was my early ecumenical interest, nurtured during my theological studies at the German state universities at Tübingen and Münster between 1965 and 1970, and later at Marquette University in Milwaukee, which led me to the search for the "historical Luther" and to offer now, in my retirement, the results of this search. My professors in Germany who indirectly inspired me to this research over the years were not church historians but dogmatic theologians, including Hans Küng, Karl Rahner, Walter Kasper, and Josef Ratzinger (now pope) whose lecture notes on ecclesiology (1968/1969) I still possess. I wish to dedicate this book to Cardinal Walter Kasper, President Emeritus of the Pontifical Council for Promoting Christian Unity and President of the Commission for Religious Relations with the Jews.

Franz Posset
Beaver Dam, Wisconsin
Reformation Day 2010

Martin Luthers Lebensbeschreibung durch Philipp Melanchthon. Deutsch-Lateinisch (Zurich: Theologischer Verlag, 2008) 14–47. (6) The English translation is not always reliable: *Luther's Lives: Two Contemporary Accounts of Martin Luther.* Translated and annotated by Elizabeth Vandiver, Ralph Keen, and Thomas D. Frazel (Manchester and New York: Manchester University Press, 2004) 14–39; *books.google.com/books?isbn=0719068029*... (accessed in February 2010).

ACKNOWLEDGMENTS

For their help, words of encouragement, and critical questions either after the oral presentation of my guest lecture at Marquette University in Milwaukee on 9 March 2010, or at the subsequent board meeting of *Luther Digest,* or after reviewing the expanded manuscript at its various stages, I thank

Prof. Mickey Mattox and Prof. Markus Wriedt, Program Directors of "Luther in Catholic Context" at Marquette University

Prof. em. Kenneth Hagen, Theology Department of Marquette University

Prof. Timothy Maschke, The Harry R. and June J. Rouse Professor of Pre-Seminary Studies and Recruitment, Concordia University of Wisconsin

Rev. David Froemming, Lancaster, Wisconsin

Rev. Dr. Richard Krause, Pewaukee, Wisconsin

Prof. Helmar Junghans (+), Germany

Prof. Theo Bell, The Netherlands

Associate Editors and Consultants of *Luther Digest*

The book team of Concordia Publishing House.

ABBREVIATIONS

ABR	*The American Benedictine Review.*
Ann 1	*Sermo in annuntiatione domini.* Saint Bernard's First Sermon on the Annunciation, edited in SBOp vol. 5, 13–29.
ARG	*Archiv für Reformationsgeschichte / Archive for Reformation History.*
CR	*Corpus Reformatorum*, vols 1–28 [Melanchthon], ed. Carolus Gottlieb Bretschneider et al., Halle: 1834–1860.
CTQ	*Concordia Theological Quarterly.*
Festschrift Pesch 2007	Johannes Brosseder and Markus Wriedt, eds., *"Kein Anlass zur Verwerfung." Studien zur Hermeneutik des ökumenischen Gesprächs. Festschrift für Otto Hermann Pesch.* Frankfurt: Verlag Otto Lembeck, 2007.
Junghans, *Der junge Luther*	Helmar Junghans, *Der junge Luther und die Humanisten,* Weimar: Hermann Böhlaus Nachfolger, 1984; Göttingen: Vandenhoeck & Ruprecht, 1985.
LB	*Luther-Bulletin. Tijdschrift voor interconfessioneel Lutheronderzoek* (The Netherlands)

LD	*Luther Digest.*
LH	*Luther Handbuch*, ed. Albrecht Beutel, Tübingen: Mohr Siebeck, 2005.
LQ	*Lutheran Quarterly.*
LuJ	*Lutherjahrbuch.*
LW	*Luther's Works*. American Edition of Martin Luther's Works. General editors Helmut T. Lehmann, Jaroslav Pelikan, and Christopher Boyd Brown, vols. 1–75, St. Louis: Concordia; Philadelphia and Minneapolis: Fortress, 1955–.
Luther	*Luther: Zeitschrift der Luthergesellschaft.*
Luther und das monastische Erbe.	Christoph Bultmann, Volker Leppin, and Andreas Lindner (eds.), *Luther und das monastische Erbe*, Tübingen: Mohr, Siebeck, 2007.
Luthers Thesenanschlag	*Luthers Thesenanschlag—Faktum oder Fiktion* (Schriften der Stiftung Luthergedenkstätten in Sachsen-Anhalt 9), eds. Joachim Ott and Martin Treu, Leipzig: Evangelische Verlagsanstalt, 2008.
Luther zwischen den Kulturen	*Luther zwischen den Kulturen. Zeitgenossenschaft—Weltwirkung*, eds. Hans Medick and Peer Schmidt, Göttingen: Vandehoeck & Ruprecht, 2004.

MBW	*Melanchthons Briefwechsel: Kritische und kommentierte Gesamtausgabe*, ed. Heinz Scheible (Stuttgart: Frommann-Holzboog, 1977–).
MDZ	Munich Digitalisation Zentrum (digital library).
NWDCH	*The New Westminster Dictionary of Church History*, vol. 1, ed. Robert Benedetto, Louisville and London: Westminster John Knox Press, 2008.
OP	Order of Preachers (Dominicans).
OSA	Order of Saint Augustine.
OSB	Order of Saint Benedict.
OSF	Order of Saint Francis.
Posset, *The Front-Runner*	Franz Posset, *The Front-Runner of the Catholic Reformation. The Life and Works of Johann von Staupitz*, Aldershot, GB, 2003.
SBOp	*Sancti Bernardi Opera*, eds Jean Leclercq, Henri Rochais, and Charles H. Halbot, 8 vols. Rome: Editiones Cistercienses, 1957–1977.
SCJ	*The Sixteenth Century Journal.*
SJ	Society of Jesus (Jesuits).
Studienausgabe	*Martin Luther Studienausgabe*, Berlin: Evangelische Verlagsanstalt, 1979–1999.

VD 16	*Verzeichnis der im deutschen Sprachbereich erschienenen Drucke des XVI. Jahrhunderts*, ed. Bayerische Staatsbibliothek München, 25 vols. Stuttgart: 1983–2000.
WA	*D. Martin Luthers Werke.* Kritische Gesamtausgabe, Weimar 1883 –. References to this edition are abbreviated in line with the following example: WA 39-II, 100, 1–5 = WA vol. 39, part 2, page 100, lines 1–5 ("Weimar Edition").
WA Br	*D. Martin Luthers Werke*. Briefe (Letters).
WA DB	*D. Martin Luthers Werke. Deutsche Bibel* (German Bible).
WA TR	*D. Martin Luthers Werke. Tischreden* (Table Talk).
ZKG	*Zeitschrift für Kirchengeschichte.*

INTRODUCTION

In PART ONE the event that made the year 1517 famous, and to be commemorated in 2017, is to be scrutinized. The first questions arise about whether the historical Luther actually spoke of "Theses" on the Indulgences, whether he numbered them himself with "95," and whether he "nailed" them to the door or not. Luther himself cannot be the source of Melanchthon's statement in this specific regard; and, nowhere else did Luther hint at a "posting" on any "door" of what he called his "talking points" (only later, they were labeled *Ninety-Five Theses*).

These questions lead us to embark on Luther research and make us take a closer look at the sources that are used. We shall see that the colorful Table Talk may not qualify unconditionally as a primary source, and that some reconsideration is in order. We shall briefly address the "legends" concerning the young Luther, as the first chapter concludes with a reminder of what is needed in Luther research in order to arrive at the historical Luther. This Chapter will also show that there are problems with Philip Melanchthon's story about the posting in 1517 which contradicts reliable documents from Luther's own pen. It would have been so much easier to accept Melanchthon's account of Luther's struggle over indulgences in 1517, if Luther himself would have told us that he had nailed *Ninety-Five Theses* on the door of the church. But such a report or any related reliable recollection does not exist. What Melanchthon narrated in this regard most likely did not stem from any information that Luther had given him.

In chapter 2 we nevertheless take Philip Melanchthon as our guide who provides a biographical sketch of Martin Luther, published as the *Preface* to Volume Two of Luther's works, edited in 1546. Melanchthon assures us that he recites "in good faith" everything he could find out about Luther during the years he and Luther were colleagues in Wittenberg. He also drew from conversations he had with others who knew Luther well (oral history). Melanchthon will indicate those cases for which he has no detailed information, but which later historiographers claim to have. For biographical information on Luther it must be read together with Luther's own *Preface* of 1545 for Volume One of the Wittenberg Latin Writings. In his reporting Melanchthon was a faithful theological secretary.[1]

The views that are displayed in the two prefaces seem to be contradictory. Researchers, however, did not take the assumed discrepancies as an opportunity to investigate the influence of Saint Bernard of Clairvaux on the young Luther,[2] but rather (unjustifiably) discredited Melanchthon's report about Bernard's influence as a legend, especially the part about Luther gaining decisive insights from an anonymous senior friar who showed him a proof text from Saint Bernard on salvation by grace alone and on consolation. The senior friar was most likely the novice master, Johann von Greffenstein (died 1520), to whom Melanchthon referred twice.[3]

As I use my own fresh translation of Melanchthon's recollections in Latin I realize that throughout the centuries, up to this day, the historians and translators have the expression *collegium* for the original *colloquium.* Furthermore, only very seldom do Luther biographers point out the significance of the *Constitutiones fratrum Eremitarum sancti Augustini* for the spiritual life and work of Luther.

Melanchthon's repeated hint at Luther's spiritual advisor at Erfurt concerning the issue of "forgiveness of sins" leads to the advice given to Luther, namely to read Saint Bernard's sermon on the Annunciation, which leads us to consider Luther in the context of the "Bernard renaissance" around 1500. Chapter 2 concludes with brief considerations of the relationship between the young Luther and three friends who are all older than he: Johann von Staupitz (ca. 1465–1524), Georg Mascov (died in 1521), and Martin Pollich von Mellrichstadt (died in 1513).

Chapter 3 focuses on the "Augustine awakening" and the "Bernard renaissance" whereby we realize that Saint Bernard of Clairvaux was of greater impact on Luther than Augustine. We shall

---

[1] See Helmar Junghans, ''Philipp Melanchthon als theologischer Sekretär,'' in *Der Theologe Melanchthon*, ed. Günter Frank (Stuttgart: Thorbecke, 2000) 129–152.
[2] As Ulrich Köpf pointed out in "Bernhard von Clairvaux im Werk Martin Luthers. Bemerkungen zur neueren Forschung." *Rottenburger Jahrbuch für Kirchengeschichte* 18 (1999) 225–233; Ulrich Köpf, "Martin Luthers Lebensgang als Mönch" in *Kloster Amelungsborn 1135–1985,* ed., Gerhard Ruhbach and Kurt Schmidt-Clausen (Hannover: Missionshandlung Hermannsburg, 1985) 187–208.
[3] As is pointed out by Weihnacht, *Melanchthon und Luther,* 64.

frame Melanchthon's very credible account about "Luther and Bernard" with some considerations about the great popularity of Bernard around 1500 including the Augustinians at Erfurt and elsewhere. Then we go into the detailed analysis of Melanchthon's account about the novice master who with his hint at a specific sermon of Bernard was of decisive help for Luther in his "consternations." We include hints at the works which Friar Martin read in his early years in the friary at Erfurt and we question the need for "Augustinianism" in the search of the historical Luther. Twice in his *Preface* Melanchthon pointed out the role of the senior Augustinian friar at Erfurt with his citation of Bernard's First Sermon on the Annunciation (*Ann 1*). This observation clearly tells us that the quotation from *Ann 1* was of central importance in Melanchthon's biographical sketch as it was the one text from Bernard's biblical theology that led Luther to what we customarily call his Reformational insight of salvation by grace alone through faith alone. The direct quotation from Bernard's sermon is important for another reason: It contains the Pauline reference of Rom 8:15–17 on the children of God who call out "Abba," which is a verse that Luther wanted to be written "with golden letters" (see Chapter 3. 9).

In this context the following question arises: how is Melanchthon himself impacted by what he learned from his interviews with Luther about the influence of Bernard's theology upon Luther? In PART TWO we investigate what effect the insight about Luther and his high esteem of Saint Bernard had on Melanchthon who apparently was directed to Bernard by Luther. We scrutinize the young Melanchthon's opinion of Bernard and his later view as we come to terms with the fact that it must have been Luther himself who caused Melanchthon to change his mind about Bernard.

In PART THREE the full text of Melanchthon's memoirs[4] is provided, i.e., Melanchthon's *Preface* to the Second Volume of Luther's Works of 1546.

The APPENDIX offers a completely new look at the chronology of young Luther's career, based upon the most recent research results.[5] In particular, Luther's journey to Rome had to be

---

[4] As Michael A. Mullett calls the *Preface* in his *Martin Luther* (London and New York: Routledge, 2004), 22.

[5] Based primarily upon Julius Köstlin (1913), Hans Schneider (2007 and 2008), and Jun Matsuura (2009).

reconfigured. Whereas the accepted opinion had been that Luther undertook his trip in 1510, compelling evidence points us to the winter semester of 1511–1512.

PART ONE

TOWARD THE ANNIVERSARY IN 2017

1. Gearing Up for the Luther Year 2017

Just about everything that concerns the life of Martin Luther was and is questioned except the fact he was born and that he died. As we approach the next jubilee year or the "Luther Year 2017" for the celebration of the 500th anniversary of the *Ninety-Five Theses* we should remember that with this so-called first "Reformation Day" we use a term (*reformatio*) that Luther himself hardly ever used, in spite of what biographers may say.[1]

The historical Luther, surprising as this may be, did not use the title "Reformer" (*reformator*) for himself as a defining self-designation.[2] This does not mean that Luther was not convinced that changes were necessary.[3] However, Luther's main goal was not the often discussed "reform of the Church" (*reformatio ecclesiae*).[4] Luther's use of the concept of "reformation of the Church" remained relatively rare. He employed it in his *Resolutiones* of 1518, saying that the Church is in need of a *reformatio*, but that it is not something to be undertaken by human beings, but by God alone.[5] Luther explicitly spoke again in terms of *reformatio* in 1528, but only once in his preface to another author's book about married priests: "I think that I stirred up a Council and a *reformation* [in German] which

[1] See, for example, James M. Kittelson, *Luther the Reformer: The Story of the Man and His Career* (Minneapolis: Augsburg-Fortress, 2003).
[2] See Heiko A. Oberman, *Luther—Mensch zwischen Gott und Teufel* (Berlin: Severin and Siedler, 1982) 84 (*Luther—Man Between God and the Devil*, trans. Eileen Walliser-Schwarzbart, New Haven: Yale University Press, 1989).
[3] See Johannes Schilling, "Geschichtsbild und Selbstverständis" in LH, 102.
[4] See *The Catholicity of the Reformation*, eds. Carl E. Braaten and Robert W. Jenson (Grand Rapids, MI: W. B. Eerdmans, 1996); Dorothea Wendebourg, "Kirche" in LH, 403.
[5] *Ecclesia indiget reformation* . . . WA 1, 627, 27–28.

makes the papists' ears ring."[6] Six years later, he spoke of "reform" in a letter of 1534. He claims that he has done more reforming with his gospel than five councils.[7] The latter two references are looking back over more than a decade, not specifically onto the so-called *Ninety-Five Theses*, but on gospel preaching and comparing himself to ecclesiastical councils.

The young Luther did not think in terms of a "Protestant Reformation" or of "protesters" against abuses.[8] The concept of a general ecclesiastical deformation that calls for reformation does not apply very well. Luther's development originally was not at all in opposition to the late medieval spirituality but was instead a product of it growing from the matrix of the Augustinian order tradition. One must then ask whether the later accounts about early events in Luther's life really correspond to the actual course of those events.[9] It is a huge, misleading exaggeration to speak of Luther's *Ninety-Five Theses* of 1517 as his "first reformation act," whereas his intent was rather to serve a purely "pastoral purpose."[10] Luther's opinions on the indulgences were given out ("issued") primarily because of pastoral care and concern, as he called for a more cautious approach in promoting indulgences as remission by the Church of temporal punishment for sins already forgiven.[11] Reforming German popular piety (*Volksfrömmigkeit*), where he saw it misdirected, was

[6] *Ich meine ia, ich hab ein Concilium angericht und eine reformation gemacht, das den Papisten die ohren klingen*; in: *Von Priester Ehe des wirdigen herrn Licentiaten Steffan Klingebeyl, mit einer Vorrede Mart. Luther*, WA 26, 530, 7–9.

[7] *Ich hab, Gott lob, mehr reformiert mit meinem Euangelio, denn sie vielliecht mit fünff Concilijs hetten gethan*; WA 38, 271, 2–4.

[8] On the notion "Protestant" see Siegfried Bäuer, "Protestierende—Protestanten. Zu den Anfängen eines geschichtlichen Grundbegriffs im 16. Jahrhundert" *Europa in der Frühen Neuzeit. Festschrift für Günter Mühlpfordt. Band 6: Mittel-, Nord- und Osteuropa*, ed. Erich Donnert (Weimar, Cologne, Vienna: Böhlau, 2002), 91–114.

[9] See Volker Leppin, "Martin Luther, Reconsidered for 2017," LQ 22 (2008): 376–377. One would expect Leppin to keep a critical attitude toward the information provided in Table Talk (in his Luther biography, *Martin Luther*; Darmstadt: Wissenschaftliche Buchgesellschaft, 2006).

[10] Heinrich Boehmer had both assertions in his *Martin Luther: Road to Reformation* (New York: Meridian Books, 1957), 186. John M. Todd, *Luther: A Life* (New York: Crossroad, 1982) in his Chapter 8 maintained that Luther's *Ninety-Five Theses* were intended only for scholarly debate.

[11] For a concise review of the issue, see Markus Wriedt's entries "Indulgences" and "Penance" in NWDCH 1, 334–335, 506–507.

permanently on his agenda. The historical Luther is the pastoral Luther.

Notably, Luther moves within the recent, general tradition of the reform efforts of pastoral care (i.e., not specific to the Augustinian order) which was under way since the fifteenth century.[12] He was concerned about the *curati* (*Seelsorger*) doing a good job in their work; he mentions them in several of the so-called *Ninety-Five Theses*.[13] The early concern for those ministering in pastoral care will live on in Luther's later career when he will reissue a book first published in 1489, half a century later, with his preface of 1540 to the *Letter on the Wretchedness of Curates*.[14] Luther's text on indulgences of 1517 was designed primarily for improving pastoral care.[15]

The seventeenth-century picture titled "Frederick the Wise's Dream at Schweinitz" (Fig. 1) shows his dream on the night preceding the day on which Martin Luther affixed his "Theses" and the outcome of their posting; it is a copperplate engraving by Conrad Grahle from Leipzig produced for the Jubilee Year 1617. Luther supposedly recounted the dream in a Table Talk.[16] The words that

---

[12] For example, the book by the humanist pastor and professor Ulrich Surgant, *Manuale curatorum* (Basel: Michael Furter, 1503).

[13] See nos. 25, 69, and 80 in *Studienausgabe*; Franz Posset, "Lehrer der Seelsorge. Das ökumenische Potential der Seelsorge-Konzeption des alten Luther," *Luther* 72 (2001): 3–17, here 7–8 with note 24; English digest in LD 12 (2004): 74–76.

[14] *Epistola de miseria curatorum seu plebanorum, aeditus anno. 1489. Cum Praefatione D. Mart. Lvth. Vittembergae* (Augsburg: Anton Sorg, 1489); WA 51, 453, 10–11; MDZ (accessed March 2010); LW 59 forthcoming in 2011; Posset, "Lehrer der Seelsorge," 7 with note 23.

[15] "Sein ganzes Wirken hat seelsorgerlichen Charakter," said Walther von Loewenich in his Luther biography: *Martin Luther. Der Mann und das Werk* (Munich: List, 1982), 340; (*Martin Luther: The Man and His Work*, trans. Lawrence W. Denef, Minneapolis: Augsburg Publishing House, 1986); Markus Wriedt, "Le réconfort aux frontières de la vie: Martin Luther, directeur d'âmes," *Positions luthériennes* 49 (2001): 122–140 (translated from the German by M. Arnold); Lothar Vogel, "Zwischen Universität und Seelsorge: Martin Luthers Beweggründe im Ablasstreit," ZKG 118 (2007): 187–212.

[16] According to Peter Manns, *Martin Luther: An Illustrated Biography* (New York: Crossroad, 1983), 71; Brian Cummings, "Luther and the Book: The Iconography of the Ninety-Five Theses" in *Papers Read at the 2000 Summer Meeting and the 2000 Winter Meeting of the Ecclesiastical History Society*, ed. R. N. Swanson (Rochester NY: Boydel Press, 2004), 222–232; LD 15 (2007): 15–17.

Friar Luther wrote with his quill onto the wooded door are *Vom Ablass* (About Indulgence). The story of the dream is a myth.[17]

Noteworthy is the observation that during the first one hundred years of the "Reformation" there are no pictorial representations of the posting of Luther's sentences on the indulgences. The first picture is not depicting the assumed act as such, but a dream of Frederick the Wise (1463–1525) about a posting at the door in the seventeenth century. In pictures relating to Luther's Reformation the Posting of the Theses was not included at all. For example, it is not found in Ludwig Rabus' book *Historien der Heyligen Außerwölten* (1556–1558), but Rabus shows Luther's encounter with Cardinal Thomas Cajetan (ca. 1468–1534), Luther at the Diet of Worms, Luther at the Leipzig Disputation with Johann Eck (1486–1543), and at the Marburg Colloquy.

The first pictorial representations of the Posting of the Theses surfaced only around 1700.[18] A 1750 image of Luther's nailing is known from an anonymous Austrian artist in the form of an ivory plaque.[19] These observations make one pause and reflect on this strange fact in the iconography of the "Posting." In contrast to the lack of early pictorial representations of the "Posting" we find early depictions of the scandalous sale of indulgences.[20] On the left of those woodcuts one may see the pulpit with a Dominican friar (Tetzel? ca. 1465–1519) who is reading the papal bull on indulgences, provided

---

[17] See Robert W. Scribner, *Popular culture and popular movements in reformation Germany* (London and Ronceverte, WV: Hambledon Press, 1987), 302; website accessed March 2010.

[18] Copper plate by Christoph Weigel, 1697; see Henrike Holsing, "Luthers Thesenanschlag im Bild" in *Luthers Thesenanschlag—Faktum oder Fiktion* (Schriften der Stiftung Luthergedenkstätten in Sachsen-Anhalt 9), eds. Joachim Ott and Martin Treu (Leipzig: Evangelische Verlagsanstalt, 2008), 141–172, with Fig. 2 showing the copperplate of 1697 ("Reformationis Lutheri initia").

[19] Depicted in LD 17 (2009): 155.

[20] See the title page of an anonymous pamphlet against the Roman indulgences: *On Aplas von Rom kan man wol selig werden;* woodcut by Heinrich Vogtherr, printed by Melchior Ramminger in Augsburg, 1520; website: www.dodedans.com/Dholbein21.htm (accessed May 2010). The same woodcut is used for another pamphlet: *Beclagung aines leyens genant Hanns schwalb über vil mißbreüch Christliches lebens, vnd darinn begriffen kürzlich von Johannes Hußsen* (1521) ("Complaint by a layman by the name of Hanns Schwalb about much abuse of Christian life . . . "); website: www.dodedans.com/Dholbein21.htm (accessed May 2010).

with five hanging seals; in the background the papal coats of arms; before the big cross is the strongbox or coffer.

Notable, furthermore, is the fact that the commemoration of the Reformation was celebrated up to the nineteenth century not on 31 October, but on 25 June which is the date of the presentation of the *Augsburg Confession*, i.e., the celebration in the south German territories.[21] This observation corresponds with the idea that the "Posting" was not always understood as the decisive event that would call for celebration.[22]

Fig. 1. "Frederick the Wise's Dream" at Schweinitz on the outcome of the posting of the *Ninety-Five Theses*.

[21] See Vinzenz Pfnür, "Die Bestreitung des Thesenanschlags durch Erwin Iserloh. Theologiegeschichtlicher Kontext—Auswirkung auf den katholisch-lutherischen Dialog" in *Luthers Thesenanschlag,* 111–126, here 123.
[22] How exactly later generations came to see 31 October as the important day, needs to be investigated yet.

1. 1. "THESES" OR "TALKING POINTS"?

Fig. 2. In 1858 King Friedrich Wilhelm IV of Prussia commissioned the *Ninety-Five Theses* to be inscribed on the bronze replacement door when the original wooden door was lost in a fire in 1760.

Whether the so-called "Theses" were actually posted is a matter of ongoing debate for half a century now.[23] Most recently, Martin Treu (1953–) believes in the authenticity of the posting whereas Volker Leppin (1966–) does not.[24] Whether the text is rightly called "Theses" (or, just "talking points" or "articles") should also be considered. We do not have Luther's original autograph of the so-called *Ninety-Five Theses*, nor an original print of October or of November 1517.[25] The earliest prints known are of December 1517 and only they included the numbering of the *propositiones*, but not "theses."

Luther himself never used the expression *Ninety-Five Theses*. He neither used the figure "95" nor the expression "Theses." Furthermore, in a different context he used the expression *propositiones* for his deliberations on the Johannine Prologue in his first known Christmas sermon (1514/1515).[26] The word "thesis" entered German vocabulary only in the eighteenth century.[27]

In following Luther's choice of words, Philip Melanchthon, too, wrote of Luther's *Propositiones* in his *Preface* to the Second Volume of Luther's works and not of "theses" nor of the number "95":

> [Luther] angered by [Johann] Tetzel's impious and execrable sermons and, burning with eagerness for piety, issued propositions concerning indulgences which are extant in the First Volume of his writings.[28]

In the German translation of Melanchthon's memoirs of 1554, the expression *Artickel* (articles) was chosen for what today is known as

---

[23] See Erwin Iserloh, *Luther zwischen Reform und Reformation: der Thesenanschlag fand nicht statt* (Münster: Aschendorff, 1966); English translation by Jared Wicks: *The Theses were not Posted: Luther between Reform and Reformation* (Toronto: Saunders of Toronto, Ltd., 1966; Boston: Beacon, 1968); Thurman L. Smith, "Luther and the Iserloh Thesis from a Numismatic Perspective," SCJ 20 (1989), 183–201 (affirming Iserloh's find);

[24] Martin Treu, "Der Thesenanschlag fand wirklich statt," *Luther* 78 (2007): 140–144; Volker Leppin, "Geburtswehen und Geburt einer Legende," *Luther* 78 (2007): 145–150; idem, *Martin Luther*, 117–126; see also their contributions in *Luthers Thesenanschlag* (2008).

[25] See *Studienausgabe* I, 174.

[26] *. . . ut sic vere sit distinctus a patre filius, qui tamen idem cum ipso Deus. Haec satis sunt de istis propositionibus*, WA 1, 22, 26–28.

[27] See *Duden: Etymologie. Herkunftswörterbuch der deutschen Sprache*, s. v. "These."

[28] CR 6, 161–162.

the "theses" and what he called *propositiones* in Latin.[29] In the previous year, 1553, Georg Major (1502–1574) also spoke of *Propositiones* in a German/Latin text.[30] In 1557 a German translator used the expression "sayings about indulgence" (*Sprüche vom Ablas*),[31] no "theses." Furthermore, the term "theses" was also not used in the collection of *Theologicae propositiones Vitebergae disputatae* (ascribed to Melanchthon, printed by Joseph Klug, Wittenberg, 1534). Luther, who wrote a preface for this work, did not use the expression "theses" here either.[32]

In his letter of May 1518 to Pope Leo X (1475–1521) Luther used the expression *schedula disputatoria*,[33] which Helmar Junghans (1931–2010) and Volker Leppin quite impressively translate into German as *Disputationszettel* (Junghans) or in the diminutive form *Disputationszettelchen* ("a little slip of paper for a disputation," Leppin).[34] Luther preferred the unusual expression of "a little slip of paper" (*schedula*) also in his own *Preface* to Volume One of his collected works in 1545.[35] Luther mentions this in the context of reporting about two letters he had sent out at that time (31 October 1517), one to Albrecht of Brandenburg (1490–1545)[36] who was

---

[29] *Melanchthon, Philipp / Ritter, Mathias: Beschreibung des Lebens und Handlungen des Ehrwürdigen Herrn D. Martini Lutheri* (Frankfurt a. M.: 1554) [VD 16 M 3426]; MDZ (accessed June 2010).

[30] See Timothy J. Wengert, "Georg Major: An 'Eyewitness' to the Posting of Martin Luther's Ninety-Five Theses" in *Luthers Thesenanschlag*, 93–97, here 95.

[31] As quoted in Wengert, "Georg Major: An 'Eyewitness' . . . ," 96.

[32] See WA 39-I, 1–8. However, the WA editors uncritically use the term under discussion in their title: *Luthers Vorreden zu den Thesensammlungen von 1534 und 1538*.

[33] WA 1, 528, 18.

[34] Helmar Junghans, "Martin Luther, kirchliche Magnaten und Thesenanschlag. Zur Vorgeschichte von Luthers Widmungsbrief zu den 'Resolutiones disputationum de indulgentiarum virtute' an Papst Leo X." in *Luthers Thesenanschlag*, 33–46, here 33; Leppin, "Geburtswehen und Geburt einer Legende," 147.

[35] *Ego contemptus, edidi Disputationis scedulam*, *Studienausgabe* V, 628, 1. The first volume is titled *TOMVS PRIMVS OMNIVM OPERVM REVERENDI DOmini* [sic] *Martin Lutheri, Doctoris Theologi[a]e, Continens scripta Triennij, ab eo tempore, quo primum controuersia de Indulgentijs mota est, uidelicit ab anno Christi M.D.XVII. usque ad annum XX. VVITEBERGAE* [sic] *Per Iohannem Lufft. 1. 5. 45.* This Preface continues to plague historians as in it Luther does not always correctly remember everything that happened.

[36] WA Br 1, 39–41 (no. 48); the original is kept in the archives at Stockholm. Bernhard Lohse, "Albrecht von Brandenburg und Luther" in *Erzbischof Albrecht von Brandenburg (1490–1545). Ein Kirchen- und Reichsfürst der Frühen Neuzeit*, ed.

archbishop of Magdeburg since 1513 and also archbishop of Mainz since 1514, a cardinal since 1518, the *primas* of Germany; the other to the local bishop Jerome Schulze (Hieronymus Scultetus, ca. 1465–1522; he was the bishop of Brandenburg from 1507 to 1522) to whose jurisdiction Wittenberg was subject. The letter to Bishop Schulze is no longer extant.[37] Luther confirmed that he "gave out a slip of paper [*schedula*] for the purpose of disputing," but he did not use the expression "theses."[38] Therefore, Melanchthon in the Second Volume did not use it either.[39]

With his choice of the word *schedula* Luther may have wanted to play down the commotion created by a "slip of paper" he had issued, namely his talking points on the indulgences. His unpretentious phrase would then mean: "I issued a slip of paper with talking points for a disputation," which is quite different from an official academic text that would be posted on a university bulletin board with the intent to use it for professorial academic purposes. His expression does not necessarily evoke the idea of a printed text. Perhaps, the *schedula* with the propositions may not refer to a printed version. In fact, the lawyer and humanist Christoph Scheurl (1481–1542) mentioned in his book on contemporary church history (*Geschichtsbuch der Christenheit von 1511–1521*) that Luther's text was "merely [hand] written."[40] Scheurl had been professor of law in Wittenberg from 1507 to 1512. The question remains: Did Melanchthon have the

---

Friedhelm Jürgensmeier (Frankfurt: Knecht, 1990), 73–83; English digest in LD 1 (1993): 108–110.

[37] See *Studienausgabe* V, 627, 9–13. Luther also sent him the manuscript of his *Resolutions* on 13 February 1518, WA Br 1, 135–141 (no. 58).

[38] *Studienausgabe* V, 628, 1. Without any qualms the English translator has it as follows: "I published the Theses," in *Martin Luther. Selections From His Writings*, edited and with an Introduction by John Dillenberger (Garden City, New York: Doubleday, 1961), 5.

[39] The English translation on the website http://www.iclnet.org/pub/resources/text/wittenberg/luther/preflat-eng.txt (accessed February 2010) renders the phrase as follows: "Therefore, finding myself despised, I published a list of theses." Whereas "list" may be an acceptable translation of *scedula*, the rendering with "theses" for *disputatio* is a later interpretation. Originally, *schedula* is the diminutive of *scheda* = strip of papyrus. By the way, the expression *schedula* gave the German language the word *Zettel*, a "slip of paper."

[40] *Bloßlich geschrieben*, as quoted in WA 1, 230; Scheurl's book was edited by Knaake (Leipzig, 1872); the expression *bloßlich geschrieben* is quoted also by Adolf Hausrath, *Luthers Leben* (Berlin: G. Grote'sche Verlagsbuchhandlung, 1904), vol. 1: 145.

handwritten or the printed text of Luther's Propositions in mind when he wrote that Luther affixed them to the "temple" (church)?

In the First Volume (to which Melanchthon in his *Preface* to the Second Volume made reference!), Luther's indulgence text speaks of "what is written below for the purpose of disputing": *hec subscripta disputabuntur*,[41] again, no "theses." The Latin header of the earliest print simply announces them as "that what is written below" (*hec subscripta*). It is assumed that this print of December came from Johann Grünenberg's press who had his workshop at the Augustinian friary (across the street).[42] It would be the print which Ulrich von Dienstedt (Dinstedt, Denstedt, ca. 1460–1525, cantor and canon of the All Saints church in Wittenberg since 1507) possessed and which he forwarded to Christoph Scheurl in Nuremberg. Luther himself had not sent his "Positions"[43] to Scheurl directly because it was not his intension to spread them as Luther explained in his letter of 5 March 1518 to Scheurl, although they had become known in Nuremberg. Luther may have sent his *Propositions/Positions* as his "disputable statements"[44] to friends and invited their comments. Luther regrets that his *Positions* were widely circulating.

The print of the *Positions* which Scheurl received from Dienstedt was handed over to the printer Hieronymus Höltzel in Nuremberg (he was active between 1500–1525) and is considered the most reliable source,[45] printed in the form of a poster by the same printer who printed Staupitz's *Constitutiones* of the Augustinian order (see Fig. 6). The two other oldest extant printed versions are also from December 1517 (and we do not know whether they were authorized by Luther): (a) Print by Jacob Thanner in Leipzig in the form of a poster (placard); (b) Print by Adam Petri in Basel in booklet form. None of those three Latin prints of December 1517 use the notion "theses." They remain with the wording "that what is written below."

---

[41] *Studienausgabe* I, 176, 1.

[42] See Boehmer 184.

[43] *Positiones meas Latinas et vulgares*; WA Br 1, 152, 6 (no. 62); see Posset, *The Front-Runner*, 216.

[44] Boehmer 191.

[45] See *Studienausgabe* I, 174; Elizabeth L. Eisenstein layed out the problem with these prints, but conceded that it cannot be solved: *The Printing Press as an Agent of Change: Communications and Cultural Transformations in Early-Modern Europe* (Cambridge and New York: Cambridge University Press, 1997; first edition 1979), 307.

The Wittenberg print of five years later (1522) by Melchior Lotter the Younger still has the same wording (*hec subscripta*) but now styled as the *disputatio de virtute indulgen[tiarum]*.

The German version was supposedly provided first at Nuremberg, by Kaspar Nuzel (Nützel, ca. 1471–1529), a member of what is sometimes called the "Staupitz sodality" at Nuremberg, also dated December 1517 or early January 1518. The German version was mentioned first in Scheurl's letter to Dienstedt of 5 January 1518 and referred to as Martin's *conclusiones*, and as *conclusiones de indulgentiis* in Scheurl's letter to Güttel of 8 January.[46] But so far no print of an early German translation surfaced. [47] The German translator's choice of words for the Latin *[pro]positiones* would have been of considerable interest.

Luther's own subsequent explanations of the *propositions* also do not employ the notion "theses" (*Resolutiones disputationum de indulgentiarum virtute*).[48] Luther had sent his original *propositions* (letter of 31 October 1517, not extant) and then also his recent *Explanations* of them to his diocesan bishop, Jerome Schulze, in February 1518.[49] His bishop attested in writing that he found the *Explanations* to be "good Catholic." The letter, now lost, was delivered personally to Luther in Wittenberg by the Cistercian Abbot Valentine Henneken of Lehnin[50] (died in 1542), i.e., of the religious order to which Saint Bernard belonged, from the monastery located northeast of Wittenberg. We know of this meeting from Luther's letter to Georg Spalatin (1484–1545) of the second half of March 1518. In it Luther confessed his surprise about the high visitor who came to him "yesterday" and he mentions that the bishop had judged

---

[46] See the editorial notes to letter 62 in WA Br 1, 152.

[47] See Reinhard Schwarz, *Luther* (Göttingen: Vandenhoeck & Ruprecht, 1986), 46; on this, see also Hans J. Hillerbrand, "The Spread of the Protestant Reformation of the Sixteenth Century: A Historical Case Study in the Transfer of Ideas," *The South Atlantic Quarterly* 67 (1968): 265–286.

[48] WA 1, 525–628. See also *Resolutiones Lutherianae super propositionibus suis Lipsiae disputatis* (Leipzig Disputation 1519), WA 1, 391–435.

[49] See WA Br 1, 135–141 (no. 58); see *Exkurs I* in WA Br 1, 113–114 (on *Propositions*) for letter no. 48; E. G. Schwiebert, *Luther and His Times. The Reformation from a New Perspective* (Saint Louis: Concordia, 1950), 321; Leppin, *Martin Luther*, 117.

[50] See Boehmer 199; Franz Posset, *Luther's Catholic Christology According to his Johannine Lectures of 1527* (Milwaukee: Northwestern Publishing House, 1988), 31.

("censored") his *Resolutiones* on the indulgences as Catholic, but disapproved of their "indiscrete" dissemination.[51]

In contrast to this episcopal reaction about Luther's catholicity, the official response from Rome in 1518, written by Sylvester Prierias OP (1456–1523), referred to Luther's presumptuous *conclusions* about the power of the pope.[52] In a way, Prierias had been programmed to frame the issue as a question of papal authority because Archbishop Albrecht of Brandenburg had forwarded Luther's propositions on 13 December 1517 to the pope in terms of an issue about papal authority.[53] All of a sudden Luther's text was an issue of papal power. This Dominican friar at the papal court appears eager to turn Luther's efforts into an issue not only of authority but also of heresy: "Whoever in regards to the indulgences says that the Roman Church is not allowed to do what she is de facto doing is a heretic."[54] This charge was not intended by Archbishop Albrecht, who in his spiritual outlook was some sort of a reform-minded follower of Desiderius Erasmus of Rotterdam (ca. 1466–1536), when he forwarded Luther's text to Rome.

What Melanchthon calls *propositiones* Luther calls *disputationes* in his cover letter with the exact date of 31 October 1517, which he sent to Archbishop Albrecht,[55] i.e., talking points. In his letter to his confrere Johann Lang (ca. 1486–1548) in Erfurt of 11 November 1517, Luther referred to them as *Paradoxa*.[56] In his letter to Spalatin of early November 1517 Luther simply calls them *positiones* (again, without giving the number "95").[57] *Positiones* sounds like what we call today a "position paper." In his letter to Jodocus Trutfetter (ca.

---

[51] *Licet enim nihil erroris in illis [resolutionibus], sed omnia Catholica esse censeret* . . . ; WA Br 1, 162, 20 (no. 67).

[52] *Responsio Magistri Silvestri de Prierio ordinis predicatorum . . . ad Conclusiones Magisti Martini Lutheri,* in *Dokumente zur Causa Lutheri (1517–1521*), ed. Peter Fabisch and Erwin Iserloh (Münster: Aschendorff, 1988), 53; see also *Studienausgabe* I, 174.

[53] See Lohse, "Albrecht von Brandenburg und Luther," 77.

[54] *Qui circa indulgentias dicit ecclesiam Romanam non esse facere id quod de faco facit, heretics est*; *Dokumente zur Causa Lutheri (1517–1521*), 56.

[55] *Meas disputationes videre vt intelligat, quam dubia res sit Indulgentiarum opinio, quam illi vt certissimam seminant*; WA Br 1, 112, 66–68 (no. 48).

[56] See WA Br 1, 121, 4 (no. 52). On the tensions between the Augustininas and Dominicans, see Chapter 2. 6.

[57] *Positiones nostras*; Luther's letter to Spalatin is not dated; it is generally agreed that it is of early of November 1517; WA Br 1, 118, 9 (no. 50).

1460–1519; called Dr. Eisenach after his native town, a doctor of theology since 1504) of 9 May 1518 Luther wrote again of his *Positiones Indulgentiarum.*[58] This letter, too, confirms the wording in Melanchthon's memoirs. Notable is the fact that the elder Luther (in 1541) still used the less provocative expression *propositiones* for his opinion about the indulgences of 1517 against *Detzel* (=Tetzel).[59] Luther never referred to his "theses." In his protestation of 1519 Luther declared that he testifies that he published some *propositiones* on the papal indulgences, not "theses."[60] One must wonder *when* the switch occurred from *"[pro]positions"* to "theses" and who made it. It was not Melanchthon. At times, inaccurate translations can have serious consequences. Translations are always also interpretations. And, one must also wonder why the testimony of Luther's bishop with respect to the catholicity of Luther's *Explanations* of the *Propositions* is largely underexposed in Reformation history. Noteworthy in this context, too, is the fact that, for instance, no printer at the important imperial city of Augsburg reprinted it, although they printed just about everything else that Luther preached.

Melanchthon, in employing a milder term, also recalls Luther's remark that he very much disliked the "commotion"[61] that accompanied his *propositiones.* Luther's original call was one for "moderation"—thus not wanting to stir "commotion" (*rhum*); no talk of "glory" here. He simply disagreed with Tetzel who presented his opinion about indulgences in his preaching as being "most certain." Tetzel had "promulgated" indulgences for sale since 22 January 1517, demonstrably, for instance, in Eisleben on 24 January 1517, in

[58] *De aliis autem Positionibus indulgentiarum prius tibi scripsi, mihi non placere earum tam vastam in vulgationem*, WA Br 1, 170, 41–42 (no. 74).
[59] *Also giengen meine Propositiones aus wider des Detzels Artickel*, WA 51, 540, 25–541, 5; see Junghans, *Der junge Luther*, 292. Print by Hieronymus Höltzel, Nuremberg 1517; first edition (Facsimile in the State Library in Berlin—Prussian cultural possession).
[60] *Propositiones aliquot contra pontificales, ut vocant, Indulgentias a me editas esse*; WA 2, 620, 3–4.
[61] *Der Rhum war mir nicht lieb*; WA 51, 540, 25–541, 5. Early New High German *Rhum* = today's German: *Rummel*, not *Ruhm* (glory, fame). The English translation of "I did not want the fame" (LW 41, 234) is misleading because it does not take the original meaning of *rhum* ("commotion") into consideration.

Leipzig in the first half of the month of February, and in Jüterbog on 10 April.[62]

Fig. 3. Indulgence Letter of 1492 issued in Rome for fundraising for the rebuilding of St. Peter Church in Rome. The indulgence document was signed by eighteen cardinals and granted the privilege to raise money from people attending St. Mary Chapel in Puchbach (near Salzburg). The document was a license to print and sell personal indulgence letters, which granted forgiveness for all sins for the duration of one hundred days to the buyer of that letter.

Melanchthon's presentation about the unwanted commotion as far as Luther was concerned and the modesty of Luther's sentences points to the fact that Luther's words were not meant to cause a revolt or a revolution. It corresponds with the observation that Johann Eck in 1519, who will be the fiercest adversary of Luther, apparently was in virtual agreement with Luther on the issue of indulgences, as

[62] *Studienausgabe* V, 627, note 30 (relying on H. Volz's research). On the developments leading up to the controversy over the indulgences, see Junghans, "Martin Luther, kirchliche Magnaten und Thesenanschlag" in *Luthers Thesenanschlag,* 33–46.

Luther himself pointed out in 1519: "We practically [almost] agreed on the indulgences."[63]

The wording in Luther's, Melanchthon's, and also Prierias' utterances in this immediate historical context thus leads to this suggestion: Whoever introduced the expression "theses" concerning the issue of indulgences (instead of remaining with the original "propositions") was interested in sharpening the contrast, in acerbating the confrontation, and perhaps in firing up the reforms.

The fact that Luther felt uncomfortable with all the commotion surrounding his talking points on the indulgences suggests that they were not meant to be used as if written for a formal, public debate to which politicians would send official observers as would be the case with the Leipzig Disputation in 1519. Rather, he planned to have informal conversations in order to reach some clarification concerning the pastoral handling of the proper promotion of the indulgences. Besides these two basic concepts of *disputatio*, Luther also used this notion in terms of individual sentences or "articles" as in a list of talking points. His ninety-five talking points were styled only later on as academic "theses" to be discussed. By translating the pastoral talking points into academic "theses" a step is taken away from the historical *Seelsorger* Luther of 1517 toward the realm of a later professorial frame of interpretation.

1. 2. Melanchthon Did Not Mention any "Door"—Luther Without Hammer, Not a Rebel

Admittedly, one aspect of Melanchthon's biographical sketch may be less reliable: The mention of the "posting" of the [*Ninety-Five*] *Propositions*. He only said that they were "affixed" to the church adjacent to the castle. Remarkably, he did not say anything about a "door":[64]

[63] *De indulgentiis pene concordamus*, in *Resolutiones Lutherianae super propositiones suis Lipsiae disputatis* (1519), WA 2, 396, 12; see Pfnür, "Die Bestreitung des Thesenanschlags," 122.

[64] Leppin, "Geburtswehen und Geburt einer Legende," 149, wrote that Georg Rörer relied on Melanchthon and his reference to the doors [plural] (*insofern er von Melanchthon die Zuspitzung auf die Türen der Schloßtür übernimmt*). Leppin overlooks the plain fact that Melanchthon did not mention any door at all. Melanchthon may have implied it, but in his memoirs he did not explicitly speak of a door, or of doors.

> And he publicly attached these [propositions] at the [to the] Temple [church] adjacent to Wittenberg Castle, on the eve of All Saints Day, in the year 1517.[65]

In his funeral oration for Luther on 22 February 1546, Melanchthon did not recall any posting of ninety-five propositions on a door.[66] At that point, to him it may not have been very important to mention something like that. Melanchthon cannot be blamed for setting in motion the legend of the "nailing on the door." He only reports in rather general terms that Luther "affixed them at the church" or "to the church" (*Templo . . . affixit*). The Latin expression *publice affixit* ("he publicly attached") appears a common expression, as also Andreas Bodenstein von Karlstadt (ca. 1480–1541) used it in his letter to Spalatin of 28 April 1517.[67] The expression referred to a "publication" of some sort. However, if the text was sent to bishops, it was not a public event.

The "door" was mentioned first by someone else in 1540, and then not just one church door, but more than one, and specifically: "on the folding-doors of the churches."[68] The man was Georg Rörer (1492–1557) who used the phrase in the 1540s in a private note of his *German New Testament*.[69] In 1522 he had come to Wittenberg with a master's degree from Leipzig. [70] Evidently Rörer was not in Wittenberg in 1517 (nor was Melanchthon). Luther himself nowhere hints at his own posting of his talking points or his so-called

---

[65] *Et has publice Templo, quod arci Witebergensi contiguum est, affixit pridie festi omnium Sanctorum anno 1517;* CR 6, 162.

[66] See *Oratio über der Leich Mart. Luthers*, German translation by Caspar Creuziger (Wittemberg: Georg Rhaw, 1546 [VD 16 M 3872]); MDZ (accessed March 2010).

[67] Heinrich Bornkamm, *Thesen und Thesenanschlag Luthers. Geschehen und Bedeutung* (Berlin: Töpelmann, 1967), 28.

[68] *In valuis temploru[m]*; the "folding-doors" (*valuae*) of the Wittenberg churches. The doors are mentioned prominently in the statutes of the University of Wittenberg as the places for official announcements by a dean; on this see Leppin, "Geburtswehen und Geburt einer Legende,"148, with note 11. Leppin is convincing when he ascribes the legend of the nailing of the *Ninety-Five Theses* to Rörer's thoughtful *Rekonstruktion*, and not to any eyewitness reports (p. 149).

[69] See Treu, "Der Thesenanschlag fand wirklich statt," with two illustrations of Rörer's note.

[70] See Manfred Eder, art. "Rörer, Georg (Rorareius)," *Biographisch-Bibliographisches Kirchenlexikon* 8 (1995), 523–526; Joachim Ott, "Georg Rörer (1492–1557) und sein Nachlass in der Thüringer Universitäts- und Landesbibliothek Jena" in *Luthers Thesenanschlag*, 47–57.

"treatise,"[71] later called the *Ninety-Five Theses*. Did Rörer converse with Melanchthon about the alleged posting in 1517? We do not know. All we know is that after Rörer's private entry in his *German New Testament* (1540s) Melanchthon reported about it in his *Preface* of 1546, but without the mention of the "door." Did Rörer and Melanchthon concoct the Posting in good faith? It looks like it. Erwin Iserloh (1915–1996) in 1961 presented his doubts about the Posting and asked: Fact or Fiction?[72] In opposition to him and his research Kurt Aland (1915–1994) in 1983 tried to defuse the presented source material and digressed from the essential problem.[73] Nevertheless, the following issue remains to be discussed: Did the historical Luther tell the truth with his own story about his talking points of 1517?

1. 2. 1. LUTHER'S STORY ABOUT HIS TALKING POINTS AS TOLD THREE TIMES IN 1518

Luther told his side of the story first to Christoph Scheurl on 5 March 1518. He wrote to him that he was unhappy about the wide dissemination of his talking points. Luther had first wanted to discuss them "with a small group here and in the vicinity," and based upon the group's judgment the theses then could have "either been condemned and destroyed or approved and then published."[74]

Luther repeated the story in essence in his letter to Pope Leo X of May 1518, that first he admonished the bishops privately and only afterwards did he think it appropriate to issue his talking points and to invite some scholars if they would want to talk with him, literally "to take apart" the discussion points with him.[75] Luther's Latin *disceptare,* which he used in this letter, is derived from *dis/captare* and may also mean to discuss something before an arbitrator; in this

---

[71] In the Introduction to the English translation of *Table Talk* (Bridge-Logos, 2004) Luther is said to have called "his 95 salient points the Treatise on Indulgences . . . Issued as a challenge to debate, he nailed a copy of his treatise to the door . . . ." The important part of this observation is the rare expression "95 salient points" ! See website (accessed in March 2010): *books.google.com/books?isbn=088270818X* . . .

[72] See Vincenz Pfnür, "Die Bestreitung des Thesenanschlags durch Erwin Iserloh. Theologiegeschichtlicher Kontext—Auswirkung auf den katholisch-lutherischen Dialog" in *Luthers Thesenanschlag*, 111–126.

[73] See ibid.

[74] WA Br 1, 152, 1–10 (no. 62); Posset, *The Front-Runner*, 215–216.

[75] . . . *mecum disceptare*; WA 1, 528, 16–26 (to Pope Leo X).

case, the arbitrators would have been the scholars whom Luther invited, just like he told Scheurl.

Finally, Elector Frederick the Wise wanted to know from Luther directly what was going on. In his long letter to Frederick the Wise of 21 [?] November 1518 Luther in his defense declared that he did not go public concerning the *disputatio* on the indulgences. He objected to the insinuation that he had acted upon the elector's exhortation and advice (*hortatu et consilio*) to write (or set up?) a disputation on the indulgences. To the contrary, Luther insisted, that nobody was aware of a disputation (i.e., a disputation text), not even his closest friends. Only the archbishop of Magdeburg and Mainz and the bishop of Brandenburg were aware of the disputation text because Luther sent it to them in "private letters." And, Luther added that he sent the two letters "before he issued the *disputatio*" (the so-called *Ninety-Five Theses*).[76]

The statements in the three documents sound like Luther did not publish anything on 31 October 1517. There is no word on a posting, but everything on sending his letters to the proper ecclesiastical authorities, namely on the same day, 31 October 1517, when supposedly he nailed the text onto the door. Luther only wrote of "issuing" by using the Latin *edere*, which does not mean that he "published in print" or "posted" something. He simply said: "I gave out"/"I issued." In his letter to Bishop Schulze of February 1518, in which he enclosed his *Resolutiones*, Luther used the Latin *emittere* ("to send out") which may or may not imply the sending of a printed text; it could be handwritten.[77] Luther also told the bishop that the planned disputation never materialized ("but nobody came").[78]

Furthermore, Luther sent his text, calling it *Paradoxa* (see above) to a friend, but not before the date of his sending of the two letters to

---

[76] *Sic enim et apud not quidam sycophantae iactaverunt, tuae Celsitudinis hortatu et consilio me ista disputasse: cum huius disputationis nullus etiam intimorum amicorum fuerit conscius, nisi Reverendissimus Dominus Archiepiscopus Magdeburgensis, et Dominus Hieronymus Episcopus Brandenburgensis. Hos enim, sicut intererat eorum ista monstra prohibere, ita privatis literis, antequam disputationem ederem, humiliter et reverenter monui, ut super oves Christi vigilarent adversus lupos istos*; WA Br 1, 236–246, here 245, lines 358–363 (no. 110).

[77] *Itaque emisi disputationem*; WA Br 1, 138, 17 (no. 58).

[78] WA Br 1, 139, 46 (no. 58). Later in the same letter Luther qualified his "issuing" of the disputation with the expression *publicitus ędere* [sic], after he felt compelled to set the record straight, namely that he wanted to offer talking points and not assertions, and that he subjected himself to the authority of the Church; lines 47–54.

the bishops. Luther insisted that it was only eleven days later, on 11 November 1517, that he sent his *Paradoxa* to Johann Lang,[79] to whom he had sent his earlier "Positions against the Scholastic theology" (on 4 September 1517).[80] Therefore, this letter of Luther to Lang confirmed what Luther told Elector Frederick, that he had not confided his disputation text on indulgences to anybody, not even to his close friends. And this letter proves his intention to keep the talking points reserved to a circle of trusted friends and to Bishop Schulze and Archbishop Albrecht. Melanchthon in his *Preface* mentioned nothing about the two official letters (to the bishop and the archbishop) or the letter to Scheurl. He did not have to repeat what Luther had written about them in his recent *Preface* to Volume One (*Nota bene*: both *Prefaces* [Luther's and Melanchthon's] need to be read together). There is also no hint in the letters to the pope, the elector, and to Scheurl about any formal, academic disputation at the University of Wittenberg.

Melanchthon did not mention anything about a connection between the criticism of the indulgences in 1517 and Luther changing the spelling of his family name. Thus, the thesis[81] cannot find any support from Melanchthon's memoirs that Luther made a conscious effort of switching his name from *Luder* to *Luther* or *Eleutherius* in order to express his Reformational conviction in the context of issuing the so-called *Theses* of 1517. Only the contemporaneous Johannes Cochlaeus (1479–1552) made something out of the various forms of spelling.[82] Much of this discussion appears to over-interpret the variations in the spelling of the family name. Perhaps Luther had in mind also the simple idea, which is not taken into consideration at all so far, that his name "Luther" is just another version of "Lothar": In his *World History* of 1541/1545, he entered in the section of the Middle Ages (1120–1130) the names *Lotharius* and *Luther Saxo* ("Lotharius," "Luther the Saxon").[83]

[79] *Ecce alia denuo Paradoxa mitto*; WA Br 1, 121, 4 (no. 52).
[80] *Misi ad te . . . positiones nostras*; WA Br 1, 103, 4 (no. 45).
[81] As proposed by Bernd Moeller and Karl Stackmann, *Luder—Luther—Eleutherius. Erwägungen zu Luthers Namen* (Göttingen: Vandenhoeck & Ruprecht, 1981). Their observations are noteworthy, but should not be over-interpreted.
[82] See *Luther's Lives*, 218.
[83] WA 53, 156.

1. 2. 2. MELANCHTHON IS NOT RELIABLE IN EVERY INSTANCE

In sum, here are the options for dealing with Melanchthon's and Luther's reliability:

1. One may leave the question open whether the historical Luther was correct in his letters to Elector Frederick the Wise of 21 [?] November 1518, to Pope Leo of May 1518, and to Christoph Scheurl in March 1518, or whether Melanchthon is correct concerning a posting on the Eve of All Saints Day 1517. The odds are against Melanchthon.

2. One is virtually compelled to take Luther's side with his story as told to the pope, to the elector, and to Scheurl in 1518. This means, however, that one is unable to harmonize Luther's story, neither with Rörer's private note (1540s) nor with Melanchthon's published *Preface* (1546) about the posting.

It all boils down to Luther's two official letters and to the one to Scheurl (all of 1518) versus Melanchthon's (and Rörer's) construct from hear-say in the 1540s. I am compelled to side with the historical Luther and his letters of 1518 because I do not think Luther was a liar when he explained himself to the pope, to his territorial lord, and to his friend Scheurl in Nuremberg. Luther's recollection expressed in the three letters is by far more trustworthy than the hear-say of what a Rörer or a Melanchthon picked up and handed on decades later (Rörer in his private note, Melanchthon in his biographical memoirs).

Luther cannot be the original source for Melanchthon's *Preface* about "affixing" a text (the so-called *Ninety-Five Theses*) "to the temple" next to the castle on the eve of All Saints Day. Perhaps the otherwise scrupulous Melanchthon picked up the idea of the "posting" from Rörer's construct (of the event of 1517) in the 1540s when Melanchthon gathered information for his biographical sketch in his *Preface* of 1546. And, why would Rörer make his private entry in the first place? Did he have a need to remind himself in the 1540s? Apparently, at that time, there were no solemn celebrations yet of the so-called "Reformation Day." There was no public commemoration of the posting in the first half of the sixteenth century; it may be a legend which Melanchthon may have accepted as bare fact.

Another questionable report in Melanchthon's *Preface* is the note that Tetzel burned Luther's "Theses":

> [Tetzel] cries aloud everywhere that this heretic must be condemned and be burned; he even publicly hurls Luther's propositions and the sermon concerning indulgences into the flames.[84]

We do not know where Melanchthon could have gotten this idea from. Since Luther did not mention it anywhere, Melanchthon must have picked it up from somebody else. Allegedly, Tetzel burned them at Jüterbog and/or Frankfurt on the Oder in early December 1517.[85]

1. 2. 3. MELANCHTHON'S SUMMARY

Concerning Luther's controversy over indulgences, Melanchthon simply summed up as follows:

> These were the beginnings of this controversy when Luther, as yet suspecting anything, would not even dream of making changes in [religious] customs, as he was not at all completely trying to get rid of [*abiiciebat*] indulgences, but only urging moderation [*sed tantum moderationem flagitabat*]![86]

Melanchthon employed the same expression *controversia* which is found in the first print of Luther's First Volume of his Latin writings, namely, a volume "in which first the controversy about the indulgences" is to be found.[87] Melanchthon's concern of presenting Luther as a moderate *Seelsorger*, not as a rebel, chimes quite well with Luther's insistence that he had wanted to work on the issue of the indulgences first with the proper authorities of the Church (the archbishop and the bishop) and by presenting talking points for the clarification of the given issues.

In the paragraph in which Melanchthon came to the summary of the controversy over the indulgences in 1517 he wanted to make sure that Luther was not perceived as a rebel or that he acted upon his lord's instigations. Melanchthon seems to take up the issue which Luther had refuted already in his letter of November 1518 to Frederick the Wise (see above) as Melanchthon continued to defend Luther; mainly that Luther was not "secretly instigated and incited by

---

[84] CR 6, 162.

[85] See the extensive note 117 in Weinacht, *Melanchthon und Luther.* 84.

[86] CR 6, 162.

[87] . . . *ab eo tempore, quo primum controuersia de Indulgentijs mota est; Studienausgabe* V, 622.

princes," which was a charge made by the "Duke of Braunschweig" who in later years was a vehement opponent of the Reformation:

> Therefore, they falsely accuse him [Luther] who say that he began under false pretenses, so that afterwards he could change the [affairs of the] state and seek power either for himself or for others. And it is far from the truth that he was secretly instigated and incited by princes, as the Duke of Braunschweig wrote [about him].[88]

With respect to the duke of Braunschweig, this was a reference to the feud in the year 1541. Duke Heinrich von Braunschweig-Wolfenbüttel (Henry II, the Younger, 1489–1568), was the notorious tyrant who became later known as the "militant leader of the Catholic league."[89] Duke Heinrich attacked Luther as an arch-heretic in May 1541. Luther counter-attacked him as "the clown" or "Jack Sausage" (*Hans Worst*). Melanchthon in his memoirs spoke here from hindsight, saying in effect that the duke recently wrote about these slanders (but he evidently was not referring to the year 1517, but to 1541).

The Ninety-Five *Propositions* themselves will not be analyzed in the following pages,[90] nor can we discuss further the fact that Luther gave no date for an alleged academic disputation at the University of Wittenberg, if he originally would have wanted one at all (which is doubtful as far as an official academic event is concerned). He looked mostly for reactions from his bishops and his friends, including his confreres Johann Lang and Johann von Staupitz.

Here we break off as we concentrate on the earlier years that Luther spent in the Augustinian Friary at Erfurt (1505–1512), i.e., the years that lead up to his criticism of the indulgences in the fall of 1517. We first need to preface all this with some considerations on what is needed in present-day Luther research.

---

[88] *Ac tantum abest, ut ab aulicis subornatus aut incitatus sit, sicut scripsit Dux Brunsvicensis*; CR 6, 162.

[89] Hartmann Grisar, *Martin Luther. His Life and Work* (Westminster, MD: The Newman Press, 1930, reprinted in 1953), 445, 539–540; Franz Petri, "Herzog Heinrich der Jüngere von Braunschweig-Wolfenbüttel," ARG 72 (1981): 122–158.

[90] See Reinhard Brandt, *Lasst ab vom Ablass: ein evangelisches Plädoyer* (Göttingen: Vandenhoeck & Ruprecht, 2008).

1. 3. Embarking on Luther Research

As we enter into the search for the historical Luther we need to be warned that we enter on a choppy "ocean."[91] When leaving behind the safe harbor in search of the historical Luther we must be prepared to leave behind also some of the familiar stories and the history that was made (*Wirkungsgeschichte*). The historical Luther needs to be distinguished from his own impact, i.e., either from an adulating Lutheran or from a vicious Catholic *Wirkungsgeschichte*.[92]

With the Catholic Luther scholar Hartmann Grisar, who is often denigrated for other reasons, one needs to remain aware that the "historical Luther has been obliterated."[93] Already one hundred years ago Grisar had written of the "historical Luther", an expression which nowadays has become standard research vocabulary, as is also the expression "the original Luther,"[94] or "the authentic Luther."[95]

---

[91] As Paul Althaus (1888–1966) warned, *Die Theologie Martin Luthers* (Gütersloh: Gütersloher Verlagshaus, 1962), 8 (*The Theology of Martin Luther*, trans. Robert C. Schultz, Philadelphia: Fortress, 1966) and as Gerhard Ebeling repeated in 1964 in *Luther: Einführung in sein Denken* (Tübingen: Mohr, 1964), 41 (*Luther: An Introduction to His Thought*, trans. R. A. Wilson, Philadelphia: Fortress, 1970; reprinted in 2007).

[92] See Gerhard Ebeling, *Umgang mit Luther* (Tübingen: Mohr Siebeck, 1983), 221. Bernd Moeller, "Luthers Erfolge" in *Luther in seiner Zeit. Persönlichkeit und Wirken des Reformators*, eds. Martin Greschat and Günther Lottes (Stuttgart, Berlin, Cologne: Kohlhammer, 1997), 89–105; reprinted in Moeller, *Luther-Rezeption. Kirchenhistorische Aufsätze zur Reformationsgeschichte*, ed. Johannes Schilling (Göttingen: Vandenhoeck & Ruprecht, 2001), 270–284.

[93] Grisar 584.

[94] See Kenneth Hagen, Preface to *Luther's Approach to Scripture as seen in his 'Commentaries' on Galatians 1519–1538* (Tübingen: Mohr Siebeck, 1993), VII: "My research, however, forced me to return to the 'original' Luther rather than use nineteenth- and twentieth-century editions and methods." See also Egil Grislis, "Piety, Faith, and Spirituality in the Quest for the Historical Luther," *Consensus* 19 (1993): 29–51; Franz Posset, "From the Corrupter of the Faith to the Father in the Faith: 100 Years of Catholic Luther Research," *Luther Study* 14 (Korea, 2000): 79–141, here 135; appeared in LD 12 (2004): 188–193; Thomas Kaufmann in his *Martin Luther* has his opening chapter titled with *Auf der Suche nach Luther* (Munich: Beck, 2006, 2nd ed. 2010); one may assume that Kaufmann meant the search for the historical Luther.

[95] Joan Skocir, "A Search for the Authentic Luther: Kenneth Hagen's Approach to Luther Studies" in *Ad fontes Lutheri*, 253–269.

1. 4. TABLE TALK AS SECONDARY SOURCE

Many Luther scholars past and present display a naïve trust in the historicity of what was said during dinner time at Luther's table in the 1530s (Table Talk).[96] I can no longer share their naiveté that Table Talk would constitute an important *primary* source for biographies of the historical Luther. Perhaps we should reckon with the possibility that the real distortion of the Luther image occurred with the Table Talk.

The real experiment in Luther biography would be to write one without relying on Table Talk. This is my *plaidoyer*! Even Lutheran Luther scholars accuse the collector Johannes Aurifaber (ca. 1519–1575) of incorporating some fabricated talks with his 1566 edition (of course, always with good intentions).[97] Aurifaber is also accused of "correcting" offensive talks and transforming them into "pious platitudes."[98]

Those who embark on the ocean of Luther research need to heed the storm warning that is issued by eminent Lutheran Luther experts, namely, that already Luther's own contemporaries had some doubts about the reliability of the Table Talk. Johannes Aurifaber was not even born when Luther published his *Propositions* in 1517. Aurifaber was guided by the honorable desire to demonstrate that Luther was a holy man of God who alone was able to lead the people out of the papist darkness.[99] At times some statements are simply false.

In search of the historical Luther one is well advised not to rely on Table Talk unless they can be corroborated from other original source

[96] "The culmination of all that is Martin Luther revealed in conversations with his colleagues and students" (on the book cover): *Table Talk of Martin Luther* (Bridge-Logos, 2004).

[97] See Walther von Loewenich, *Martin Luther. Der Mann und das Werk*, 273–274 (*Martin Luther: The Man and His Work*, trans. Lawrence W. Denef, Minneapolis: Augsburg Publishing House, 1986); Karl Dienst, "Martin Luther als Tischredner. Eine Tischrede," *Luther* 70 (1999): 145–50, here 146.

[98] See Karl Dienst, "Geistliches und Weltliches. Martin Luther im Spiegel seiner Tischreden," *Blätter für pfälzische Kirchengeschichte und religiöse Volkskunde* 63 (1996): 327–341; Helmar Junghans, "Die Tischreden Martin Luthers" in *Spätmittelalter, Luthers Reformation, Kirche in Sachsen. Ausgewählte Aufsätze*, eds. Michael Beyer and Günter Wartenberg (Leipzig: Evangelische Verlagsanstalt, 2001), 155–176; English digest in LD 12 (2004): 52–55.

[99] See Junghans, "Die Tischreden Martin Luthers," 156; idem, art. "Aurifaber, Johannes (1519–1575) in *Theologische Realenzyklopädie* 4 (1979), 752–755.

material such as Luther's own letters and writings. A very simple example of false information that was handed down through them was a Table Talk of the summer of 1540. Luther supposedly said that he stayed at the Augustinian friary at Augsburg in 1518, at the time when he was interrogated by Cardinal Cajetan.[100] The people who recorded this obviously did not know that no such friary existed at Augsburg. Luther stayed at the monastery of the Carmelite friars where his friend Johann Frosch (ca. 1480–1533) was the prior. A statement from a Table Talk without the backing from an authentic source from Luther's own works or letters remains suspicious. In addition, one must remember that the Table Talk began rather late, i.e., with the year 1531, after the *Augsburg Confession* of 1530.[101]

Who knows how much German beer was consumed while some student stenographers penned down their notes! Altogether there are more than 7,000 entries (including duplicates) into the records of Table Talk in six fat volumes. All the entries need to be questioned for their credibility, in particular when events prior to 1530 are mentioned and interpreted from hindsight. On our ocean cruise, we may relax, perhaps with a *stein* of good German beer, and read the Table Talk for our entertainment,[102] but not for a serious guide or compass to locate the historical Luther or to find his *ipsissima verba.* For the most part Table Talk is "secondary literature"[103] and displays at times a distorted image of Luther. And, who knows what was mixed into the notes from conversations when Luther was gone, when Luther had to be absent, and had appointed a substitute.[104] Therefore, methodologically we exclude Table Talk from the investigation.

---

[100] *Cum veni Augustam, diverti ad Augustinianos*, WA TR 5, 79, 1 (no. 5349, Summer 1540).

[101] The *Confession* was meant to be a Catholic document from the perspective of the Wittenberg Christians.

[102] Junghans: *zur Erbauung und Unterhaltung*, in "Die Tischreden Martin Luthers," 176. A vivid picture of Table Talk is provided by Rudolf K. Markwald and Marylynn Morris Markwald in *Katharina von Bora: A Reformation Life* (St. Louis: Concordia, 2002).

[103] Franz Posset, "Goldene Worte: Augustinus und Bernhard in der Sicht des alten Luther (1531–1546)," *Catholica. Vierteljahresschrift für ökumenische Theologie* 54 (2000): 220–239, here 221; English digest in LD 11 (2003): 54–56.

[104] That this was his practice is stated by Markwald 129.

1. 5. Some Rethinking Is Needed

1. 5. 1. LUTHER WITH AND WITHOUT HALO

Fig. 4. *Martin Luther inspired by the Holy Spirit.* Woodcut by Hans Baldung Grien (ca. 1485–1545); created in the aftermath of the Diet of Worms in 1521.

It is a known fact that the Luther image of the later sixteenth century and subsequent centuries within the German Lutheran camp[105] was different from what we know from the reliable sources of Luther's time. Nevertheless, the glorification of Luther set in early on and this earliest phase is of interest for our purposes here.

A not very well known text about recommendations for living as a priest, which is an undated text attributed to Luther, has the title "Blessed Dr. Luther's Brief Pastoral Instruction" (*Des seel[igen] D. Lutheri kurze Pastoralinstruktion*).[106] Remarkable is the notion "blessed Dr. Luther" in the title. If the editor's dating is correct, who associated the text with a letter of spring 1519, then it would perhaps be the earliest document that referred to Luther as "blessed" as in "Blessed Virgin Mary."

Another early document showing the veneration for Luther was the portrait of him (Fig. 4) which appeared in 1521 on the title page of the book *Acta et res gestae D. Martini Lutheri in Comitijs Principum Vvormaciae*, published in Strasbourg.[107] We see a nimbed Friar Luther holding a Bible in his hands. He is inspired by the Holy Spirit who is represented by the dove hovering over his head. The portrait came into existence in the southwest of German speaking lands, i.e., Alsace, not Wittenberg or Saxony, by an artist who is not known to have become a staunch Lutheran. It was Hans Baldung (called Grien,

---

[105] See Johannes Mathesius (1504–1565), *Historien von des ehrwirdigen in Gott seligen thewren Manns Gottes Doctoris Martini Luthers Anfang, Lehr, Leben und Sterben*, (Nürnberg [no printer name given] 1566, VD 16 M 1490); MDZ (accessed June 2010). These sermons were reprinted fifty times according to Wolfgang Brückner, "Luther, heiliger Mann oder falscher Prophet? Legende und Antilegende zwischen 1517 und 1630" (see note in the Introduction); Hans Volz, *Die Lutherpredigten des Johannes Mathesius. Kritische Untersuchung zur Geschichtsschreibung im Zeitalter der Reformation* (Leipzig: Heinsius, 1930); Wolfgang Hermann, "Die Lutherpredigten des Cyriacus Spangenberg," *Mansfelder Blätter* 39 (1934/1935): 7–95 (Spangenberg, 1528–1604); Joachim Kruse, *Luthers Leben in Illustrationen des 18. und 19. Jahrhunderts* (exhibition catalogue, Veste Coburg) (Coburg 1980). The most comprehensive study still is the one by Ernst Walter Zeeden, *The legacy of Luther; Martin Luther and the Reformation in the estimation of the German Lutherans from Luther's death to the beginning of the age of Goethe*, trans. from the original German by Ruth Mary Bethell (Westminster, Md.: Newman Press, 1954) = *Martin Luther und die Reformation im Urteil des deutschen Luthertums. Studien zum Selbstverständnis des lutherischen Protestantismus von Luthers Tode bis zum Beginn der Goethezeit*, 2 vols (Freiburg: Herder, 1950–1952).

[106] WA 1, 395–399; the text is appended to Luther's letter to Spalatin of 16 May 1519.

[107] See, for example, Kaufmann, 24.

ca. 1485–1545),[108] who is well known for his pictorial representations of witches and of the Virgin Mary.[109] The image of "Saint Luther" was not restricted to adamant ["Lutheran"] supporters.[110] Baldung's woodcut of *Martin Luther inspired by the Holy Spirit* was possible only from the matrix of Catholic spirituality. Baldung, who was a student of Albrecht Dürer (1471–1528), most likely was guided by his master's view of Luther as a "man inspired by the Holy Spirit."[111] The same motif of the inspired Luther was employed in the woodcut of Lucas Cranach (1472–1553) of 1529 in which Luther is shown as the Evangelist Matthew, who is the inspired evangelist, with the Holy Spirit in the form of a huge dove hovering over Luther at his desk.[112]

Luther's public persona was wide-spread, but one did not have to be a convinced Lutheran to see saintly qualities in Luther. Being reform-minded, conservative Catholics may have welcomed the Luther of 1520. It was also in other parts of southern Germany, especially in the Augsburg region where sympathizers of Luther (who remained Catholic) saw in Luther around 1520 the Apostle and Savior of Germany.[113] Michael Stiefel (Stifel, Styfel, ca. 1487–1567) of the southwestern friary of the Augustinian order at Esslingen, later a Lutheran mathematician at the University of Jena, welcomed Luther as a "Christian Angel" being sent by God to disclose the subtle deceit of the Antichrist.[114]

---

[108] From the fact that Baldung produced the woodcut of "Saint Luther" one cannot automatically conclude that he was a Protestant.

[109] See Sibylle Weber am Bach, *Hans Baldung Grien (1484/5–1545): Marienbilder in der Reformation* (Regensburg: Schnell & Steiner, 2006).

[110] This narrow view is held by Mark U. Edwards, Jr., "Luther as Media Virtuoso and Media Persona," in *Luther zwischen den Kulturen,* 102–115, here 107.

[111] *Mit dem heyligen geist erleuchteten mahn* [*Mann*]; Dürer, *Tagebuch der niederländischen Reise*, 1521; *Sketchbook of His Journey to the Netherlands, 1520–21: With Extracts from His Diary*; translated and commented by Philip Troutman (London: Elek, 1971).

[112] See Peter-Klaus Schuster, "Individuelle Ewigkeit: Hoffnungen und Ansprüche im Bildnis der Lutherzeit" in August Buck (ed.), *Biographie und Autobiographie in der Renaissance. Arbeitsgespräch in der Herzog August Bibliothek Wolfenbüttel vom 1. bis 3. November 1982: Vorträge* (Wiesbaden: Harrassowitz, 1983), 121–173, here 166 (Fig. 18).

[113] For example, in December 1522 the Benedictine monk Vitus Bild called Luther the "savior of our Germany"; see Franz Posset, *Renaissance Monks: Monastic Humanism in Six Biographical Sketches* (Leiden and Boston: Brill, 2005), 149.

[114] See Stiefel, *Von der Christformigen, rechtsgerundeten leer Doctoris Martini Lutheri* (Strasbourg, 1522); Edwards, Jr., "Luther as Media Virtuoso," 107.

Soon the veneration of Luther crept everywhere into the camp of what was later to be called "Lutheran." Luther's father confessor, Johann Bugenhagen (1485–1558), who was the pastor of Wittenberg, identified Luther as the angel of Rev 14:6–8 in his funeral oration of 22 February 1546. [115] Hans Sachs (1494–1576) in his versified *epitaphium* for Luther called him "a true apostolic warrior."[116] The Lutheran preacher at Nordhausen, Anton Otho (ca. 1505–ca. 1565) spoke of the "holy father Luther" in a letter to Justus Jonas (1493–1555) of ca. 1550.[117]

As to the historical Luther, we need to see him as less heroic and less holy, without the "golden background" [118] of medieval iconography. But one must remember that the concepts of "golden background" and "halo" are elements of traditional Catholic iconography. Contemporary characterizations of the deceased Luther, including Melanchthon's, show aspects of what is known from medieval lives of saints.[119] If we want to get to know the historical Luther, present-day "Protestant triumphalism"[120] needs to be toned down.

1. 5. 2. A FRIAR WITH MORAL INTEGRITY

In opposition to the saintly Luther image, early Catholic scholars left Luther without any moral integrity. The demythologization of their

---

[115] *Denn er war on* [ohne] *zweiffel der Engel / dauon in apocalypsi xiiij. cap. steht*, folio 11, in *Eine Christliche Predigt, vber der Leich vnd begrebnis, des Ehrwirdigen D. Martini Luthers* (Wittemberg: Georg Rhau, 1546) [VD16 B 9274]; MDZ (accessed June 2010); on this, see Herbert Immenkötter, "Von Engeln und Teufeln: Über Luther-Biographien des 16. Jahrhunderts" in *Biographie und Autobiographie in der Renaissance. Arbeitsgespräch in der Herzog August Bibliothek Wolfenbüttel vom 1. bis 3. November 1982: Vorträge*, ed. August Buck (Wiesbaden: Harrassowitz, 1983), 91–102, here 94.

[116] *Ein recht apostolischer krieger*, in *Ein epitaphium oder klag-red ob der leych D. Martini Luthers*, as quoted by Immenkötter, "Von Engeln und Teufeln," 95.

[117] *S[anctus] pater Luther*; in *Briefwechsel Justus Jonas*, 300 (no. 913): website: books.google.com/books?id=4nUOAAAAYAAJ . . . (accessed May 2010); quoted by Franz Peter Sonntag, "Luther in katholischer Sicht," *Die Zeichen der Zeit* 39 (1985): 195–204, here 198.

[118] Gottfried Seebaß, "Ein Luther ohne Goldgrund—Stand und Aufgaben der Lutherforschung am Ende eines Jubiläumsjahres" in Otto Hermann Pesch, ed., *Lehren aus dem Lutherjahr. Sein Ertrag für die Ökumene* (Freiburg: Katholische Akademie, 1984), 49–85.

[119] See Immenkötter, "Von Engeln und Teufeln," 93.

[120] Heiko A. Oberman, *The Two Reformations. The Journey from the last days to the New World*, ed. Donald Weinstein (New Haven: Yale University Press, 2003), 1.

negative view is over-ripe because they presented much of the German Reformation as "the result of one deformed, over-sexed, constipated, neurotic German."[121] We come closer to the real Luther if we keep the following things in mind: First, let us employ the working hypothesis that Luther is neither exclusively and consistently a rebel or heretic nor exclusively and consistently a saint.[122] Secondly, Luther might be consistently inconsistent or "contradictory" (*widersprüchlich*).[123] The either-or-mentality does not look promising.

1. 5. 3. "LEGENDS" CONCERNING YOUNG LUTHER

[1] Caught in a thunderstorm [near Stotternheim], at a critical juncture in his university studies, he was so terrified by a lightening bolt that he uttered a compulsive vow to become a monk.

[2] His years in the monastery were fraught with brooding about how he might become justified in the eyes of an angry God. At last his evangelical breakthrough came, i.e., the Tower Experience, when he discovered his doctrine of salvation by grace alone.

[3] On All Saints' Day in 1517, Martin Luther nailed upon the door of the castle church in Wittenberg his *Ninety-Five Theses* against papal indulgences, thus initiating the Protestant Reformation.[124]

[4] When called before the Diet of Worms in April of 1521, he held steadfast in his faith, declaring before emperor and the assembled imperial estates, "Here I stand, I can do no other. God help me. Amen."[125]

---

[121] Kenneth Hagen, *Foundations of Theology in the Continental Reformation Questions of Authority* (Milwaukee, 1974; copyright Kenneth Hagen), 11.

[122] See Hans Friedrich Geißer, *Weder Ketzer noch Heiliger. Luthers Bedeutung für den ökumenischen Dialog* (Regensburg: F. Pustet, 1982), 175–200; Horst Herrmann, *Martin Luther: Ketzer wider Willen* (Munich: C. Bertelsmann, 1983).

[123] Humbert Fink, *Martin Luther: der widersprüchliche Reformator* (Munich: Molden Seewald, 1982).

[124] On this issue see Hans Volz, *Martin Luthers Thesenanschlag und dessen Vorgeschichte* (Weimar: H. Böhlaus Nachfolger, 1959); Iserloh's study (see above with note 20).

[125] On the Diet of Worms, see Fritz Reuter, ed. *Der Reichstag zu Worms von 1521: Reichspolitik und Luthersache.* (2d ed., Cologne: Böhlau, 1981); De Lamar Jensen, *Confrontation at Worms: Martin Luther and the Diet of Worms. With a complete*

According to Harry G. Haile (professor emeritus of Germanic Languages and Literatures), "every one of the statements above may well be false. Most of them almost surely are. None can be proved by contemporary documents (or disproved)."[126] As to [2] it is evident that Grisar coined the history-making idea of Luther's "discovery in the tower," located it in the toilet (*cloaca*) and dated it for the winter of 1518/1519. His idea is based on Table Talk.[127]

1. 5. 4. DID THE REFORMATION START IN THE CONFESSIONAL?

Legend no. 3 is fed by a tenacious, subsidiary legend that lets the Reformation start in the confessional—not with Luther going to confession—but with Luther as hearing confessions, as the father confessor himself. This legend presupposes that Luther was licensed to hear confessions and that he became increasingly upset with what people supposedly told him in the confessional about the effects of the indulgences. This idea was put forth by Friedrich Myconius (1490–1546), a former Franciscan friar, who as a later Lutheran wrote the "History of the Reformation" covering the years 1517 to 1542. Himself a father confessor, he projected his own experiences from hearing confessions onto Luther as a father confessor and declared that Luther was irritated by the devastating spiritual results with which he was confronted in the confessional as a result of Tetzel's unqualified promises.[128] This is a seductive theory, but cannot be demonstrated from the sources.[129] It is fed from the correct

---

English translation of the Edict of Worms (Provo, Utah: Brigham Young University Press, 1973). A colored woodcut of 1557 is extant with handwritten caption and the embellishment: *Intitulentur libri. Hir stehe ich / Ich kan nicht anders. Got hilffe mir. Amen;* website: wikimedia.org/wikipedia/commons/0/04/Luther-in-Worms (accessed October 2010).

[126] Harry G. Haile, Prolog in *Luther: An Experiment in Biography* (Garden City, N.Y.: Doubleday, 1980; Princeton University Press, 1983), 1. See also Johannes Luther, *Legenden um Luther* (Greifswalder Studien zur Lutherforschung 9) (Berlin: de Gruyter, 1933) who investigated primarily the issues of "Here I stand" and also the "ink spot" at Wartburg Castle.

[127] See Grisar 105–110.

[128] See *Historia Reformationis vom Jahr Christi 1517 bis 1542* (Leipzig: Weidmann, 1718), 22 as posted on website: books.google.com/books?id=hyNBAAAAcAAJ . . . (accessed May 2010).

[129] See Wilhelm-Ernst Winterhager, "Ablasskritik als Indikator historischen Wandels vor 1517: Ein Beitrag zu Voraussetzungen und Einordnung der Reformation," ARG

understanding that the issue was essentially one of pastoral concern (*Seelsorge*), but goes too far into projecting Luther as father confessor. Melanchthon did not know of such a motivation for Luther's criticism of the indulgence business. Apparently, Luther did not mention anything to him in this regard that would have compelled Melanchthon to incorporate it into his memoirs.

1. 6. Needs and Warnings Concerning Luther Research

First, relying on English translations such as *Luther's Works* is helpful, but only to the beginner.

Second, knowledge is needed of the languages in which the historical Luther communicated: Early New High German and Latin. If you think your knowledge of contemporary German would suffice, think again because Luther's German may occasionally sound as alien as the next foreign language and the sixteenth-century German spelling makes it worse.[130] Equally necessary is some familiarity with the ancient languages: the Latin of Saint Jerome and his Bible translation (the Vulgate), the ecclesiastical Latin in general, the Latin mannerisms of contemporary humanists, and last, but not least, biblical Hebrew and Greek. As noted earlier, it remains an open question why the WA editors and the translators refer without hesitation to Luther's original talking points as "theses," whereas Luther himself carefully distinguishes between *probationes / disputationes / propositiones* on the one hand and (dogmatic) assertions on the other, as he wrote to his bishop in 1518: "I dispute, I say, not assert." [131] Disputations are meant to clarify whereas assertions are fixed statements that may lead to the charge of heresy. Luther is too smart to fall into that trap.

Third, one would think that one could rely on all the hard work that goes into the "critical edition" of the many volumes of Luther's works in the *Weimar Ausgabe* (WA). More than 125 years of intense research went into this edition, from 1883 to 2009, and is now

90 (1999): 6–71; Vogel, "Zwischen Universität und Seelsorge: Martin Luthers Beweggründe im Ablasstreit" ZKG 118 (2007): 187–212.

[130] See Joachim Schildt, "Zum Verständnis der Luthersprache" in *Studienausgabe* I, 13–28.

[131] *Disputo, Inquam, non assero*; WA Br 1, 140, 72 (no. 58).

finished with its more than 120 volumes. A captain of an ocean journey of Luther research knows that parts of the WA are flawed. Even seasoned sailors did and still do put their trust uncritically in the critical edition thinking that they would be close to the historical Luther, until such over-confidence was dampened, for instance, by the demonstration that Luther's so-called "Writings about the Jews" (*Judenschriften*) may not be what the editorial label insinuates.[132] Even Johannes Cochlaeus, Luther's adversary, saw it differently. If the WA editors would have read Cochlaeus they may have come to a different understanding of Luther's writing about Jesus truly born a Jew. Cochlaeus said that in this pamphlet Luther was more anti-papal than anti-Jewish: "Even though in that pamphlet he [Luther] piled the heaviest possible slanders upon the Catholics and praised the Jews with many flattering words, nevertheless he did not convert a single Jew to Christ."[133]

More flaws of the WA come to light. They pertain at times to misleading and derailing editorial annotations[134] and to the wrong placement and insertions of quotation marks. We encounter these mistakes especially when investigating Luther's hundreds of hints to and quotations from the work and life of Saint Bernard of Clairvaux.[135] Nevertheless, WA certainly remains the standard reference of Luther's works.[136]

---

[132] An examination of the texts themselves reveals a picture that is different from that which the WA conveys. The classification *Judenschriften* in WA is a modern invention which distorts the genres in which Luther wrote; see Kenneth Hagen, "Luther's So-Called *Judenschriften*: A Genre Approach," ARG 90 (1999): 130–138.
[133] *Luther's Lives*, 133.
[134] For example: Luther in 1515 assumed Saint Bernard to be the author of an adage; the WA editors of WA 1 and WA 4 failed to identify the correct source (namely, Bernardinus de Siena [1380–1444]); see Franz Posset, "Luthers Predigt von 1515 gegen das Laster der Verleumdung und seine mittelalterliche Quelle," *Luther* 75 (2004): 142–149; English digest in LD 15 (2007): 31. Furthermore, the editorial reference to the Pseudo-Bernardine sermon *De duobus discipulis euntibus in Emmaus*, as in the note to line 72 in WA 55-II, 178 (published in 2000) is misleading. The more appropriate, authentic Bernard text to be considered is Bernard's *Ann 1* of which Melanchthon reported; see Franz Posset, "Bernhard von Clairvauxs Meditation zu Psalm 31,2 bei Martin Luther" in LuJ 69 (2002): 71–78; English digest in LD 13 (2005): 15.
[135] See below, Chapter 3.
[136] See Helmar Junghans, "The History, Use and Significance of the Weimar Luther Edition," *Theology and Life* 25 (2002): 43–71; reprinted in LQ 17 (2003): 267–287. Select texts are available in the improved *Studienausgabe*.

Fourth, in search of the historical Luther one needs to know more than just Luther's immediate works. What do they know of Luther who *only* know Luther, and not also his spiritual and theological sources and context?[137] One needs to go to the sources as articulated in the programmatic title of the *Festschrift* for Kenneth Hagen: *Ad fontes Lutheri: Toward the Recovery of the Real Luther*![138] We need to go to Luther's text and context, and to the original sources from which he himself drank.

As to method: I employ the historical critical method for my Luther research which involves, as said, some rethinking. This approach helps most of all to find the *Sitz im Leben* (setting in life) and thus helps to contextualize events in Luther's life.

Furthermore, the historical critical approach lets me take a closer look at *Formgeschichte*, i.e., the genre of source materials, such as Melanchthon's biographical memoirs of Martin Luther (i.e., the *Preface*), written likely also related to the genre of a commendation (*laudatio*),[139] first printed on 1 June 1546. In utilizing Melanchthon's *Preface* or "memoirs" for biographical information about Luther we do not want to be all too side-tracked by questions such as the following: Did the humanist rhetorician, Melanchthon, provide the real "story," a "historical biography," or perhaps more of a "commendation"/ *laudatio* in terms of a "hagiography"? The issue is rather complex, and cannot be treated here satisfactorily because it involves investigations into the genre of "biography," which is not clearly defined neither in antiquity, the Middle Ages, nor in Renaissance humanism.[140] It also would require looking into the nature of "hagiography" (*legenda*, as in *The Golden Legend*) and whether the inclusion of prayers would constitute it. Melanchthon

---

[137] See E. Gordon Rupp in 1957: "What do they know of Luther, who only Luther know?" as quoted by Else Marie Wiberg Pedersen, "The Significance of the Sola Fide and the Sola Gratia in the Theology of Bernard of Clairvaux (1090–1153) and Martin Luther (1483–1546)," LB 18 (2009): 20–43, here 20.

[138] Edited by Timothy Maschke, Franz Posset, and Joan Skocir, Joan, *Ad fontes Lutheri: Toward the Recovery of the Real Luther. Essays in Honor of Kenneth Hagen's Sixty-Fifth Birthday* (Milwaukee: Marquette University Press, 2001).

[139] See *Melanchthon deutsch,* vol. 2, eds. Michael Beyer, Stefan Rhein, and Günther Wartenberg (Leipzig: Evangelische Verlagsanstalt, 1997), 169.

[140] See Jozef Ijsewijn, "Die humanistische Biographie" in *Biographie und Autobiographie in der Renaissance. Arbeitsgespräch in der Herzog August Bibliothek Wolfenbüttel vom 1. bis 3. November 1982: Vorträge*, ed. August Buck (Wiesbaden: Harrassowitz, 1983), 2.

actually did include a prayer of thanksgiving to God that by the ministry of Martin Luther God removed the filth and poisons in order to restore the pure doctrine of the Church. Would Melanchthon's commemorative eulogy and prayer qualify as a distorted perspective due to the veneration he had for Luther? Or, did Melanchthon's account suffer the transformation into a "hagiography" shortly afterwards with the book title of 1555: History of the Life and Deeds of the Most Reverend Man D. Martin Luther, Doctor of the True Theology, Written in Good Faith by Philip Melanthon [sic] (*Historia de Vita et actis reverendissimi viri D. Martini Lutheri verae Theologiae Doctoris, bona fide conscripta a Philippo Melanthone*)?[141] This much is fairly clear: Melanchthon wanted to write about the real Luther who started out wanting to save souls, his own and others', but ended up in church-political controversies over ecclesiastical authority and with a Church split apart. For now, I work with the concept of "memoirs" as a reliable designation for his text.

The historical-critical method as applied in my Luther research leads me to some sort of source analysis (*Quellenscheidung*) as it makes no sense to prefer Table Talk that were first published in 1566 (by Aurifaber who was born in 1519) over Melanchthon (1497–1560) and his carefully assembled notes which he kept from personal interviews with Luther. Instead of constructing a Luther biography based upon, at times dubious, if not totally mistaken, Table Talk, it is more reasonable to build one on Melanchthon's memoirs, without trusting him blindly in everything.[142] Both, the Table Talk and Melanchthon's account, are based upon Luther's retrospectives. But, when it comes to weighing which one to trust, one may give more credence to the careful and cautious (at times, scrupulous) Melanchthon than to recollections of students during meals. Also, Melanchthon may have consulted Georg Major concerning Luther's text on the indulgences of 1517 as "it would not be unreasonable to assume"[143] that, if not Luther himself, Major could even have been the source for some of Melanchthon's recollections. Yet, in our search for

[141] On this issue, see, for instance, Wolfgang Brückner, "Luther, heiliger Mann oder falscher Prophet? Legende und Antilegende zwischen 1517 und 1630" in *Mythen Europas: Schlüsselfiguren der Imagination 4. Renaissance*, ed. Christine Strobl (Regensburg: Pustet, 2006), 37–57.

[142] On mistakes Melanchthon made, see Bornkamm, *Thesen und Thesenanschlag Luthers,* 24–40.

[143] Wengert, "Georg Major: An 'Eyewitness'," 93.

the historical Luther we do not rely on Table Talk, although Luther scholars will not likely disregard them completely.[144] If taken as "secondary literature" (see above) Table Talk has its place in Luther research when it corroborates points made in the primary sources.

[144] See Theo Bell, *Divus Bernhardus. Bernhard von Clairvaux in Martin Luthers Schriften* (Mainz: Philipp von Zabern, 1993), 341.

2. PHILIP MELANCHTHON'S MEMOIRS AS GUIDE

Fig. 5. Philip Melanchthon in 1526 at the age of 36, by Albrecht Dürer.

After having reflected on the issue of sources in Luther research and on the ways in which the 95 Theses entered the public arena, we now turn to the best available source for biographical data, i.e., Melanchthon's memoirs, in order to learn about his views of Luther's life and work.

Our knowledge of Philip Melanchthon seems limited.[1] One may see him as a faithful "theological secretary"[2] of the Reformation (which is not meant to minimize his role). I do not join those who claim that Melanchthon's biographical research on the young Luther resulted in a "monastic tale" (*Klosterlegende*).[3] It is not a dubious legend about an old man in the Erfurt friary who set Luther on the right path to a theology of penance. Melanchthon's "biographical memoirs" were used, after all, as the *Preface* to the Second Volume of Luther's collected works of 1546. They were taken very seriously already by earlier Luther researchers such as the Lutheran Julius Köstlin (1826–1902), who held that Luther already at Erfurt had become familiar with Saint Bernard's teaching.[4] This view seemed to contradict, at first glance, Luther's own *Preface* of 5 March 1545 to the First Volume of his works. Protestant researchers, however, did not take the assumed discrepancies as an opportunity to investigate Saint Bernard's influence on Luther. They rather spent much time in discrediting Melanchthon's report as a legend.[5] Luther himself in his own *Preface* of 1545 to the edition of his works recognized Melanchthon (after having worked with him for more than a quarter

---

[1] See Predigerseminar der Lutherstadt Wittenberg (ed.), *"Man weiß so wenig über ihn." Philipp Melanchthon, ein Mensch zwischen Angst und Zuversicht* (Wittenberg: Drei-Kastanien-Verlag, 2004; 2nd edition).

[2] See Junghans, "Philipp Melanchthon als theologischer Sekretär." It should be noted, however, that Junghans in characterizing Melanchthon in this way did not take Melanchthon's memoirs into consideration.

[3] Melanchthon's account would suffer from *perspektivischer Verzeichnung*, i.e., from a distortion of history from a certain perspective and that his report is supposedly a *wunderliche Anekdote*, an "odd anecdote" (the dictionary also offers "queer" and "strange" as a translation of *wunderlich*), Bell, *Divus Bernhardus*, 36–38.

[4] Julius Köstlin, *Life of Luther* (New York: Scribner's, 1913) (on internet, accessed February 2010), based upon the German original *Luthers Leben* (Leipzig: Fues, 1887).

[5] As Ulrich Köpf pointed out in "Bernhard von Clairvaux im Werk Martin Luthers. Bemerkungen zur neueren Forschung" and in "Martin Luthers Lebensgang als Mönch" in *Kloster Amelungsborn 1135–1985* (see note in Introduction).

of a century) as his theological partner who, too, was God's instrument.[6]

Another older researcher was the Lutheran systematic theologian Carl Stange (1870–1959) who as a rare exception interpreted Luther as a disciple of Saint Bernard along the outline of Melanchthon's memoirs. For the celebration of the Bernard Year 1953, Stange declared that Luther gained essential insights from a senior spiritual director in Erfurt who showed him "Bernard's Sermon for the Day of the Annunciation."[7] Reinhard Schwarz (1929–), a highly respected Lutheran Luther scholar, took up the scholarly insights of Stange,[8] and so did Ulrich Köpf (1941–). We may follow their direction.[9]

Before doing that, one may take issue with a recent, brief introduction about "Philip Melanchthon and the historical Luther" (2002) for an English translation of Melanchthon's report.[10] One may have reservations with respect to the observation that Melanchthon "presents Luther's life in a noticeably Melanchthonian fashion" by creating a Luther who rises heroically from the "dregs of late medieval Catholicism."[11] Unfortunately, this sounds more like a distortion than a help in the search of the "historical Luther." In reality, according to Melanchthon, Luther was made aware of the great, authentic theology of a medieval monk (no dregs here). Nor was there an "ism" then as in "Catholicism." Rather, Melanchthon presents a Luther deeply inspired by the Catholic saint, Bernard of Clairvaux.

---

[6] See Junghans, "Philipp Melanchthon als theologischer Sekretär," 149.

[7] See his *Bernhard von Clairvaux: Studien der Luther-Akademie* (Berlin: Alfred Töpelmann, 1954), 5; Posset, *Luther's Catholic Christology*, 120; Bell, *Divus Bernhardus*, 30.

[8] Referring to Melanchthon, CR 6, 159. Schwarz's comment: *In seiner Begegnung mit Bernhard hat es sich Luther eingeprägt, daß der Glaube auf den gekreuzigten Christus blicken soll, um der Barmherzigkeit Gottes inne zu werden. Der wahre Glaube stütze sich in persönlicher, vom heiligen Geist gewirkter Gewißheit auf die Vergebung in Christus; nur in der persönlichen Aneignung des Glaubensangebotes werde der Mensch vor Gott gerecht*; in "Martin Luther (1483–1546)" in *Große Mystiker: Leben und Wirken*, ed. Gerhard Ruhbach and Josef Sudbrack (Munich: Beck, 1984), 185–202, note 11.

[9] On the issue, see *Reformation und Mönchtum. Aspekte eines Verhältnisses über Luther hinaus*, eds. Athina Lexutt, Volker Mantey, and Volkmar Ortmann (Tübingen: Mohr, Siebeck, 2008).

[10] Ralph Keen's introduction in *Luther's Lives*, 7–13.

[11] Ibid., 12.

The same disregard of the Bernard factor in Luther's life (as mirrored in Melanchthon's memoirs) is to be observed when Luther is viewed between God and the devil and Bernard not being taken into consideration. It is not enough to point out with Melanchthon that Luther was an "instrument of God" (Melanchthon certainly was convinced of that),[12] but one must recognize also the concrete setting in life and what Melanchthon had to say about Luther's time at the Erfurt friary and the positive experience he had under the spiritual guidance of a senior friar who directed him to Saint Bernard.

2. 1. "We Shall Recite in Good Faith"

> [Luther] himself would have exposed [*exposita*] these things, wholly and copiously set forth and commemorated. For even if evil wishers were to reproach with that common saying, *He toots his own horn* [in Greek letters], nevertheless we know there was so much seriousness in him that he would have related the account with the utmost fidelity. And many good wise men are still living, to whom it would have been ridiculous for another account to be mixed in, as sometimes happens in poems, since he knew they were aware of the order of these events. But because his day of death turned aside the publication of so important an account, we shall recite in good faith about the same matters those things which partly we heard from the man himself, partly those which we ourselves saw.[13]

In the year 2010, which was to insiders a "Melanchthon Year" celebrating the 450th anniversary of his death on 19 April 2010, one should give this man a chance and allow him to become the compass and guide on the ocean journey to the historical Luther. However, the anniversary as such cannot be the only reason for taking this course; it is just the occasion. Melanchthon's view of Luther may be the closest in time and needs to be taken seriously. With Melanchthon one may counteract the most recent Luther biographies by younger German

---

[12] See Irena Backus, "Luther: Instrument of God or Satan's Brood. Main Developments in Luther Biography, 1546–81," in *Life Writing in Reformation Europe: Lives of Reformers by Friends, Disciples and Foes* (Aldershot: Ashgate, 2008), 1–46. The author did not work from Melanchthon's memoirs as edited in CR 6, but from Neander's 1841 edition of Luther's life.

[13] CR 6, 156.

Lutheran church historians.[14] They have some general remarks, for instance, on Bernard, but Melanchthon's account about the senior friar being in conversation with Luther about Bernard's teaching is not brought into play at all.[15]

Melanchthon was a Hellenist (Grecian) and a Hebraist, a rising humanist, a theologian (not ordained) who since 1518 was Luther's younger colleague at Wittenberg. Melanchthon arrived in Wittenberg on 25 August 1518. He can lead us to the historical Luther to a greater, but limited, degree of certainty. Here, too, one should not rely only on English translations, but work from the available, original source material. And, in relying on Melanchthon one must pay close attention to his humanist Latin.[16]

The relationship between Luther and the "real Philip Melanchthon" was part of the celebrations of the 500th anniversary of Melanchthon's birth in 1997.[17] It could still be celebrated after the 450th anniversary of Melanchthon's death (on 19 April 2010).[18] Melanchthon remains an important contemporary source for a biography of the historical Luther,[19] although he was often dismissed

---

[14] Thomas. Kaufmann (born 1962, Professor at the University of Göttingen, Luther biography of 2006; 2nd ed. 2010); Volker Leppin [born 1966; Professor at the University of Tübingen; Luther biography of 2006, 2nd ed. 2010).

[15] Even a critical thinker like Leppin relies heavily on the Table Talk; in his *Martin Luther* he quoted or referred to Table Talk more than 120 times; some of the sayings are quoted several times, one of them six times (no. 116) on Plautus, Virgil, and the Bible bound in red leather. See his position expressed in LQ (2008) as noted above.

[16] For instance, he used for "preaching" the Latin *concio* instead of *sermo* and "temple" for a "church building."

[17] See Timothy J. Wengert, "Beyond Stereotypes: The Real Philip Melanchthon," in *Philip Melanchthon: Then and Now (1497–1997); Essays Celebrating the 500th Anniversary of the Birth of Philip Melanchthon, Theologian, Teacher and Reformer*, eds. Scott H. Hendrix and Timothy J. Wengert (Columbia, SC: Lutheran Southern Seminary, 1997). Timothy J. Wengert, "Melanchthon and Luther / Luther and Melanchthon," in LuJ 66 (1999): 55–88; idem, *Der Theologe Melanchthon* (2000).

[18] Melanchthon, too, may have to be liberated from the distortions of his own history of impact (*Wirkungsgeschichte*). Siegfried Wiedenhofer, "Zum katholischen Melanchthon-Bild im 19. und 20. Jahrhundert," *Zeitschrift für Katholische Theologie* 102 (1980): 425–454.

[19] See Eike Wolgast, "Biographie als Autoritätsstiftung: Die ersten evangelischen Lutherbiographien" in *Biographie zwischen Renaissance und Barock: zwölf Studien*, ed. Walter Berschin (Heidelberg: Mattes, 1993), 41–71, here 51–60. Wolgast pointed out that due to Melanchthon's interest in history one may give him credence on issues such as Luther's birth in 1483 and the issue of the *Theses*. However, Wolgast failed to point out that Melanchthon did not speak of a "door" for the posting.

as unreliable. Grisar criticized Melanchthon's biographical sketch as written "with closed eyes to the defects of Luther's character."[20] This might be partly true. Yet, Luther's character flaws were not Melanchthon's topic or the center of his attention when he sketched Luther's life and work, in the way Grisar would have preferred it. Such a criticism is not a good enough reason to throw out Melanchthon's account altogether. Melanchthon's partial Luther-biography was given its final touch after Luther's death, but it is based upon notes from earlier interviews with Luther. At Luther's death rumors circulated that demons had seized the reformer on his deathbed and dragged him off to hell. Melanchthon took the opportunity to set the record straight.

Melanchthon's *Preface* to Volume Two is parallel to Luther's *Preface* to Volume One. Luther's is meant as an *introduction* to his Latin works that are published in the First Volume, not as an *autobiography.* Melanchthon in his memoirs in the Second Volume wanted to complement, however, what Luther said in the First Volume. Melanchthon appears to concentrate on filling the "gap" with information which Luther in Volume One did not cover, the years from his birth to 1517. Melanchthon presents all that he had learned from Luther himself in somewhat chronological order since Luther in Volume One had not intended to give a chronology of his life, but to provide some insights on the contents of the reprinted Latin texts. Therefore, Luther's *Praefatio* can hardly be used as a proof text for a chronology of his so-called "Reformation Discovery."[21]

2. 1. 1. THE TIME WHEN MELANCHTHON GATHERED BIOGRAPHICAL DATA

It is not clear when Melanchthon began to collect data for a Luther biography. But it is rather clear from the data in his *Preface* that they were not hastily and carelessly cobbled together shortly after Luther's death. One may surmise that Melanchthon started his collection of material for a Luther biography (or, for his own memoirs) as early as 1521 because his chronology in the *Preface* did not cover much beyond the year 1521.

---

[20] Grisar 580.

[21] See *Studienausgabe* V, 622

A clue for perhaps a penultimate draft of his biographical sketch of Luther may be found in Melanchthon's mention of the duke of Braunschweig: "And it is far from the truth that he [Luther] was secretly instigated and incited by princes, as the duke of Braunschweig wrote."[22] This reference to the mutual attacks of the duke and Luther in 1541 may be the only clue for the approximate date for his composition. It may still have been a draft. Or, his draft came into existence still later, perhaps around 20 October 1545, when Luther pursued the duke "with implacable hatred," as Hartmann Grisar put it.[23]

Up to this point we discussed the merits of Melanchthon's memoirs for Luther research. Now we turn to Luther's life as Melanchthon actually described it, starting with the information he had received from Luther's mother about the day and year of birth.

2. 1. 2. LUTHER'S MOTHER WAS UNCERTAIN OF THE YEAR OF HIS BIRTH

The year of his birth is somewhat uncertain.[24] His mother was not sure about the year, but she was adamant about the day. Melanchthon repeatedly had inquired about Martin's birthday. His inquiries show us how meticulously he proceeded. He published this report:

> . . . She remembered the day and hour exactly, but she was uncertain of the year. However she affirmed that he was born the night of 10 November after eleven o'clock, and the name Martin was given to the infant, because the next day, on which the infant was brought into the Church of God through Baptism, had been St Martin's Day. His brother Jacob, an honest and upright man, said the family believed that the year of his birth was A.D. 1483.[25]

The fact that Melanchthon reports that he had asked Luther's mother about "the time" (*de tempore*) of his birth "several times" (*aliquoties*) is peculiar. He wanted to be absolutely certain about the time because this factor is important for casting a person's horoscope,

---

[22] *Ac tantum abest, ut ab aulicis subornatus aut incitatus sit, sicut scripsit Dux Brunsvicensis,* CR 6, 162.

[23] Grisar 528.

[24] See Leppin, *Martin Luther,* 16.

[25] CR 6, 156. Jens Bulisch, "Wie alt ist Martin Luther geworden? Zum Geburtsjahr 1482 oder 1484," LuJ 77 (2010): 29-39.

and Melanchthon was a strong scholar of astronomy and astrology (which in his time were linked subjects).[26] Martin Luther's birth chart was to become a focus of debate amongst astrologers who wanted to establish whether he was sent by God or the Antichrist. Incidentally, Melanchthon wrote a speech on the dignity of astrology.[27]

2. 2. THE STUDENT AT ERFURT: INTERESTED IN THE CLASSICS—AND AN UNEXPLAINED EVENT

2. 2. 1. NOTE ON LUTHER'S INTERESTS

Melanchthon was told that Martin as a student at Erfurt read the ancient authors on his own initiative, as the Latin *ipse* in this context indicates.[28]

> And since his mind was eager for learning, he sought more and better things, and he himself on his own [*ipse*] read the many writings of the ancient Latin writers, Cicero, Virgil, Livy, and others.[29]

2. 2. 2. "I DO NOT KNOW THE CIRCUMSTANCES"

On our cruise on the ocean we may by-pass Stotternheim. Landfall at this overrated "holy ground" is optional because the story of the thunderstorm of Stotternheim is probably more legend than legitimate historiography. Melanchthon did not mention the town at all.[30] His

---

[26] See Stefano Caroti, "Melanchthon's Astrology" in Paola Zambelli (ed.), *'Astrologi hallucinati.' Stars and the End of the World in Luther's Time* (Berlin and New York: Walter de Gruyter, 1986), 109–121; Exhibition Catalogue: *Melanchthons Astrologie: Der Weg der Sternenwissenschaft zur Zeit von Humanismus und Reformation* (Lutherhalle Witttenberg, 1997); Markus Wriedt, "Zwischen Angst und Zuversicht: Melanchthon als Mensch des 16. Jahrhunderts" in *"Man weiß so wenig über ihn." Philipp Melanchthon, ein Mensch zwischen Angst und Zuversicht,* 9–32, here 17; Claudia Brosseder, "The Writing in the Wittenberg Sky: Astrology in Sixteenth-Century Germany, " *Journal of the History of Ideas* 66 (2005): 557–576.

[27] *De dignitate astrologiae*, CR 11, 261–265.

[28] See Junghans, *Der junge Luther,* 90.

[29] CR 6, 157.

[30] Nor does Luther's adversary, Johannes Cochlaeus, in his book about Luther's life, "The deeds and writings of Martin Luther from the year of the Lord 1517 to the year 1546 related chronologically to all posterity by Johannes Cochlaeus," in *Luther's Lives,* 55. Michael Weichenhan, "Luther und die Zeichen des Himmels"; Andreas Lindner, "Was geschah in Stotternheim? Eine problematische Geschichte und ihre problematische Rezeption" in *Luther und das monastische Erbe*, eds. Christoph

memoirs only say the following in the context of speaking about Luther's anxieties:

> [Luther] He felt those terrors either from the beginning or most sharply in that year when he lost a companion [*sodalem*]—I do not know the circumstances.[31]

Apparently, Luther gave Melanchthon no detailed information worthwhile to report. A new tour guidebook of 2006 by a German Lutheran publishing house no longer provides an entry on "Stotternheim"—despite the author's suggestive book title of offering a walk to Luther places in Luther's footsteps: *Auf Luthers Spuren*.[32]

There was no drama at Stotternheim, at least not according to Melanchthon who based his account on interviews with Luther. However, the issue of "death" was an important one. Luther confessed that he was driven by the terror over a sudden death, according to his autobiographical account in *On the Monastic Vows* of 1521. He, however, did not mention the name Stotternheim either.[33] The town became famous only because of its mention in Table Talk.[34] What could the reference to "death" mean? It may be a hint not so much concerning his fear for his own life, but for that of another student, whose death Luther may have witnessed in January 1505. Unfortunately, Melanchthon mentions no details.[35] If the frightening death situation was not a fatal duel, the fear of fatal

---

Bultmann, Volker Leppin, and Andreas Lindner (Tübingen: Mohr, Siebeck, 2007), 57–92 and 93–110.

[31] *Illos terrores seu primum, seu acerrimos sensit eo anno, cum sodalem, nescio quo casu interfectum, amisisset*; CR 6, 158. "*Nescio quo casu*" seems to be a standard expression; Schwiebert, 143, wrote: "Another experience of Luther's college days which left a deep impression upon him was the sudden death of a friend [CR 6, 158]. Melanchthon knew of and mentioned the event but added that he did not know the circumstances of its occurrence. But he considered it of parallel importance with the thunderstorm in its effects upon Luther."

[32] See Reinhard Dithmar, *Auf Luthers Spuren. Ein biographischer Reiseführer* (Leipzig: Evangelische Verlagsanstalt, 2006). He mentions Stotternheim in his introduction to the Erfurt friary, see 75.

[33] *Et ego de coelo terroribus me vocatum assererem, neque enim libens et cupiens fiebam monachus, multo minus vero ventris gratia, sed terrore et agone mortis sibitae circumvallatus vovi coactum et necessarium votum: 'Utinam (aiebas) non sit illusio et praestigum'*; 8, 573, 31–574, 2.

[34] See WA TR 4, 440, 8 (no. 4707).

[35] CR 6, 158 *Luther's Lives*, 14–16.

pestilence makes good sense which had broken out in Erfurt in 1505[36] and Luther would have fled from it, going home to Mansfeld on 20 June. If this is the case, much speculation about Luther's surprise visit at home is superfluous. At that occasion Luther may have informed his parents and relatives that he planned to join a religious order. Be that as it may, he returned on 2 July from Mansfeld to Erfurt and on 17 July entered the Augustinian friary at Erfurt, which maintained a college there.[37] Whether or not this was the only option or the only alternative available to him is an intriguing issue. Some monasteries accepted only members of noble families.[38]

2. 3. LUTHER CAME TO A *COLLOQUIUM* AND PETITIONED FOR ADMISSION

Luther apparently did not mention anything to Melanchthon about the marriage plans Martin's father had for him and that he may have wanted to flee from it into a religious order.[39] Neither the idea of a flight *from* any marriage plans (Volker Leppin, Thomas Kaufmann) nor the flight *into* the cloistered solitude (Richard Marius, 1933–1999, see below) is convincing; nor did Luther secretly and during the night slip away into the friary.[40] Melanchthon turns the reader's attention to a *colloquium* before entering the friary at Erfurt. Melanchthon's Latin wording is generally ignored, namely, that an initial *colloquium* took place (not: *collegium* [college], as an English translator assumes).[41] Melanchthon apparently must have heard Luther mention that he first went to the friary and had to go through some sort of a "qualifying entrance examination" for becoming an Augustinian at Erfurt.

---

[36] See Junghans, *Der junge Luther*, 44.

[37] Josef Pilvousek, "Martin Luther und Erfurt," in *Luther in Erfurt und die katholische Theologie*, ed. Josef Freitag (Leipzig: St. Benno Verlag, 2001), 13–27, here 15; the date is based upon the hint in Table Talk no. 4707: *In die Alexii,* WA TR 4, 440, 8–11.

[38] See Schwarz, *Luther*, 12.

[39] Leppin, *Martin Luther,* 28–34, makes Martin's rejection of his father's plan for him the main motivation for Luther to run away into a religious order.

[40] As the report of Justus Jonas would have it, dated 28 January 1538; Schwiebert 137.

[41] Frazel, 2004, as posted on Books.google.com/books?isbn=0719068029 . . . (accessed July 2010).

Luther with his master's degree in philosophy, at the age of twenty, had begun to study law, but then changed his mind at the age of twenty-one:

> But a short time later, when he was twenty-one, suddenly, against the opinion of his parents and relatives, he came to a *colloquium* with the Augustinian friars at Erfurt, and petitioned for admission.[42]

Apparently, the Erfurt friars did not accept just anybody who walked in. They first wanted to take a closer look at this potential postulant.[43]

In stark contrast, the legendary version lets Luther swear on July 2, 1505, while he was caught in a terrible thunderstorm: "St. Anne, help me! I will become a monk." The phrase containing the so-called "vow" of Stotternheim is based solely upon a Table Talk of 1539.[44] Oddly enough, the feast day of St. Anne is celebrated not on 2 July, but on 26 July. The date of the talk is thirty-four years removed from Luther's decision to join the friars at Erfurt. Richard Marius got this story about right, but his idea of a "flight" into the solitude of a monastery is flawed.[45] A critical examination of the Table Talk shows that Luther said that God understood his "vow" as spoken in the Hebrew language because "Anna" in Hebrew means "under grace."[46] *[H]anna* derived from the Hebrew root *hen*. Yet, is such a linguistic and religious self-interpretation from hindsight in agreement with reality? One may have doubts. Luther at that time did not have an inkling of Hebrew. How could he have "spoken the vow in the Hebrew language"? Luther did not want to make a historical-biographical, but a theological, statement. What he wanted to say is this. His life's journey is the outcome of God's grace. This is exactly what Luther told Melanchthon in different words (on 9 September 1521) when he confessed to Melanchthon that he is no longer sure in

---

[42] . . . *venit ad colloquium Monachorum Augustinianorum Erphordiae seque recipi petit . . . ;* CR 6, 158.

[43] See Todd's biography, Chapter 2.

[44] . . . *ut in terrore dixisset: Hilff du, S. Anna, ich wil ein monch werden! Sed Deus tum Hebraice meum votum intellexit: Anna, id est, sub gratia, non legaliter;* WA TR 4, 440, 8–11 (no. 4707).

[45] Harvard professor emeritus and novelist, with his biography *Martin Luther: The Christian between God and Death* (Cambridge, Mass.: Belknap Press of Harvard University Press, 1999).

[46] See Angelika Dörfler-Dierken, "Luther und die heilige Anna. Zum Gelübde von Stotternheim," LuJ 64 (1997): 19–46; Posset, *The Front-Runner*, 95.

which mental state he had made the promise. In any case, Luther told him that he was convinced that God wanted him to join the friars: *Gott hat es so gewollt*![47] This statement squarely fits with the notorious Table Talk about St. Anne and Stotternheim—however, only if understood theologically, that his becoming a religious occurred under God's grace. The suggestion that Luther called upon St. Anne because she is the patron saint of the mountain miners[48] is not essential. Melanchthon did not mention it nor did he hint at any terrifying lighting during the thunderstorm at the place by the name Stotternheim, nor did he use the notion "vow." Melanchthon only held up the suddenness of Luther's decision and that it was made to the surprise of his parents and relatives. Why then make so much of this legend? The Lutheran church historian Walther von Loewenich (1903–1992) mistakenly spoke of Luther swearing the *Mönchsgelübde* in the *Schreckensstunde*[49] (monastic vows in the hour of terror). Whatever Luther may have uttered when he was frightened was a serious promise, but not a formal "monastic vow." If it had happened it would have been more of a private promise to God (which nobody else would have heard).

2. 3. 1. BECOMING A MONK?

The English translation of Melanchthon's account has Luther becoming an "Augustinian Monk," which is an oxymoron because the so-called "Hermits of Saint Augustine" are actually friars. Routinely, English translators make the mistake of making him a "monk." They naively render the German *Mönch* with "monk," as they are seduced by the linguistic and phonetic similarity of German *Mönch* and English *Monk*. Unfortunately, they do not utilize the neat distinction which the English language offers: the differentiation of monks and friars. Such translating proves the wisdom of the saying that translations always are also interpretations. In this case a bad one.

By making Luther a "monk" the historians and their translators steer their readership and audience in the wrong direction. They set them on the wrong track and set them up for everlasting misconceptions. Time and again one reads in English translations that

---

[47] See WA Br 2, 384, 79 (no. 428).
[48] See Bernhard Lohse, Martin Luther. *Eine Einführung in sein Leben und sein Werk* (third edition, Munich: Beck, 1997), 37.
[49] Loewenich 53.

Martin Luther was a "monk."[50] One may assume that this flawed expression has its *Nachleben* also in the foreign translations, for instance, of a popular Luther biography, being carried over into the Korean, Chinese, Portuguese, Finnish, and Estonian editions.[51] The constant repetition of a flawed translation does not make it right. There is a big difference between monks and friars.

Translators often do not seem to know that the German language is too simplistic in this case as it provides only one word for the variety of professed religious men in religious orders, be they Benedictine, Cistercian, or Carthusian monks on the one hand and Augustinian, Dominican, and Franciscan friars on the other hand. "Monks" properly understood are permanent residents at the abbey or monastery of their choice. Their life is governed by the Rule of Saint Benedict which includes the life-long attachment to the one location they have chosen and are then bound to adhere to the *stabilitas loci*. The historical Luther was not attracted to the contemplative life which monks offer in their (normally) remote abbeys and monasteries that are established in the Benedictine tradition. Monks under the Rule of Saint Benedict, properly understood, are primarily concerned with "Pray and Work" (*Ora et Labora*), with prayerful Bible reading (*lectio divina*), meditation, and contemplation as they seek union with God in prayer, and as they are working with their own hands for their livelihood.

The city of Erfurt offered Luther a choice from among several abbeys and friaries. This city was then one of the largest ones in German speaking lands, nicknamed "Little Rome."[52] There were not only the two Benedictine abbeys, one on Peter's Hill (founded in 1059) and one called *Schottenkloster* (founded in 1136 by Irish monks), but also the Carthusian monastery in the southern part of the

[50] For example: Roland H. Bainton, *Here I Stand* (Chapter 1) (New York: Abingdon Press, 1950); James M. Kittelson (1941–2003), whose recent reprint (2003) of the 1986 biography keeps the expression "Augustinian monk"; Helmar Junghans, "Luther's Wittenberg" in *The Cambridge Companion to Martin Luther*, ed. Donald K. McKim (New York: Cambridge University Press, 2003), 20–36. Rightly Jared Wicks wrote of "Brother Martin, Augustinian Friar," in *Lutheran Forum* 42 (2008): 33–36; so does Kenneth Hagen, "So You Think Luther Was a Monk? Stop It," *Logia* 19 (2010): 35–37.

[51] On the foreign translations of James Kittelson's book, see Carter Lindberg, "In memoriam James M. Kittelson" in LuJ 73 (2006): 12.

[52] Loewenich 44.

city (founded in 1371). Was Luther driven by the desire to become a contemplative monk, and perhaps by the desire to join the most severe monastic life style available to him in his days? No. The historical Luther did not seem to have sought out the strictest or harshest religious order he could find, as a well-known, older Lutheran Luther biographer once proposed.[53]

Unlike the monks, the friars were used to moving around from city to city and are accustomed to being ordered around in order to take on pastoral assignments in the cities where they were needed most. Luther was easily transferred back and forth from Erfurt to Wittenberg. In contrast to friars, monks by definition were not *Seelsorger* (pastors, German: *Seelsorger,* Latin: *curati*) for others outside their monastic walls. Monks are not even always priests. They normally did not *seelsorgen*, to use a verb which Luther employed.[54]

Luther was not necessarily attracted by the ordination to the priesthood or becoming a liturgist celebrating Masses like a parish priest (German: *Leutpriester*, Latin: *plebanus*). When or if the historical Luther sorted out his options,[55] as to the monastery or friary in Erfurt, he evidently did not make a decision based upon the names of the founders of the orders such as Saint Benedict or Saint Augustine. Under the latter's name priests at Erfurt had organized themselves as the Augustinian canons (*Augustiner–Chorherren*) at the church of the regulated priests (*Reglerkirche*).

There were four different mendicant orders at Erfurt: The Dominicans had a friary on the left bank, the Franciscans on the right bank of the Broad Creek. A third option would have been the Servites, or "Servants of the Holy Virgin" (*Marienknechte*), on the eastside of town.[56] "Mendicants" evokes at times some strange connotations of "beggars" roaming the medieval streets. The term has a specific meaning as to the way these mendicant friars earned their living.[57] The word "mendicant" (begging) means primarily that the friars depended on donations or on temporal monetary contracts for

[53] See Heinrich Boehmer (1869–1927), 36.

[54] Luther's expression *seelsorgen* is a verb: "to do pastoral care." It is no longer in use in contemporary German; Posset, "Lehrer der Seelsorge," 6–7.

[55] Leppin, *Martin Luther,* 34 and 36, works with the assumption that Luther had a choice—something which is not that clear-cut.

[56] See Boehmer 36.

[57] On the difference between monks and mendicant friars, see Posset, *The Front-Runner*, 8.

their preaching activities in certain, clearly defined, determined areas. For the storage of food and wine donations they used buildings at a branch office in a given town or region where they were allowed to preach; such as location was called a *terminus*. The friar in charge of collecting and storing goods that were donated or delivered to a *terminus*, usually the preacher himself, was called a *terminarius*. The friary at Wittenberg had grown out of a branch office (*terminus*) of the friary of Herzberg, located south-east of Wittenberg.[58]

Independently from the English translation issue (monk/friar), the distinction of monk and friar *is* important and should not be played down in assuming that in Luther's days such a differentiation was "blurred."[59] Such a thesis would be hard to prove. Admittedly, Melanchthon, the young layman who was likely not familiar with the various versions of monastic life, made no mention of any potential options Luther may have had for the religious life. Yet, to Luther it must have been important that the Augustinian friars were not monks (who by definition were not involved in pastoral care outside their own abbeys). In contrast, Augustinians are a fraternal organization of highly educated preachers and curates who knew how to shepherd souls, including troubled ones. Luther obviously experienced personally the preaching activities of the Erfurt Augustinians. They held prestigious preacher positions not only at the cathedral, the main church of Erfurt (the *Dom*), but also at other churches in the city. We know them as preachers at the oldest Benedictine Abbey, the one on Peter's Hill. Apparently, the Benedictine monks had no well-trained preachers from their own ranks. It was customary for abbeys and cathedrals to hire friars to fill the full-time preacher positions which were securely financed from endowment funds. We also know that the local Cistercian nuns hired Augustinian friars as preachers for their St. Martin church.[60]

---

[58] See Posset, *The Front-Runner*, 74. The Augustinians of Munich had a *terminus* at Salzburg (not a friary as such). Staupitz (in Salzburg in 1510) had to make sure that certain goods were handed over to his order's branch office; see Posset, *The Front-Runner*, 134.

[59] Without offering evidence, this thesis is promoted by Leppin, *Martin Luther,* 35. Even if it could be proved that the distinction was blurred, it would not excuse the English translators from making the distinction between monk and friar in English publications.

[60] See Christoph Burger, "Der Augustinereremit Martin Luther in Kloster und Universität bis zum Jahre 1512" in *Kloster Amelungsborn 1135–1985,* 170. In

Luther was drawn to the Augustinians. Melanchthon explicitly mentions the "College of the Augustinians" as part of the university system of Erfurt. Melanchthon may have implicitly provided an answer to the question why Luther shortly after the beginning of his study of law decided to join the Augustinians. Luther may have wanted to be more like the known preachers in town, men who could articulate spiritual matters, help troubled consciences, and interpret the Scriptures well. Luther surely was familiar with them. The fact that the Augustinians had a college in Erfurt was appealing to the graduate student, who, as we know, had already developed a desire to read the whole Bible even before he entered the order of the Augustinians.[61] The aspect of a biblical spirituality for which Augustinians were known appears more significant and relevant than the idea that Luther was interested in the seamless continuation of his philosophical-theological studies with which he had become familiar in his pre-monastic years at the faculty of arts of the University of Erfurt.[62]

With his interest in the Bible Luther impressed the Augustinians and in turn their order looked attractive to the budding humanist.[63] They were in the process of opening up to humanism—not to the version of later Erasmian anthropology, but to one that wanted to return *ad fontes*, to investigate the original meaning of the Scriptures in Hebrew and Greek.

2. 3. 2. THE BUDDING HUMANIST BECOMES A BIBLICAL HUMANIST WITHIN THE FRIARY

One could have expected that he joined the Franciscans. The prior at the Franciscan friary of Eisenach was Johann Braun (1470–1516), a good friend of Luther. In the fifteenth century the Saxon Franciscans had a very famous Bible scholar in Matthias Doring (Thoring, Döring, ca. 1390–1469). If indeed as a student in Erfurt Luther was already interested in the Scriptures he could have come across the

---

Luther's days other monasteries for women at Erfurt were the three that belonged to the Benedictine order. There also were nunneries of the Cistercians, the Augustinians, and the Ursulines (*Magdalenerinnen*).

[61] See Heinz Endermann, "Martin Luther in Erfurt: Student. Mönch und Wissenschaftler," *Luther* 72 (2001): 83–95, here 94. See below on Luther and Trutfetter.

[62] As Lohse, 38, assumed.

[63] See Leppin, *Martin Luther,* 24–28.

name of Doring who had been a professor at the University of Erfurt. His contributions to the late-medieval Latin Bible commentaries in the form of *Responses* were always included in the Bible editions of that time. Doring was also known as the defender of the *Postils* of his Franciscan confrere Nicholas of Lyra (1270–1349) against the criticisms (called *Additions*) of Bishop Paul of Burgos (1351–1435) who was a Thomist (but not a member of the Dominican order). This historical context (the tradition of Franciscan Bible commentaries) makes the question even more pressing as to why Luther did not enter the order of Saint Francis, but the order of Saint Augustine.

Melanchthon in his memoirs made no mention of any possible choices from among the religious orders. The question is important, though. There are some good educated guesses as to why the Augustinians looked attractive to Luther: (a) He was inwardly already well prepared to become a religious (not so much a parish priest). Whatever happened to Luther prior to his entry into the religious order must have accelerated his considerations of becoming a religious. (b) Luther had come to know the Augustinian friars from their pastoral work and preaching at Erfurt's major churches.[64] (c) The Erfurt Augustinian friary was the largest and most significant friary in the Saxon Province and it housed the order's college that was integrated into the University of Erfurt. The Augustinian friary "excelled all others in learning and practical activity."[65] (d) The Augustinian friars were in the process of opening up to humanism. Notably, Luther was allowed to bring books with him into the friary. He felt he could not part with two books of pagan writers, the comedian Plautus and Virgil.[66] (e) Perhaps, Luther was aware of the order's *Constitutions* that just came off the press (in 1504, see Fig. 6) with their focus on Scripture studies. (f) Luther may have wanted to continue his search for truth with friars who influenced his previous studies. The combination of these motifs represents a strong pull toward the Augustinians at Erfurt, rather than to the Franciscans be

---

[64] See Adolar Zumkeller, "Martin Luther und sein Orden," *Analecta Augustiniana* 25 (1962): 254–290, here 256–25; Loewenich 52–53; Lohse 37.

[65] Grisar 23.

[66] See Junghans, *Der junge Luther*, 13 and 80; Reinhard Schwarz, "Beobachtungen zu Luthers Bekanntschaft mit antiken Dichtern und Geschichtsschreibern," LuJ 54 (1987): 7–22; based on Table Talk no. 116, WA TR 1, 44, 21–23 (1531, Veit Dietrich).

they at Eisenach or at Erfurt. Luther himself did not provide any clues as to why he joined the Augustinians.[67]

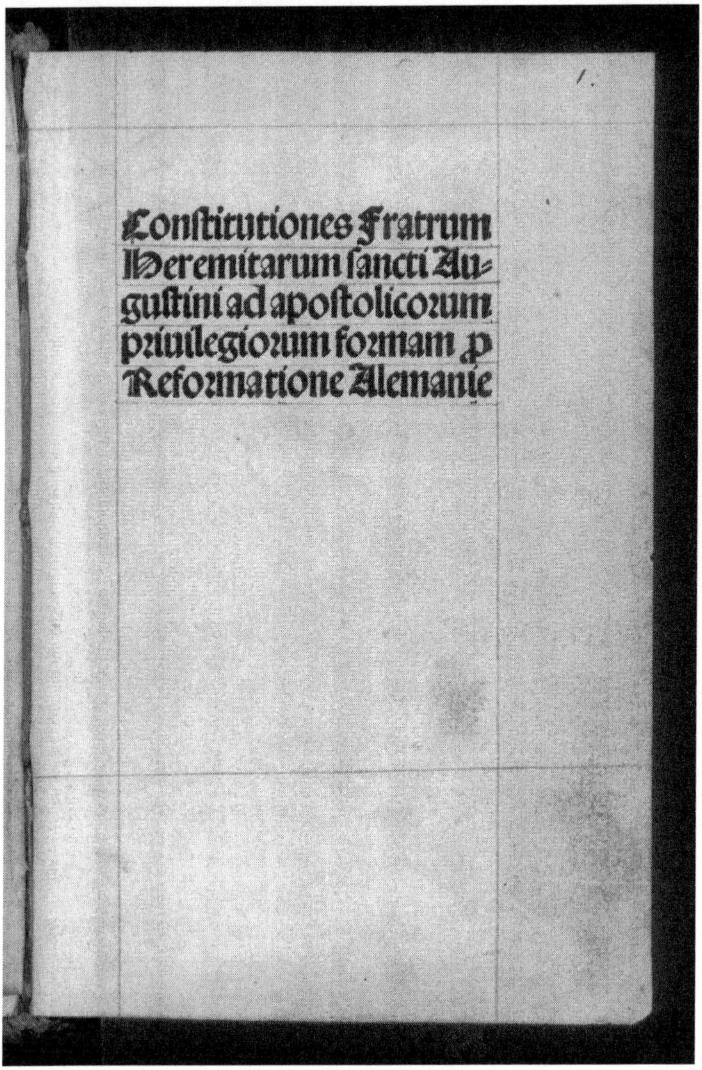

Fig. 6. The first print of the *Constitutions of the Augustinian Order*, 1504.

[67] See Köpf, "Martin Luthers Lebensgang als Mönch," 190; Burger 169; Josef Pilvousek, "Askese, Brüderlichkeit und Wissenschaft" in *Luther und das monastische Erbe*, 39–92; Leppin, *Martin Luther,* 35.

Still, one of the most recent German biographers simplistically wrote of Luther's "Conversion to monasticism."[68] One may find this way of describing Luther's entry odd considering the fact that Melanchthon did not use this kind of language at all. He pointed out, however, that it was definitely not the mendicant element in the Augustinian order that attracted Luther: "Not poverty but eagerness for piety led him into this mode of monastic life."[69] This means that Luther either was not aware or ignored the aspect of "mendicant," which was changing and which gave the mendicant orders a less favorable image. Those for the most part highly educated friars were lumped together with ordinary "beggars" as the Alsatian satirist Sebastian Brant (1457–1521) ridiculed them as begging vagabonds in his 1494 *The Ship of Fools*.[70]

2. 3. 3. THE POSTULANT IN THE FRIARY (FROM 17 JULY TO THE BEGINNING OF SEPTEMBER 1505)

Evidently, the initial *colloquium* turned out in Luther's favor, as he was admitted "for the observation of 'the state of his soul'," [71] which must have lasted until early September 1505. Apparently the historical Luther was able to convince the friars that his decision was in accord with the will of God. The prior of the friary was Winand von Diedenhofen (Dydenhofen, no dates known), who together with other friars determined Luther's suitability for their order. He became a novice for one year (up to September 1506). Within eight months he was ordained a priest (April / May 1507).[72]

2. 3. 4. IN HIS FIRST YEAR IN THE ORDER: READING THE DISPUTATION BETWEEN ARIUS AND ATHANASIUS

Luther mentioned in 1531 that in "his first year" at the Erfurt friary, i.e., 1505/1506, he eagerly had read the disputation between Arius

[68] Kaufmann 32.

[69] CR 6, 158.

[70] See Christopher Ocker, "'Rechte Arme' und 'Bettler Orden'. Eine neue Sicht der Armut und die Delegitimierung der Bettelmönche" in *Kulturelle Reformation: Sinnformationen im Umbruch 1400–1600*, eds. Bernhard Jussen and Craig Koslofsky (Göttingen: Vandenhoeck & Ruprecht, 1999), 129–158.

[71] Schwiebert 146; see Boehmer 41.

[72] See Todd, Chapter 2. Ordination happened rapidly (by our standards), but probably not so at that time.

and Athanasius, *D. Athanasii libri contra idolatriam Gentium, & de fide Sancte Trinitatis.*[73] He did this upon recommendation by his superior who himself had made a copy of it. In his Preface of 24 November 1531 to Johann Bugenhagen's edition of this fictitious disputation Luther did not mention the superior's name, but one may assume that it was the novice master Johann von Greffenstein (more on him in Chapter 3). In 1531 Luther was very happy to write the preface for Bugenhagen's edition because in this text the pure doctrine of the Holy Trinity is preserved and defended.[74] Luther was always impressed by Athanasius as an exemplary bishop and teacher of the Church and his struggle against Arius.[75] However, Athanasius' teaching played no significant role in Luther's further development. Such lack of impact is mirrored in the fact that Athanasius is not mentioned in Melanchthon's memoirs about Luther's life—quite in contrast to the significance of Bernard of Clairvaux whose role Melanchthon brilliantly lifts up in his biographical sketch, as we shall see.

2. 4. LUTHER BEING PREPARED FOR "SCRIPTURE ALONE"

2. 4. 1. "ONE OWES FAITH TO SACRED SCRIPTURE ALONE"

One point (e) needs to be lifted up: Prior to entering the religious order (1501–1505) Luther was taught by his professor of philosophy in Erfurt, Jodocus Trutfetter who was open to humanism and was a respected representative of the "modern way" [*via moderna*]).[76] From

---

[73] See WA 30-III, 530, 5–531, 2; see *Vigilius von Thapsus, "Die Disputation zwischen Arius und Athanasius." Luthers erste Klosterlektüre. Ein Beitrag zur Lutherforschung*, eds. Theobald Beer and Alma von Stockhausen (Weilheim-Bierbronnen: Gustav-Siewert-Akademie, 1999). However, Beer's interpretation is untenable and unacceptable that the young Luther had entered the order with his preconceived, fixed, heretical thinking for which not even his reading of Athanasius versus Arius made any difference (29).

[74] . . . *vt iste articulus de trinitate purus & integer, in Ecclesia Dei, seruetur & defendatur*; WA 30-III, 531, 4–5.

[75] See Bernhard Lohse, "Luther und Athanasius" in *Auctoritas Patrum. Zur Rezeption der Kirchenväter im 15. und 16. Jahrhundert*, eds. Leif Grane, Alfred Schindler and Markus Wriedt (Mainz: Philipp von Zabern, 1993), 97–115.

[76] He taught at Wittenberg from 1507 to 1510; see Martin Treu, "Die Leucorea zwischen Tradition und Erneuerung. Erwägungen zur frühen Geschichte der Universität Wittenberg" in *Martin Luther und seine Universität. Vorträge anläßlich*

him Luther learned that one "owes faith to the Sacred Scripture alone." Luther pointed this out, not in a Table Talk, but in his letter of 9 May 1518.[77] Luther is prepared for his later advocacy of "Scripture Alone" through Trutfetter's teaching, i.e., to place one's faith in the "canonical Scriptures alone." All this happened prior to his entry into the Augustinian order. As an aside, on the eve of the "Reformation" there was a canonistic tradition supporting the assertion of the supreme authority of Scripture over councils or ecclesiastical authorities.[78]

The *Tendenz* to downplay Trutfetter's impact on young Luther in this regard needs to be questioned. The argument goes as follows: because of the mere fact that Trutfetter was a scholastic teacher he could not have taught the "Reformation Principle."[79] I beg to differ. Trutfetter was a representative of the peaceful co-existence of scholasticism and humanism,[80] or "Scholastic Humanism."[81] In terms of *Sola Scriptura* there was a continuum from Trutfetter via Luther, the undergraduate student in the faculty of arts, prior to his entry into the order, to Luther's later applications of the Scripture principle to

---

des 450. Todestages des Reformators, ed. Heiner Lück (Cologne, Weimar, Vienna: Böhlau, 1998), 31–51, here 40.

[77] *Ex te primo omnium didici, solis canonicis libris deberi fidem*; letter to Trutfetter of 9 May 1518; WA Br 1, 169–171 (no. 74), here 171, 72–73. On Trutfetter, see Wolfgang Urban, "Die 'via moderna' an der Universität Erfurt am Vorabend der Reformation, in *Gregor von Rimini: Werk und Wirkung bis zur Reformation*, ed. Heiko A. Oberman (Berlin and New York, de Gruyter, 1981), 311–330.

[78] Hermann Schuessler, "Sacred Doctrine and the Authority of Scripture in Canonistic Thought on the Eve of the Reformation," in *Reform and Authority in the Medieval and Reformation Church,* eds. Guy Fitch Lytle and Uta-Renate Blumenthal (Washington DC: The Catholic University of America Press, 1981), 55–68.

[79] *"Allein schon die Tatsache, dass Luther dies auf seinen scholastischen Lehrer zurückführt, macht deutlich, dass etwas anderes gemeint ist als das reformatorische Schriftprinzip."* Leppin, *Martin Luther*, 377, note 133. Leppin seems to follow Oberman who opined that Trutfetter's maxim on Scripture alone should not be understood as the later "Protestant maxim" because "after all *sola scriptura* is the fundamental principal [sic] of the entire scholastic disputation tradition." Oberman confirmed the principle as essential in scholasticism while at the same time he does not want to connect it to the "later Protestant maxim." See his "Martin Luther Contra Medieval Monasticism: A Friar in the Lion's Den" in *Ad fontes Lutheri*, 182–213, here 186.

[80] See Grisar 28; Junghans, *Der junge Luther*, 42 and 188.

[81] See Herbert Rommel, *Über Luthers Randbemerkungen von 1509 bis 1510* (Thesis [Kiel, 1931]), as referred to by Schwiebert 135.

pastoral care and theology. In between, there was his training in the friary.

Melanchthon did not mention the maxim of Luther's professor Trutfetter concerning "Scripture alone," nor did he give a hint that the young Luther was open to humanist ideas at the time when Luther came to the friary with two pagan books under his arms, nor did he mention that Luther received a complete Bible (either upon arrival or, at the beginning of his novitiate). The myth that in Luther's early days the Bible lay hidden under a bench[82] supposedly unused may easily be debunked.

2. 4. 2. THE NOVICE WAS DIRECTED TO READ THE BIBLE AVIDLY

"Meanwhile, the impressionable young brother of twenty-one was feeding on the rich diet of the Bible, both in choir and his cell. He had a copy for his own use with a red cover to it, as he recalled in later years."[83] The Augustinian order appeared quite "liberal" in its openness to the new movement of humanism. Humanism was actively promoted from the top down by the order's general in Rome, Egidio da Viterbo (1469–1532, Giles of Viterbo), and locally by Johann von Staupitz in Saxony, leader of the Reformed Saxon Augustinians and a professor of the Sacred Page in Wittenberg. Staupitz was particularly open to humanism.[84] Luther moved from the *bursa*, the student dormitory with its humanistic orientation,[85] into a friary that was receptive to humanism, not an illogical step, but easy to understand. Luther himself worked toward the humanistic ideal of the polyglot humanists and he was quickly accepted as one of them.[86]

---

[82] See Grisar 25.

[83] Todd, Chapter 2, based on Table Talk no. 116 (the same that Leppin used so often) insinuates in one and the same train of thought that "here the friars gave him a Bible bound in red leather." *Nullos secum in monasterium abstulit praeter Plautum et Virgilium. Ibi monachi ei dederunt bibliam rubro corio tectam*; WA TR 1, 44, 21–24 (no. 116).

[84] Junghans, *Der junge Luther*, 49–56 (*Der Humanismus bei den Augustinereremiten)*; Posset, *The Front-Runner*, 96–102 (Staupitz: open to humanism).

[85] Junghans, *Der junge Luther*, 32–33; idem, "Bibelhumanistische Anstöße in Luthers Entwicklung zum Reformator," *Revue d'Histoire et de Philosophie Religieuses* 85 (2005): 17–42; Endermann 86.

[86] See Franz Posset, "Polyglot Humanism in Germany circa 1520 as Luther's Milieu and Matrix: The Evidence of the 'Rectorate Page' of Crotus Rubeanus," *Renaissance and Reformation* (Canada): 27 (2003, issued in 2004): 5–33; appeared in LD 14

Spalatin, one of Luther's humanist friends, was the first who used the Graecized family name, Eleutherius, for the heading of Luther's Latin text on the Lord's Prayer of 1516: *Oratio dominica enarratore F[fratre] M. Eleutherio Aureliano MDXVI.* [87] Luther sent his *Propositions* which he called *Paradoxa* on 11 November 1517 to his confrere, the humanist Johann Lang in the Erfurt friary, and signed the cover letter with the Graecized humanist name *Eleutherius*,[88] "the freed one" or "the freer,"[89] notably in the immediate context of the coming into existence of the Ninety-Five *Propositions*. But perhaps there is no deeper meaning than Luther wanting to parade his knowledge of Greek to the friend who taught him this language. Luther used this Graecized name in his correspondence only between 1516 and 1519.[90]

Another indication that Luther was a humanist was his eager reading of the Italian monastic humanist, Johannes Baptista Mantuanus (1448–1516), a Carmelite friar.[91] When the young Luther at Erfurt was reading Augustine's *The City of God*, he made a reference to this well known monastic humanist.[92]

The Erfurt friary of the Augustinians belonged to the Saxon Reform Congregation which claimed (justified or not) a stricter observance of their Rule and proper adherence to their *Constitutions* than non-reformed Augustinian friaries. The leader of the Reformed

---

(2006): 97–103; Helmar Junghans, "Der Einfluss des Humanismus auf Luthers Entwicklung bis 1518," LuJ 37 (1970): 37–101. Christiane Maass and Annett Volmer, eds., *Mehrsprachigkeit in der Renaissance* (Heidelberg: Winter, 2005).

[87] WA 59, 23, 1–2, with note 1. *Aurelianus* is a hint at Luther as a member of the order of Aurelius Augustinus.

[88] *Ecce alio denuo Paradoxa mitto . . . . F. Martinus Eleutherius, imo dulos et captivus nimis*; WA Br 1, 121, 4 and 122, 56 (no. 52); Posset, *Luther's Catholic Christology*, 29.

[89] See Leppin, *Martin Luther,* 124–125, who sees in this name change, including from *Luder* to *Luther*, the real significance of the happenings in the fall of 1517, and not the often retold Nailing of the Theses on the door of the castle church. Kaufmann 17 takes a similar position.

[90] See Moeller und Stackmann in *Luder—Luther—Eleutherius.* 26, 36–37.

[91] See Morimichi Watanabe, "Martin Luther's Relations with Italian Humanists: With Special Reference to Ioannes Baptista Mantuanus," LuJ 54 (1987): 23–47; Franz Posset, "'Heaven is on Sale'. The Influence of the Italian Humanist and Carmelite Friar Baptist Mantuanus on Martin Luther," *Carmelus* 36 (1989): 134–144.

[92] *Vide baptis[tam] Mant[uanum]* . . . ; Jun Matsuura, *Erfurter Annotationen 1509–1510/11. Archiv zur Weimarer Ausgabe der Werke Martin Luther* (Weimar, Cologne, Vienna: Böhlau, 2009), 619.

Congregation for a long time had been Andreas Proles (1429–1503) who died two years before Luther entered the order. Staupitz succeeded him. When considering the real Luther, one cannot disregard Luther's specific membership in the reformed branch of the order of Saint Augustine which became known for its study of the Scriptures.

We do not know whether every novice in the Augustinian friary received a Bible or whether it was just Luther who had shown great interest in Bible reading (being prepared by Trutfetter) and for that reason received one. It appears rather extraordinary that a novice would have had a complete Bible at his disposal. Be this as it may, Luther's pre-monastic interest in the Bible[93] was happily matched by the Augustinian order's strong emphasis on the centrality of the Bible, as the *Constitutions* of the order prove.[94] Its printing conspicuously coincided with the time when Luther joined the reformed friary at Erfurt (summer 1505). An original print of the *Constitutions* is extant at the library of Jena.[95] These *Constitutions* date back to the late thirteenth century (1287/1290). In Chapter 17 of the Augustinians' *Constitutions* the following directive is given which suggests the meaning of the maxim of Scripture Alone, *sola scriptura*:

> [A friar] is to read the Sacred Scripture avidly, listen to it devoutly, and learn it fervently. *Sacram scripturam avide legat, devote audiat et ardenter addiscat.*[96]

---

[93] See Grisar 25.

[94] *Constitutiones fratrum Eremitarum sancti Augustini ad Apostolicorum privilegiorum formam pro reformatione Alemanniae* (Nuremberg: Höltzel, 1504) in *Johann von Staupitz: Gutachten und Satzungen. Sämtliche Schriften,* vol. 5, ed. Wolfgang Günter (Berlin and New York: Walter de Gruyter, 2001), 144–319; see Posset, *The Front-Runner,* 88 and 96; idem, "Sola Scriptura—Martin Luther's Invention? Commemorating the 500th Anniversary of the Printed Edition of the *Constitutions* of the Order of St. Augustine in Nuremberg in 1504–1506," *Augustiniana* 56 (2006): 123–127; appeared in LD 17 (2009): 57–58.

[95] See Jena University Library, Signatur: 8 Hist.eccl.VIII, 10. A real cause of ecumenical celebration should have been the year 2004 for the 500th anniversary of the first printing of their *Constitutions* which Johann von Staupitz arranged in 1504, for commemorating the Augustinian order's adherence to the priority of the Scriptures and its impact on Luther.

[96] Günter ed., *Johann von Staupitz: Gutachten und Satzungen*, 194, 38–39. Richard D. Balge, "Martin Luther, Augustinian," in Edward C. Friedrich, Siegbert W. Becker, David P. Kuske, eds., *Luther Lives. Essays in Commemoration of the 500th Anniversary of Martin Luther's Birth* (Milwaukee: Northwestern Publishing House,

Luther is the personification of this medieval directive. This directive is the matrix for Luther's biblical theology and hermeneutics.

Although the directive about intensive Bible studies may easily be drowned out by all the other rules and regulations in this particular chapter, it is indeed contained in them. The fervent study of the Sacred Scripture is the noblest task for the friars, a kind of divine service.

The notions "Scripture principle" and "Scripture alone" are often used as watchwords to distinguish Protestants from Catholics. However, the notion "Scripture principle" is an invention of the nineteenth century[97] and "Scripture alone" as a fundamental concept is much older than Luther, although known primarily as a post-Reformation slogan.[98] As to Luther's biblical theology that follows from the focus given by his order's *Constitutions,* one should not get trapped in the later theological debate about Scripture and Tradition at the Council of Trent. For the historical Luther the issue was not so much Scripture versus Tradition, but biblical theology versus philosophical theology.

The expression "Scripture Alone" is not found verbatim anywhere in the historical Luther's vocabulary. The young friar simply faithfully obeyed the directive that was given him through the *Constitutions*. The priority of the Scriptures has a long pre-Lutheran tradition inside and outside of his order. What was new with the developing Reformer is his determination and also his radicalism in the handling and employing of the Scripture principle which he had inherited from the tradition in his religious order, with its practice of Scripture meditation to which any young novice was introduced.[99]

1983), 7–20, here 8. Adolar Zumkeller, "The Augustinian School of the Middle Ages," in John E. Rotelle, ed., *Theology and History of the Augustinian School in the Middle Ages* (n. p., Augustinian Press, 1996), 11.

[97] See Walter Sparn, Art. "Sola scriptura" in *Dictionary of the Reformation*, eds. Klaus Ganzer and Bruno Steimer, trans. Brian McNeil (New York: Crossroad, 2004) (based on the German *Lexikon für Theologie und Kirche*).

[98] See Anthony N. S. Lane, "Sola Scriptura? Making Sense of a Post-Reformation Slogan" in *A Pathway into the Holy Scripture* eds. Philip E. Satterthwaite and David F. Wright (Grand Rapids: Eerdmans, 1994), 297–327.

[99] See Chapter 2 (*Meditation bei den Augustinereremiten*) in Martin Nicol, *Meditation bei Luther* (Göttingen: Vandenhoeck & Ruprecht, 1984), 30, note 28, with reference to the *Constitutions'* emphasis on spiritual, not exegetical Bible reading.

The real Luther wanted to read the Bible without philosophical (Scholastic) filters, and thus without a specific hermeneutics: "Luther demanded for the interpretation of the Scriptures quite a special theory of understanding—namely none."[100] Luther wanted to read the Bible "with closed eyes" (*clausis oculis*), i.e., closed to any philosophical speculation or other influences such as private revelations, etc., in strictly following the monastic tradition of reading the Sacred Page in the prayerful way of *lectio divina*, reading it "avidly, listening to it devoutly, and learning it fervently."

He was convinced that Scripture can interpret itself. The eminent Lutheran theologian Gerhard Ebeling (1912–2001) clarified what Luther meant by "Scripture alone" (even as it is not verbatim Luther's own slogan). He meant to express with this concept the self-sufficiency and clarity of the biblical message that brings us life as it is the living, spoken Word of God.[101]

He did not want a "rational" but an "orational approach," praying over the Scriptures instead of reasoning about them (*ratio)*. Luther himself used the paradoxical expression of "reading" the Scriptures *clausis oculis* and to chew (*ruminare*, ruminate) on the Word of God alone. Luther was thinking of Saint John, his favorite evangelist, and declared that with closed eyes Saint John sees farther than we do as he remains with the Word of God alone.[102]

In the intellectual climate of Erfurt, which was shaped by humanism outside and inside the Augustinian friary, the budding humanist became a respected humanist in the cloister and through it then also a biblical humanist. The concentration on the study of the Sacred Scriptures was shared by the Erfurt humanists outside the

---

[100] This is a *bon mot* of F. Hahn, "Luthers Auslegungsgrundsätze und ihre theologischen Voraussetzungen," *Zeitschrift für Systematische Theologie* 12 (1934/1935): 168, quoted in Franz Posset, "Bible Reading 'With Closed Eyes' in the Monastic Tradition: An Overlooked Aspect of Martin Luther's Hermeneutics," ABR 38 (1987): 293–306, here 293. For Luther's wrestling theology away from philosophy, see Wilhelm Link, *Das Ringen Luthers um die Freiheit der Theologie von der Philosophie* (Munich: Chr.Kaiser Verlag, 2nd ed. 1955).

[101] Gerhard Ebeling, "Luther und die Bibel," *Lutherstudien* I (Tübingen: Mohr, Siebeck, 1971), 286–301. On "Scripture alone" see Gerhard Ebeling, *The Word of God and Tradition: Historical Studies Interpreting the Divisions of Christianity*, trans. S. H. Hooke (Philadelphia: Fortress Press, 1964), 102–47.

[102] See Posset, "Bible Reading 'With Closed Eyes' ", 296, with reference to 1 John 2, WA 20, 689, 11–12.

monastery and by the friars inside the Augustinian monastery[103] so that a common interest manifested itself which Luther must have found attractive. Notable is the observation that Cochlaeus, the fierce opponent of Luther, had to admit from his research about the young Luther that as an Augustinian novice at Erfurt Luther was a good servant of God: "After a year's probation, his profession of that order was made legitimate and there in his studies and spiritual exercises he fought strenuously for God for four years."[104] This was the one positive note about Luther which Cochlaeus had to concede. Cochlaeus, however, did not mention that Luther learned his focus on the Scriptures from observing the order's *Constitutions*.

2. 4. 3. TRAINED IN THE AUGUSTINIAN ORDER LUTHER WILL BE DISOBEDIENT TO ECCLESIASTICAL AUTHORITY BASED UPON THE AUTHORITY OF THE SCRIPTURES

Being trained in the Augustinian order tradition of studying the Sacred Page had far-reaching ramifications when Luther in the Augustinian cowl stood before the emperor and the representatives of the empire at Worms in 1521, when he refused to recant "unless I shall have been refuted by the testimony of the Scriptures."[105] There is no need to amplify his "stand" with the non-historical embellishment of "Here I stand!" It had slipped into the first *printing* of the account about the events at Worms in 1521.[106] Melanchthon, himself not present at Worms, depended on this slightly embellished printed report, whereas according a direct, unsympathetic eye witness, i.e., Cochlaeus, Luther only said this to the emperor:

> Since your Holy Majesty and your Lordships seek a simple answer, I will give it, neither horned nor toothed, in this manner. Unless I shall have been refuted by the testimony of the Scriptures, or by evident reason . . . I am convinced, by the Scriptures that I have brought forward and by my conscience which is bound by the word of God, that I neither can nor wish

[103] Junghans called it an *Interessengemeinschaft* in *Der junge Luther*, 85.
[104] *Luther's Lives*, 55; see Sonntag, "Luther in katholischer Sicht," 197.
[105] WA 7, 838 (Latin); WA 7, 876–877 (German).
[106] The early print has the line in the German report by Spalatin: *Ich kan nicht anderst, hie stehe ich, Gott helf mit, Amen.* In: *Reychs tag tzu Wormbs gewest, ergangen ist, auffs kurtzest begriffen, Item die geleytcz brieff D. M. gegeben hyr yhnn auch begryffen seynt* [Wittenberg], [1521] [VD 16 S 7418].

> to recant anything, since to act against my conscience is neither safe nor honest. *Got Helff mir* [this phrase is printed in the original German, meaning "God help me"] Amen."[107]

Cochlaeus' testimony is to be preferred primarily because he was an eye-witness who evidently offered a very precise description of the event. However, his words were not quite as dramatic as the famous exclamation of "Here I stand!" would have it.

As to the issue of authority (and only as an aside), Luther's stand on the role of the Scriptures is usually perceived as being disobedient and unwilling to recant before the political assemby, whereas it is usually ignored or forgotten that his own territorial lord, the pious Frederick the Wise, was the real political and ecclesiastical rebel (of course, having been persuaded by Luther and others that the authority of the Scriptures as the salient point is to be obeyed). Frederick first had refused to have Luther delivered up to Rome. He sent him instead to Augsburg (in October 1518) in order that he could be interrogated there by Cardinal Cajetan. Frederick's second disobedient act was three years later, when he acted against the young emperor by completely disregarding his Edict of Worms in 1521. [108] In Melanchthon's memoirs, Frederick the Wise comes across as the pious prince who was obedient most of all to the Word of God:

> This man [Frederick] did what many other pious and wise men did; he yielded to God, and he carefully read those things which were written, and those which he judged to be true he did not want to do away with.[109]

2. 4. 4. MELANCHTHON'S REASONING FOR LUTHER'S ENTRY INTO AN ORDER: EAGERNESS FOR PIETY

Melanchthon stressed the severity of discipline in the friary but did not mention its *Constitutions*. He nevertheless explicitly used the same expression in his Latin memoirs that is found in the order's *Constitutions*, "avidly reading the Scripture" as he described Luther's focus on Scripture reading during his first years as a friar (referring to

---

[107] Cochlaeus, *Luther's Lives*, 86; based on LW 32, 113 (the speech of Dr. Martin Luther, April 18).

[108] See Rolf Decot, "Reichstage und Religionsgespräche: Zur reichspolitischen Behandlung der Religionsfrage" in *Festschrift Pesch 2007*, 110–139, here 114–115.

[109] CR 6, 162–163.

a time when the formal study of theology was not on the horizon for him at all). Melanchthon offered the following reasoning for Luther joining the religious order: (a) the pursuit of piety and (b) the pursuit of the knowledge of God. Both reasons were meant to help Luther in his anxieties:

> A favorable opportunity for entering this kind of life [in the friary] which he [Luther] deemed more suitable for piety and for the studies of the teachings about God, was the following as he himself told [us] and as many do know:[110] Often, when he thought more intently about the wrath of God or the awesome examples of punishments, great terrors so suddenly terrified him that he almost died.

Melanchthon interrupted his recollection of Luther's narration and entered his own eyewitness report about Luther's behavior when those anxiety attacks occurred, apparently after 1518 when Melanchthon was living in Wittenberg:

> And I myself saw him, when he was overcome by tension in a disputation about a certain doctrine, go into a nearby room and lay on the bed, where he repeatedly called upon God and mixed the following sentence [Bible verse] into his prayer: "For God delivered all to disobedience, that he might have mercy upon all" [Rom 11:32].[111]

Melanchthon continued with a reminiscence that went back to the pre-monastic days, which he must have heard from Luther, about the death of a friend. "He felt those terrors either from the beginning or most sharply in that year when he lost a companion [*sodalem*]—I do not know the circumstances" (see Chapter 2. 3.). Melanchthon concluded that it was Luther's "eagerness for piety" that led him into this mode of religious life.[112]

Melanchthon pointed out that Luther went along with everything he was supposed to study in scholasticism, but continued his private

---

[110] *Occasio autem fuit ingrediendi illud vitae genus, quod pietati et studiis doctrinae de Deo existimavit desse convenientius, haec fuit, ut ipse narrabat, et ut multi norunt*; CR 6, 158.
Cum sodalem, nescio quo casu interfectum, amisisset; CR 6, 158. A reference to what is associated with Stotternheim?
[111] CR 6, 158.
[112] CR 6, 158.

Bible studies which he pursued "avidly." When Melanchthon reported about Luther's Bible studies he referred to this avid reading of the Scriptures as the "heavenly doctrine" using the wording (*avide*) of the order's *Constitutions*:

> Meanwhile he himself avidly read the sources of heavenly doctrine, i.e., the writings of the Prophets and the Apostles, in order to have an erudite mind about the will of God and in order to support his reverence [*timor*, fear of God] and faith from firm testimonies [of the Scriptures].[113]

Melanchthon's Latin *timor* must be understood positively from the immediate context as the reverent "fear of God" (German: *Gottesfurcht*), not the fear of an imagined "angry God." Luther's "avid" reading of the "sources of the heavenly doctrine" was purposeful. Melanchthon reported: "in order to have an erudite mind about the will of God." This aspect of Luther's spiritual life is important to Melanchthon and worthwhile to be reported in his memoirs because Melanchthon himself is directed by this same purpose in all of his scholarly work: All aspects of letters and science, including language studies, natural sciences and philosophy, serve the purpose of gaining insight into the will of God[114] and of supporting piety in terms of human reverence of and faith in God. The passage about Luther's "avid" reading of the biblical sources for the purpose of erudition and piety perfectly echoes Melanchthon's two-fold purpose of life: *Pietas* and *Eruditio*.[115]

2. 4. 5. NEITHER SUBJECTIVISM NOR PAULINISM

On the solid foundation of the *Constitutions* of the Augustinian order with its priority of studying the "Scripture avidly, . . . devoutly, and . . . fervently" it was virtually impossible that Luther should have

[113] *Interea fontes doctrinae coelestis avide legebat ipse, scilicet scripta prophetica et apostolica, ut mentem suam de Dei voluntate erudiret, et firmis testimoniis aleret timorem et fidem;* CR 6, 158.

[114] See Wriedt, "Zwischen Angst und Zuversicht: Melanchthon als Mensch des 16. Jahrhunderts" in *"Man weiß so wenig über ihn,"* 15–17.

[115] On this, see Markus Wriedt, "Pietas et Eruditio. Zur theologischen Begründung der bildungsreformerischen Ansätze bei Philipp Melanchthon unter besonderer Berücksichtigung seiner Ekklesiologie" in Johanna Loehr (ed.), *Dona Melanchtoniana. Festgabe für Heinz Scheible zum 70. Geburtstag* (Stuttgart: Frommann-Holzboog, 2001), 501–520.

become a "subjectivist" since he was exposed to the entire Bible in his devout reading. Luther's drive to reforming Bible studies and pastoral care was not caused by "subjectivism," a typical Catholic charge, leveled by Grisar,[116] which was repeated by other Catholic scholars like Joseph Lortz and Hans Küng (in 1961) with their psychologizing Luther-interpretations.[117] Joseph E. Vercruysse (1931–) rightly advocated that such a charge should be left behind.[118] The issue deserves to be discussed in terms of hermeneutics, but not of psychology. The historical Luther was not a partial hearer of the Word of God, who allegedly restricted himself to Saint Paul's letters, which supposedly made him a Paulinist.[119] Luther was led to Paul because he was first advised to read Bernard. Notably, Bernard's works contain "several thousand quotations" from Saint Paul.[120] The mass of quotations does not make Bernard a Paulinist, nor is Luther.

In his own preface to Paul's Letter to the Romans Luther actually used Saint John's theology for interpreting the biblical concepts of sin and faith! Luther explained the "classical definition"[121] of "faith" with Johannine wording of what Paul means by faith: Faith is a divine work in us which changes us and gives us new birth from God [*aus Gott*], killing the old Adam.[122] "Scripture interprets itself" (or better:

---

[116] "The tragic schism, cause by subjectivism in breaking away from the ancient and venerable universal church, is all that remains . . . ;" Grisar 188.

[117] See Posset, "Bible Reading 'With Closed Eyes'," 302; see also Otto Hermann Pesch, "Theologische Überlegungen zum 'Subjektivismus' Luthers" in *Zum Gedenken an Joseph Lortz (1887–1975). Beiträge zur Reformationsgeschichte und Ökumene*, eds. Rolf Decot and Rainer Vinke (Stuttgart: Steiner, 1989), 106–140; Hagen, *Luther's Approach to Scripture as seen in his 'Commentaries' on Galatians 1519–1538*, 28–29 with note 72.

[118] Joseph E. Vercruysse, "The Catholic View of Luther Five Hundred Years After His Birth" in *Pro Mundi Vita. Europe. North American Dossier* 21 (1983), 2–22.

[119] Leppin, *Martin Luther,* 192, appears to remain with the concept of Luther as a Paulinist.

[120] Denis Farkasfalvy, "The Use of Paul by Saint Bernard as Illustrated by Saint Bernard's Interpretation of Philippians 3:13" in *Bernardus Magister: Papers Presented at the Nonacentenary Celebration of the Birth of Saint Bernard of Clairvaux*, Kalamazoo, Michigan. Sponsored by the Institute of Cistercian Studies Western Michigan University 10–13 May 1990, edited by John R. Sommerfeldt (Cistercian Publications and Cîteaux: Commentarii Cistercienses, 1992), 161–168, here 161.

[121] Oswald Bayer, "Das paulinische Erbe bei Luther" in *Festschrift Pesch 2007*, 171–183, here 178.

[122] *Aber glawb ist eyn gotlich wreck ynn vns, das vns wandelt vnd new gepirt aus Gott, Johan. 1. vnd todtet den allten Adam;* WA DB 7, 10, 6–7.

Scripture is its own interpreter; *scriptura sui ipsius interpres*) is at work here. Luther also did not want to bring new personal solutions to the doctrine of Christ. He repeated the old dogma.[123] He believed in the creed of Athanasius. And, the authentic Luther insisted that one must not alter the Word of God to one's own taste.[124] Notably, Luther's themes of his earliest known sermons are not Pauline, but Johannine. The sermon he wrote for Georg Mascov has 1 Jn 5:4 as its topic and his Christmas sermon of 1514 unfolds Jn 1 (see Chapter 2. 6. 2.).

Luther's life as a friar and his specific membership in the reformed congregation of the Augustinians and not as a Franciscan or a Dominican has further ramifications. He and fellow friars in his order disliked the competitive Dominicans who followed Saint Thomas Aquinas (ca. 1225–1274), prince of scholasticism. Because of their philosophical theology Luther called them "Sow Theologians."[125] He also seems to have disliked the Franciscans although he highly esteemed their Saint Bonaventure (see below).

---

[123] See Theodosius Harnack, *Luthers Theologie. Luthers Lehre von dem Erlöser und der Erlösung* (2 vols [1862–1885], new print 1927), here vol. 2,150. Yves Congar, "Regards et réflexions sur la christologie de Luther" in *Das Konzil von Chalkedon. Geschichte und Gegenwart III*, ed. Alois Grillmeier and Heinrich Bacht (Würzburg: Echter Verlag, 1954), 457–486, here 485; referred to by Klaas Zwanepol, *Een menselijke God. De betekenis van Christus voor Luther* (Zoetermeer: Boekencentrum, 2001), 29. Congar in English: "Considerations and Reflections on the Christology of Luther," in *Dialogue between Christians* (Westminster, 1966), 372–406; for Yves Congar's revised position, see his "Nouveaux regards sur la christologie de Luther," *Revue des Sciences philosophiques et théologiques* 62 (1982):180–197; reprinted in Congar, *Martin Luther: Sa foi, sa réforme. Etudes de théologie historique* (Paris: Les Editions Du Cerf, 1983); Markus Wriedt, "Theologiesche Innovation und konservatives Beharren bei Martin Luther und Philipp Melanchthon," in *Luther und die Freiheit*, ed. Werner Zager (Darmstadt: Wissenschaftliche Buchgesellschaft , 2010), 59–80.

[124] *Non est verbum dei zu endern secundum fidem illius vel alterius*; Sermon on 9 February 1528 (on Sunday Septuagesima), WA 27, 44, 9–10 (no. 12) (stenograph by Georg Rörer).

[125] *O Sawtheologen!* WA 56, 274, 14.

2. 5. JOHANN VON STAUPITZ, GEORG MASCOV, MARTIN POLLICH, AND MARTIN LUTHER AT WITTENBERG

Luther never mentioned the date of his ordination. Was it not important to him? He may not have mentioned it to Melanchthon, nor did it seem important to Melanchthon to inquire about it and include it in his biographical sketch.[126]

We know the date of his First Mass on 2 May 1507. More important to the young Luther was obviously the date of his doctoral promotion at Wittenberg. This degree was almost a prerequisite for becoming a good preacher in the tradition of the order of Saint Augustine (but, of course, not a requirement). The date of the promotion is known: 18/19 October 1512, about five or six years after his ordination to the priesthood.[127]

2. 5. 1. JOHANN VON STAUPITZ COMMANDS LUTHER TO TAKE THE DOCTOR'S DEGREE

Likely Luther had been proposed for the doctorate in theology during the order's chapter meeting in Cologne in May 1512.[128] Melanchthon reported:

> At this time Reverend Staupitz, who had helped with the beginnings of the Academy [University] of Wittenberg, was eager to stimulate the study of theology in the new academy. He had confidence in Luther's intelligence and learning and for this reason he transferred him to Wittenberg, in 1508, when Luther was twenty six years old.[129]
>
> And so that you might see that the doctor's degree was conferred on him for his maturity of judgment, you should know that this was the thirtieth year of Luther's life. He himself told us that he was ordered by Staupitz, even though he

[126] The ordination may have taken place in the spring of 1507; see Junghans, *Der junge Luther*, 43.
[127] See Pilvousek, "Martin Luther und Erfurt," 16.
[128] See Grisar 56.
[129] CR 6, 160.

> was quite opposed to the idea, to allow [himself] to be decorated with this [graduate] degree.[130]

This wording is strange. We know nothing of Luther writing a doctoral dissertation to earn the degree. Apparently, no doctor's thesis was required. How did he "earn" it? All we know is what Melanchthon reported: The doctor's degree was conferred on him for his maturity of judgment when he was thirty years old. Luther was ordered to accept the honor, as he should become both a professor and a preacher. From Table Talk we learn that the conversation with Staupitz took place under a pear tree, probably in September 1511.[131]

The bestowing of the doctor's degree must have something to do with his performance as a friar and a leader in his order ("for his maturity of judgment"). Luther did not give up, however, his doctor title when he left the order. On the contrary, the only thing he was proud of was his doctorate in theology, which "in his eyes" was "the anchor of his credibility and legitimacy as a teacher, preacher, and critic of the Roman hierarchy."[132] Melanchthon did not say this in such a direct way, but it is noteworthy how clearly Melanchthon stressed the doctorate (rather than, let's say, the ordination to the priesthood).

In this context one must not forget that Luther was not only appointed to lecture on the Bible but was also called almost simultaneously to fill the preacher position at the parish church of Wittenberg, starting most likely in 1514.[133] The two functions were always closely connected. The *lectura in Biblia* was a key position in the faculty and was by contract reserved to the Augustinians. Staupitz—who was preoccupied with extensive business trips on behalf of the order, with visitations and supervising the reformation of the friaries in Saxony and in the Holy Roman Empire—was very happy to have found Friar Martin to succeed him. This arrangement was to Luther's liking and happened to be in full agreement, of

---

[130] [Luther] *ipse narrabat sibi admodum defugiendi et recusanti mandatum esse a Staupicio, ut hoc gradu ornari se sinerat*, CR 6, 160.

[131] See Posset, *The Front-Runner*, 112–113.

[132] Scott H. Hendrix, "Luther's Loyalties and the Augustinian Order" in *Augustine, the Harvest, and Theology (1300–1650). Essays Dedicated to Heiko Augustinus Oberman in Honor of his Sixtieth Birthday*, ed. Kenneth Hagen (Leiden, New York, Copenhagen, Cologne: Brill, 1990), 236–258, here 248.

[133] See Lohse 44.

course, with the proper calling of the Augustinians as curates of souls and preachers, all of which was always a great concern to Staupitz.

Luther followed Staupitz not only in the professorial chair but also in the practice of good preaching. Staupitz was a popular preacher and knew how to use good imagery. We come close to the historical Luther when we believe Luther's own words that he owed just about everything to Dr. Staupitz, his fatherly friend.[134] This may have meant not only that Luther had been ordered by Staupitz to take up the study of theology in order to become a good preacher, but also that he owed everything to Staupitz's Christo-centric spirituality and biblical theology, which was geared always toward pastoral care. It may also have meant that Luther came to know in Staupitz a man who raised some serious doubts about the indulgences [135] and that in this superior Luther experienced a viable alternative to late-medieval scholasticism.[136]

The late-medieval preaching about the passion of Christ is heavily influenced by Bernard, even though preachers may not always make explicit reference to him when they preach on this subject. This was the case with Staupitz's Lenten Sermons of 1512 at Salzburg. His sermons of the eve of the Reformation prove Luther's comments about him (although preserved in Table Talk) that he (Luther) received everything from the Christ-centered teaching of Staupitz: "My good Staupitz said, 'One must keep one's eyes fixed on that man

---

[134] See WA TR 1, 80, 16–17 (no. 173), as reported by Veit Dietrich in 1532; Markus Wriedt, *Gnade und Erwählung: Eine Untersuchung zu Johann von Staupitz und Martin Luther* (Mainz: Philipp von Zabern, 1991).

[135] Staupitz voiced his criticism in an Advent sermon of 1516 in Nuremberg and in a sermon dated early 1517; see Posset, *The Front-Runner*, 211. On the history of the criticism of the indulgences, see Wilhelm-Ernst Winterhager, "Ablasskritik als Indikator historischen Wandels vor 1517: Ein Beitrag zu Voraussetzungen und Einordnung der Reformation," ARG 90 (1999): 6–71. The indulgence campaigns of Cardinal Peraudi from 1486 to 1503 were initially highly successful, but soon declined sharply. The sale of indulgences was openly questioned. Luther's criticism of indulgences drew on these sentiments. A study of the indulgence problem reveals a far-reaching, general change in the mental climate in Germany during the decades before 1517.

[136] See Lohse 43; Berndt Hamm, "Johann von Staupitz (ca. 1468–1524)—spätmittelalterlicher Reformer und 'Vater' der Reformation," ARG 92 (2001): 6–42; Markus Wriedt, "Via Augustini—Ausprägungen des spätmittelalterlichen Augustinismus in der observanten Kongregation der Augustinereremiten" in *Luther und das monastische Erbe*, 9–38. Notably, Luther's second disputation theses are those *contra scholasticam theologiam* (September 1517); WA 1, 224–228.

who is called Christ.' Staupitz is the one who started the teaching [of the gospel in our time]" (no. 526).[137] These statements from Table Talk concur with authentic sayings in Luther's correspondence about his superior in the Augustinian order: Staupitz was a "preacher of grace and cross."[138] In a letter of 27 March 1545 Luther wrote to Elector John Frederick (1503–1554): "He [Staupitz] has been, first of all, my father in this doctrine and he has given birth to me in Christ."[139] These recollections show how Luther thought of himself as a Staupitzian. It is thus difficult to accept the denial of any essential impact of Staupitz on Luther.[140]

2. 5. 2. GHOSTWRITER FOR GEORG MASCOV

One of Luther's first jobs after his return from Rome was to be a ghostwriter for a higher prelate in the diocese, Georg Mascov (Mascow, died in 1520), who was the prior of the Premonstratensian monastery at Leitzkau in Brandenburg. Melanchthon's account is silent on this issue and on this man who was not crucial for his Luther biography. Evidently, Luther's talent was known to Mascov who also may have learned that the Augustinian chapter assembly of Cologne in May had designated Luther for graduate studies; i.e., in theology, in order to become a well prepared preacher.

Prior Mascov asked Luther to write the sermon for him, which was scheduled for the diocesan assembly on 22 June 1512.[141] It was a reform synod which Bishop Jerome Schulze had summoned to his residence of Ziesar Castle, in Brandenburg. Its purpose was the *reformatio* of morale and ethical behavior of the clergy, but also of the laity. Luther's theme was "Whoever is begotten by God conquers the world" (1 Jn 5:4).[142] We do not know whether this theme was given to Luther or whether he chose it himself. In any case, Luther's

---

[137] See Franz Posset, "Preaching the Passion of Christ on the Eve of the Reformation," CTQ 59 (1995): 279–300.

[138] WA Br 2, 264, 48 (no. 376).

[139] *Das[s] er erstlich mein Vater ynn dieser lere gewest ist vnd ynn Christo geboren hat*; WA Br 11, 67, 7–8 (no. 4088). Only with these authentic words in mind may one trust the Table Talk of 1539: "Doctor Staupitz incited me against the Pope;" WA TR 4, 440, 18–19 (no. 4707); Posset, *The Front-Runner*, 214–215.

[140] As found in Martin Brecht, *Martin Luther, His Road to Reformation 1483–1521* (Minneapolis: Fortress, 1985), 230.

[141] See Hausrath, *Luthers Leben*, vol. 1, 105–107.

[142] See WA 1, 10–17.

sermon made the prelate speak about *reformatio* in the contemporaneous sense of clergy reform and reform of morals among the laypeople since the diocesan assembly was to deliberate about the status of the *reformatio* of both, clergy and laity.[143]

Luther and Mascov kept up their correspondence. A fragment of Luther's letter to Mascov, assumed to have been written in fall of 1516, is extant. Luther recommended patience in dealing with subordinates in Mascov's monastery.[144] The same issue was the subject of Luther's reply on 17 May 1517 to his Premonstratensian friend. Mascov had asked for Luther's advice on how to deal with a subordinate's violation of the religious vows. Luther did not see himself in the position to make a recommendation because he was not familiar, as he wrote, with the statutes of the Premonstratensian order.[145] In 1520 Prior Mascov is reported to have written to Luther that he would not recognize the ban against Luther and he would rather give up his ecclesiastical position than carry out the ban.[146]

2. 5. 3. MARTIN POLLICH'S PREMONITION

Melanchthon not only pointed out Luther's relationship with Staupitz, but also recalled what Martin Pollich von Mellerichstadt (Mellerstad, Mellersted), the first rector of the University of Wittenberg and the elector's personal physician,[147] said about Luther's early time in Wittenberg:

> Here [at Wittenberg], amidst the daily exercises of the school and preaching, his intelligence began to shine even more. And since wise men, such as Doctor Martin [Pollich von] Mellerstad and others, would listen to him attentively, Mellerstad often said that there was so great a power of intelligence in that man that he clearly foresaw that he would

[143] . . . *pro utriusque status reformatione*; WA 1, 12, 9–11.
[144] See WA Br 1, 59–60 (no. 23).
[145] See WA Br 1, 97–98 (no. 40).
[146] See Hausrath, *Luthers Leben,* vol. 1: 106 and 368.
[147] See Theodor Grüneberg, "Martin Pollich von Mellerstadt, der erste Rektor der Wittenberger Universität" in *450 Jahre Martin-Luther-Universität Halle-Wittenberg* (Halle: Universität Halle-Wittenberg, 1952), vol. 1, 87–91; Helmut Schlereth, "Pollich, Martin. gen. Mellerstadt," *Neue Deutsche Biographie* 20 (Berlin: Duncker & Humblot, 2001), 605–606.

change the traditional form of learning, which was the only one being employed in the schools at that time.[148]

Fig. 7. Martinus Pollychius Mellerstad (Pollich von Mellrichstadt). The text under the portrait indicates that he was a learned man in the humanities, medicine, and theology.

---

148 CR 6, 160.

2. 6. AUGUSTINIANS CONTRA DOMINICANS

Melanchthon called attention to the religious order affiliation of Johann Tetzel. He referred to him as "the Dominican" in the context of his references to Luther's humanist language studies, and the sale of indulgences, using the following words:

> Luther began to dedicate himself to the study of Greek and Hebrew, so that having learned the peculiar quality of a language and its diction, and the doctrine drawn from its sources [*ex fontibus doctrina*] he might all the more be able to make better judgments.
>
> When Luther was in this course of study, indulgence [papers] were on sale and were circulated in these regions by Tetzel the Dominican, a most shameless deceiver.[149]

This reference to Tetzel leads us to the historical animosities between the mendicant orders. Historically, the Augustinian preachers had to compete primarily with the Dominicans whose official name is the "Order of Preachers" (*Ordo Praedicatorum*). In many cities only the mendicants preached.[150] To prepare their friars in this competition, the superiors in the Augustinian order usually assigned friars to preaching positions only if they first earned a doctoral degree in theology. The main purpose was to offer superior pastoral care through preaching. Only then were their friars qualified and in the position to compete for the most important, and most lucrative preaching positions in the major cities of the empire in those days. Luther must have shown great potential as a biblical preacher.

The traditional Augustinian animosities toward the Dominicans were likely fanned by Staupitz who experienced such competition first hand at Tübingen under Duke Eberhard the Bearded (1445–1496).[151] Such competition and animosity was part of the "historical context," which had real ramifications in Luther's later career. The contemporaneous Dominicans of Cologne, led by Friar Jacob Hoogstraeten (Hochstraten, ca. 1460–1527) were involved in the on-going "Reuchlin Affair" (Johann Reuchlin, 1455–1522) in which the

---

[149] . . . *Tecelio Dominicano impudentissimo sycophanta*; CR 6, 161–162.

[150] See O.C, Edwards Jr.: *A History of Preaching* (Nashville: Abingdon Press, 2004), 210ff.

[151] See Posset, *The Front-Runner*, 24.

Augustinian order from the top down (Egidio da Viterbo in Rome) appears to have sided with the Swabian humanist and Hebraist.[152] Luther used one of the best sources available at the time, i.e., Reuchlin's book of 1512 on the Hebrew/Latin Penitential Psalms[153] as the basis for his first own publication, in the spring of 1517, written in German for pastoral purposes.[154] Furthermore, the late-medieval Dominicans were known as promoters of the rosary, whereas the Augustinians were not. Likely instigated by Staupitz,[155] Luther took up the issue of the proper praying of the rosary against the Dominican theologian Marcus von Weyda (Weida, 1450–1516).[156]

Probably instigated and again supported by Staupitz, Luther picked a fight with another Dominican concerning the proper interpretation and advertising of the indulgences, when in 1517 he challenged Johann Tetzel on this issue. Archbishop Albrecht had entrusted the gainful preaching on the indulgences to the Dominicans.[157] The animosity and envy between the two religious

---

[152] See Posset, *The Front-Runner,* 204.

[153] In 1512 Reuchlin published his booklet of about 100 printed pages, including the attachment of the seven psalms in Hebrew with a literal, word for word, Latin translation directly from the Hebrew: *In septem psalmos poenitentiales hebraicos interpretatio de uerbo ad uerbum, & super eisdem commentarioli sui, ad discendum linguam hebraicam ex rudimentis* (I used the michrofiche edition of the *Thrivent Reformation Research Program* of the Luther Seminary Library in Saint Paul, MN). MDZ has its copy on display, website: *Ioannis Revchlin Phorcensis LL. doctoris in septem psalmos poenite[n]tiales hebraicos interpretatio, de uerbo ad uerbum, & super eisdem commentarioli sui, ad discendum linguam hebraicam ex rudimentis, Tubingae, 1512* [VD 16 B 3406]**.** Strangely, the highly respected expert on Reuchlin, Hans Rupprich (1898–1972), assumed that there was only a manuscript version of Reuchlin's booklet of the Seven Penitential Psalms; see Hans Rupprich. "Johannes Reuchlin und seine Bedeutung im europäischen Humanismus," first published in *Johannes Reuchlin. Festgabe seiner Vaterstadt Pforzheim zur 500. Wiederkehr seines Geburtstages. Im Selbstverlag der Stadt Pforzheim*, 1955; reprinted in *Johannes Reuchlin 1455–1522: Nachdruck der 1955 von Manfred Krebs herausgegebenen Festgabe, neu herausgegeben und erweitert von Hermann Kling und Stefan Rhein,* 10–34; reprinted in *Ängste und Auswege. Bilder aus Umbruchszeiten in Pforzheim Band II. Pforzheim zur Zeit Reuchlins. Beiträge zur Stadtgeschichte* (Heidelberg, Ubstadt-Weiher, Basel: Verlag Regionalkultur, 2005), 115–162, here 141.

[154] WA 1, 158–220.

[155] See Posset, *The Front-Runner*, 261–262.

[156] Weyda had published *Zum Spiegel hochlöblicher Bruderschaft des Rosenkranzes Mariae* in 1515; see Franz Posset, "Martin Luther OSA und Markus von Weida OP: Auseinandersetzung um das Rosenkranzbeten," LB 13 (2004): 45–62; English digest in LD 15 (2007): 79–80.

[157] See Sonntag, "Luther in katholischer Sicht," 197.

organizations of preachers, i.e., the Dominican and the Augustinian orders, became a major factor in the entire controversy, something that Cochlaeus had observed early on.[158]

It was the Dominican order that quickly set in motion the heresy charges against Luther who was summoned before the Dominican Cardinal Cajetan in 1518. The Dominican Sylvester Prierias at the papal court in Rome had turned the whole controversy into an issue of ecclesiastical authority and heresy. The Dominicans in Rome made a Martin-in-effigy out of paper and burned, cursed, and execrated it in a public square. Luther was well aware of this incident.[159]

In sum, Melanchthon in his Preface of 1546 is the first to make mention of a "posting" of (Ninety-Five) *Propositions*. He noted that they were "affixed" to the church adjacent to the castle. However, he did not say anything about a "door" either here or in his funeral oration for Luther on 22 February 1546. Obviously, Luther himself cannot be the source for Melanchthon's statement in this specific regard, because nowhere else did Luther hint at a "posting" on any "door" of what he called his "talking points" (labeled later on as the *Ninety-Five Theses*). Melanchthon himself summed up the matter by writing that at the beginning of this "controversy" Luther had not tried to get rid of indulgences altogether, but only urged "moderation." Melanchthon included his prayer of thanksgiving to God that by the ministry of Martin Luther God removed the filth and poisons in order to restore the pure doctrine of the Church.

Having reviewed some of the aspects of the *Sitz im Leben* of the young Luther, let us go back to the first years of the sixteenth century and to Luther in the Erfurt friary. Luther's membership in the Augustinian order may suggest that he also was supposed to prefer their patron, Saint Augustine. But here one must be careful. Becoming an Augustinian friar did not mean that one automatically became a reader of the church father's works or a representative of late medieval Augustinianism.[160]

---

[158] See Cochlaeus, *Luther's Lives*, 61.

[159] *Dicitur mihi papyraceus Martinus in Campo flore publice combustus, execratus, devotus*; Luther's letter to Martin Glaser (Augustinian prior at Ramsau) of 30 May 1519, WA Br 1, 408, 13–14 (no. 182); see Posset, *The Front-Runner*, 25.

[160] See Junghans, "Luther's Development from Biblical Humanist to Reformer," 9.

3. In the Context of the Late Medieval "Bernard Renaissance"

Fig. 8. The Crucified Embraces Saint Bernard; Master of the Altar of the Augustinian Church in Nuremberg, Altar of Saint Vitus; end of the fifteenth century. Photo: Bayerische Staatsgemäldesammlungen, Munich.

3. 1. LESS "AUGUSTINE AWAKENING" AND MORE "BERNARD RENAISSANCE"

Here is the historical context: Around 1500 there was actually not just an "Augustine awakening" (as the late Heiko Oberman [1930–2001] articulated),[1] in which Luther's superior Staupitz and others were very much involved,[2] but also, and more so, something of a "Bernard renaissance" that was emerging in connection with the late medieval "theology-for-piety." Berndt Hamm (1945–) once pointed out in a study of a leader of the reformed Augustinians of Erfurt, Johann von Paltz (Jeusser, ca. 1444–1511), that there was a "Bernard renaissance."[3] Paltz was a theology professor there from 1485 to 1495 and occasionally preached in the vernacular before the Elector Frederick the Wise.[4] He was the best known Erfurt Augustinian at the beginning of the sixteenth century.[5] But Hamm, unfortunately, did not pursue this important research any further. Others have pointed out that Bernard of Clairvaux, the twelfth-century spiritual authority, was the most popular spiritual writer in the later Middle Ages,[6] more popular than Augustine.

---

[1] See Heiko A. Oberman, "'Tuus sum, salvum me fac'. Augustinreveil zwischen Renaissance und Reformation" in *Scientia Augustiniana. Studien über Augustinus, den Augustinismus und den Augustinerorden. Festschrift P. Dr. theol. Dr. phil. Adolar Zumkeller OSA zum 60. Geburtstag*, ed. by Cornelius Petrus Mayer and Willigis Eckermann (Würzburg: Augustinus-Verlag, 1975), 349–394. Markus Wriedt doubts that a particular Augustinianism—as could be related specifically to the Augustinian Friars—would be at work in Luther's development; see his "Via Augustini—Ausprägungen des spätmittelalterlichen Augustinismus in der observanten Kongregation der Augustinereremiten" in *Luther und das monastische Erbe*, 9–38.

[2] See Franz Posset, "Pater et Doctor Meus Est, Immo Sanctae Ecclesiae, Intellectu Profundissimus," *Collectanea Augustiniana: Augustine: Mystic and Mystagogue*, edited by Frederick Van Fleteren, Joseph C. Schnaubelt, OSA, Joseph Reino (New York etc: Peter Lang, 1994), 513–43 (on Augustine's influence on late medieval Dominicans and Augustinians).

[3] See Berndt Hamm, *Frömmigkeitstheologie am Anfang des 16. Jahrhunderts. Studien zu Johannes Paltz und seinem Umkreis* (Tübingen: Mohr Siebeck, 1982), 193.

[4] See Posset, *The Front-Runner*, 12.

[5] See Schwarz, *Luther*, 12.

[6] See Giles Constable, "The Popularity of Twelfth-Century Spiritual Writers in the Late Middle Ages" in *Renaissance Studies in Honor of Hans Baron*, eds. Anthony Molho and John A. Tedeschi (DeKalb: Northern Illinois University Press, 1971), 5–28; Hellmut Zschoch, *Klosterreform und monastische Spiritualität im 15.*

The "Bernard renaissance" comprises a large number of pseudepigraphy under Bernard's name. Whether the influence on later generations of spurious works, be they pseudepigraphic or mistakenly ascribed to Saint Bernard, might perhaps be greater than Bernard's genuine works, is a good question, but is not our immediate concern here.[7] About three hundred editions of Bernard's works are known between the 1460s and 1500,[8] which is more than the 187 prints of various works of Augustine.[9] It may come as a surprise to some that "no firm conclusions have been drawn regarding the reception of Augustine during the Reformation."[10]

Traces of Bernardine theology, not mysticism, show up in Staupitz and Luther, and make the "Bernard renaissance" in the Augustinian order manifest. With Theo Bell (1945–) we may point out that Luther joined the "Bernard renaissance" of the fifteenth century.[11] Luther made use of the Bernardine concept of the "right to heaven" in 1513 in his First Lectures on the Psalms without, however, giving credit to Bernard. Later on Luther employed it as Bernard's concept on a regular basis, especially in his sermons from 1520 up to 1538.[12] Staupitz in his Advent sermons at Nuremberg in 1516 also used Saint Bernard's concept of the "right to heaven," but did not give credit to him. The concept is based upon Bernard's sermon on the Canticle 61.5 and upon a sermon on the seven gifts of the Holy Spirit, processed into a story of *The Golden Legend* about Bernard:

Jahrhundert: Conrad Zenn OESA (+1460) und sein Liber de vita monastica (Tübingen: Mohr Siebeck, 1988), 90.

[7] This question looms since Werner Höver had brought it up already in 1978 in his entry "Bernhard von Clairvaux," in *Die deutsche Literatur des Mittelalters. Verfasserlexikon* (Berlin and New York: De Gruyter, 1978), 754–762, here 760.

[8] See Leopold Janauschek, *Bibliographia Bernardina* (Vienna 1891; reprint: Hildesheim: G. Olms, 1959); Constable 13.

[9] See *Gesamtkatalog der Wiedendrucke* (Leipzig: Hiersemann, 1925–), nos. 2862–3048.

[10] Hans Ulrich Delius, entry "Augustine" in *Oxford Encyclopedia of the Reformation* (New York: Oxford University Press, 1996), 1: 99. "However much they cited Augustine, Martin Luther, Ulrich Zwingli, and John Calvin did not draw their original inspiration from him," wrote John Monfasani, entry "Augustine" in *Encyclopedia of the Renaissance* (New York: Scribner in association with the Renaissance Society of America, 1999), 1: 156.

[11] See Bell, *Divus Bernhardus*, 249–250.

[12] See Posset, *Pater Bernhardus*, 298–307; Wriedt, *Gnade und Erwählung*, 16–18, 37, 42, 46–47; 63–65, 142, 200, 206–209.

> My Lord has won the kingdom by a twofold right [*duplice iure*], namely, by inheritance from his Father and the merits of his passion. The first he has reserved for himself, but the second he gives to me.[13]

Besides the open and the more subtle influence of Bernard on late medieval spirituality just outlined, there is the great impact of Bernard's work *On Consideration*. Staupitz made use of it in one of his Tübingen sermons at the end of the fifteenth century,[14] and Luther would recommend it in his Lectures on Romans in 1515/1516 and on Hebrews in 1517/1518 and, later on, so would Erasmus in 1521.[15]

Luther's interest in Saint Bernard has something to do with the senior friar at Erfurt (as said, it was most likely Johann von Greffenstein) who introduced Luther to the monastic theology of the medieval Cistercian, as we shall see. Recent Luther biographies fail because they do not take Melanchthon's memoirs into serious consideration. They ignore Melanchthon's account about "Luther and Bernard." [16] Unfortunately, even when scholars recognize the significance of Melanchthon's memoirs, they usually disregard the Bernard factor. The German historian Eike Wolgast (1939–) looked at Melanchthon's account only in terms of its role in making Luther a Lutheran authority without ever mentioning the name of Bernard and Greffenstein's role for Luther's theological development. [17] The British historian Michael A. Mullett used Melanchthon's "biographical memoirs" extensively, but never mentioned Melanchthon's emphasis on Bernard's impact on Luther.[18]

Before we proceed any further, we need to illustrate the fact that there was, indeed, a "Bernard renaissance." One of the best indicators

---

[13] See Franz Posset, "The 'Double Right to Heaven': Saint Bernard's Impact in the Sixteenth Century," *Cistercian Studies Quarterly* 38 (2003): 263–273.

[14] *Bernardus ad eugenium libro De consideratione: 'Tu, pastor, procedis . . . .' Pasce oves meas*; Sermon 19.

[15] See Franz Posset, "Recommendations by Martin Luther of St Bernard's On Consideration," *Cistercian Studies* 25 (1990): 25–36; Theo Bell, "'De Consideratione' van Bernard van Clairvaux in de optiek van Martin Luther," *Cîteaux* 48 (1998): 235–257.

[16] Including, for instance, Dietrich Korsch, *Martin Luther. Eine Einführung* (Tübingen: Mohr Siebeck, 2007).

[17] See Wolgast, "Biographie als Autoritätsstiftung: Die ersten evangelischen Lutherbiographien" (1993), see note in Chapter 2.

[18] See Mullett, *Martin Luther* (2004).

of the "Bernard renaissance" is the Bernard iconography of the Middle Ages with almost one thousand extant images of Bernard from the twelfth century to 1530.[19] In the fifteenth century, pictorial representations of Saint Bernard were so popular that they found dissemination well beyond Cistercian monasteries, a remarkable phenomenon. The Augustinian friars at Nuremberg had an altar painting that was dedicated to Saint Bernard and to his love for the crucified Lord (not to his Marian devotion!). The painting of 1487 shows the crucified Christ taking his arms from the cross in order to embrace Bernard (*Amplexus Bernardi*).[20]

Let us fast forward for a moment to Wittenberg and see how the "Bernard renaissance" took hold there. A woodcut may demonstrate what we mean: The "Bernard renaissance" is perfectly illustrated by the image called *S. Bernhards Betrachtung* (Saint Bernard's Meditation, Adoring the Man of Sorrows), a woodcut of ca. 1515 by Lucas Cranach the Elder in Wittenberg, showing a half-figure of Bernard kneeling and praying. Between them is a heart pierced by an arrow. Bernard has taken off his abbatial miter and placed it in front of him, lying on top of his crosier. In the upper right corner the coat of arms of Electoral Saxony is depicted. The original image carries the header *S. Bernhards Betrachtung.*[21] Cranach's woodcut was used more than thirty years later for the book *Hortulus animae* printed in Wittenberg (by Georg Rhaw [Rhau], 1547/1548) and is thus a testimony to the ongoing "Bernard renaissance" in Wittenberg. A similar woodcut with the very same header, styled in part after

---

[19] See James France, *Medieval Images of Saint Bernard of Clairvaux* (Kalamazoo: Cistercian Publications, 2007), with compact disk; Franz Posset, "Saint Bernard of Clairvaux in the Devotion, Theology, and Art of the Sixteenth Century," LQ 11 (1997 [dedicated to Oliver K. Olson]): 306–352; appeared in LD 8 (2000): 140–143; Gabriel Hammer, *Bernhard von Clairvaux in der Buchmalerei. Darstellungen des Zisterzienserabtes in Handschriften von 1135–1630* (Regensburg: Schnell and Steiner, 2009).

[20] See Franz Posset, "Amplexus Bernardi: The Dissemination of a Cistercian Motif in the Late Middle Ages and the Reformation Time," *Cîteaux* 54 (2003): 251–400, here 264–265 (on the Augustinians). Bell, *Divus Bernhard*, 345, calls the *Amplexus* motif a "generally known concept" (*allbekannte Vorstellung*). The painting is included on the disk of J. France, PA 009.

[21] The image is kept today in the National Gallery of Art in Washington, Rosenwald Collection, Inv. B-5940, with the title "Saint Bernard Adoring the Man of Sorrows." See also Michèle Hébert, *Inventaire des Gravures des Écoles du Nord, 1400–1550* (Paris: Bibliothèque nationale, 1982), vol. 5: 191 (no. 885); J. France's compact disk, EN 37 (see above note 19).

Albrecht Dürer’s “Man of Sorrows at Rest” was used for Lutheran literature in the later sixteenth century.[22]

It is rather conspicuous that at Wittenberg a woodcut showing Saint Bernard came into existence just about the time (ca. 1515) when Luther came to speak of Saint Bernard during his early lectures. It is the very time when Luther in his lectures on the Psalms (on Ps 31:2) feels moved to tell his audience: “Bernard meditates beautifully in a certain sermon.”[23] Luther had the passage from *Ann 1* in mind, which the novice master in Erfurt had shown him, as Luther’s paraphrase of it during his lecture demonstrates.

We do not know the circumstances or the motivation for Cranach to create this woodcut, or who ordered it and paid for it (the court of Electoral Saxony?); or, whether Cranach was inspired to produce it because he knew of Luther’s love for Bernard. But we do know that the woodcut came into existence in Wittenberg at the height of the “Bernard renaissance.”

3. 2. Luther Overcomes His Consternations with Fraternal Help

Back to Erfurt: Earlier, at the Augustinian friary at least one senior member had read Bernard’s sermons and mediated the liberating insights to the young Luther, as we shall see now.

Melanchthon’s perspective on Luther’s *consternationes* is crucial. How Luther overcame them is evident as the young friar learned more about the significance of Saint Bernard. Melanchthon remembers, after he had pointed out that the young friar had been heavily engaged in Bible studies (“avidly reading the sources of heavenly doctrine . . . ”) that Luther was stirred by his “own sorrows and anxieties” which moved him to seek counseling from a senior who strengthened him. Melanchthon wrote:

> [Luther’s] continued striving after this study [of the heavenly doctrine] was motivated by his sorrows and fears. And he narrated that he was often strengthened by the words of a

[22] See Posset, “Saint Bernard of Clairvaux in the Devotion, Theology, and Art of the Sixteenth Century,” Figures 5 and 8 (both with the header *S. Bernhards Betrachtung*).
[23] See Posset, *Pater Bernhardus*, 168–169.

senior [friar] in the Augustinian College at Erfurt to whom he exposed his confused fears.[24]

Luther, according to Melanchthon's memoirs, mentioned the "sorrows and fears" and the "consternations" (confused fears) only in the immediate context of being liberated from them. *Nota bene* that the Latin expressions he used are *dolor, pavor, consternationes*, but not the more famous one, *tentatio* (temptation, *Anfechtung*).[25] Luther described them vividly from hindsight, but one must take them not as if Luther had meant all his years in the monastery. Luther brought these "consternations" with him into the cloister as he said in retrospect about his state of mind prior to his entry into the religious order and on the motivation to seek the religious life. This autobiographical statement is given together with the famous question: "How do I get a gracious God?" *Wie kriege ich einen gnädigen Gott*?[26] This often quoted question was supposedly asked by the young Luther.[27] However, it is not retrievable for the early Luther. It cannot be located in any texts of the young friar. Luther posed it in 1534, in a sermon on baptism of 1 February (sermon no. 73). Three years later Luther used similar language in his sermon/exposition on Jn 14 and 15 (in 1537), saying that he and others ("we") ran to cloisters and churches and made pilgrimages in order to make peace with God or to get a "gracious God."[28]

Luther referred here to early *consternationes* from which, according to Melanchthon, he was freed by an anonymous *senex* at Erfurt.[29] The senior was probably not Johann von Staupitz because

---

[24] *Hoc studium ut magis expeteret illis suis doloribus et pavoribus movebatur. Et senis cuiusdam sermonibus in Augustiniano Collegio Erphordiae saepe se confirmatum esse narrabat, cui cum consternationes suas exponeret*; CR 6, 159. "Pangs of conscience" (*Gewissensqualen*) would be too strong a translation and an over-interpretation.

[25] *Tentatio* as in "and lead us not into temptation" of the Lord's Prayer in Latin.

[26] *Denn ich bin selbs funffzehen jar ein Moench gewest . . . noch hab ich mich nie koennen ein mal meiner Tauffe troesten, Sondern jmer gedacht: O wenn wiltu ein mal from werden und gnug thun, das du einen gnedigen Gott kriegst? und bin durch solche gedancken zur Moencherey getrieben . . .* ; WA 37, 661, 20–25.

[27] See Lohse 38.

[28] *Da lieffen wir alle winckel aus durch cloester, kirchen, walfarten etc. das wir moechten gottes friede oder einen gnedigen Gott erlangen*; WA 45, 626, 33–35.

[29] Unfortunately Leppin does not mention Melanchthon's "senior" friar, but acknowledges only in general the helpful role the friars played in time of spiritual

Staupitz never lived in the Erfurt friary. Likely it was the novice master Johann von Greffenstein who died in 1520.[30] In that year Luther fondly remembered Greffenstein by referring to him by name, and concerning his own, very early time in the friary, i.e., before thinking about becoming a priest.[31] Years later (1532) Luther still remembered his "pedagogue" who strongly advised (*iussit*) him to hope in God. The friar's voice moved him to have "a little bit" faith in the absolution of sin.[32] In 1540 Luther still had fond memories of him to whom he referred as "my teacher [*preceptor*] in the cloister, a fine old man."[33] This very much sounds like what Luther had told Melanchthon about the "old man" (*senex*) at Erfurt. There is no established Latin terminology for the position of the "novice master." From the monastic tradition we know that the person in charge of novices was simply called a *senex* who is versed in winning souls for the order.[34]

There is another autobiographical passage from the elder Luther (1533). It, too, is usually over-interpreted. Luther wrote in retrospect (decades later) about his very early time in the friary, that he felt "the most wretched man on earth, passing whole nights in weeping" and, as he said, bathed and baptized in "my monkery" "because I did not know Christ except as a stern judge . . . ."[35] First of all, only the much older Luther mentioned this state of mind, and it was from hindsight.

---

need: *Das Gespräch unter Brüdern brachte also tatsächlich Entlastung*; *Martin Luther 2006,* 44.

[30] See Franz Posset, "Frater Augustinus (Martin Luther) in Erfurt und seine Lektüre geistlicher Autoren, insbesondere Bernhards. Zum Gedächtnis des 850. Todestags des heiligen Bernhard von Clairvaux im Jahr 2003," LB 11 (2002): 30–47, here 32.

[31] *Wie ich den[n] gehort hab von meynem institutor, Johan. Greffenstein, gelereten und frumen man,, wilchen ich nu wol mag nennen, die weil er todt ist, und ichs zu der zeit von yhm horet, da ich nach gar wenig gedacht priester, schweyg docter zu werden*; *Von den newen Eckischenn Bullen und lugen* (1520), WA 6, 591, 17–20.

[32] *Semel audivi verbum a Pedagogo meo: Ach, quid facis? Ipse iussit sperare in se! Das war vox quae me movebat credere aliquantulum absolutionem*; *Enarratio* Ps 51 (*Miserere mei*) of 1532 (manuscript version); WA 40-II, 411, 14–412, 1.

[33] *Mein Praeceptor Im Closter, ein feiner alter Man*, Letter to Elector John Frederick of 10 June 1540; WA Br 9, 133, 40–41. Brecht, *Martin Luther, 1483–1521*, 61; Leppin, *Martin Luther,* 36 with note 46 and 78 with note 60.

[34] *Regula Benedictina* 58; Terrence Kardong OSB kindly provided this information.

[35] *Kleine Antwort auff H. Georgen*, as featured by Schwiebert 153, and repeated, for instance, by Leroy A, Dobberstein, "Luther's Legacy of Doctrinal Integrity" in *Luther Lives. Essays*, 145–156, here 146–147, based upon *Erlanger Ausgabe* XXXI, 279. It is edited also in WA 38, 148, 6–12.

Secondly, his words make good sense only with respect to his time before he was "strengthened" by the older, anonymous friar in Erfurt. Every other generalizing interpretation seems to be blowing the statement out of proportion. It is not legitimate to assume that Luther's consternations lasted during his *entire* time in the friary because, if one would assume that, one would find oneself in flagrant contradiction to Luther's own letter of 17 March 1509 to his Franciscan friend, Johann Braun, at Eisenach.[36] The letter was sent from Wittenberg where Luther was stationed temporarily from the fall of 1508 to the fall of 1509. In it he wrote that God indeed did provide very well for him: "This is how our God is: He reigns in sweetness and in eternity."[37] No connotation of any agonizing questioning or mention of an angry God can be found in this autobiographical note. His letter to Father Braun correlates actually quite well with what Melanchthon reported, that Luther had told him that he was spiritually "strengthened" by the novice master's counseling at Erfurt. We may now debunk the grave exaggeration that the young Luther spent most of his time before and during his time in the cloister in brooding and depression.[38] He would rather study the Scriptures. The same letter also shows that Luther was not fond of having to lecture on philosophy. By "philosophy" he meant the teachings of Aristotle.[39] Luther was directed to the Scriptures, especially to Saint Paul as he was interpreted by Bernard of Clairvaux.

---

[36] See Junghans, *Der junge Luther*, 66.

[37] *Hic est Deus noster, ipse reget in suavitate et in saecula*, WA Br 1, 17, 45–46 (no. 5); Posset, *The Front-Runner*, 94.

[38] See Todd, Chapter 2.

[39] On this, see Willigis Eckermann, "Die Aristoteleskritik Luthers: ihre Berdeutung für seine Theologie," *Catholica* 32 (1978): 114–130; Theodor Dieter, *Der junge Luther und Aristoteles. Eine historisch-systematische Untersuchung zum Verhältnis von Theologie und Philosophie* (Berlin and New York: Walter de Gruyter, 2001); Jared Wicks, "Luther And 'This Damned, Conceited, Rascally Heathen' Aristotle: An Encounter More Complicated Than Many Think," *Pro ecclesia* 16 (2007): 90–104.

3. 3. How Exactly Did Luther Find Help? A Senior Friar Showed Him the Page in Saint Bernard's Sermon

Melanchthon wanted to set the record straight about the real Luther and his becoming aware of Saint Bernard's theology as a decisive insight into how forgiveness of sins (theology of penance) works. Melanchthon wrote:

> He [Luther] heard him [senior friar] discuss many things about the faith, and he said that he was led to the Creed [*ad symbolum*], in which is said, "I believe in the forgiveness of sins." [The senior friar] had interpreted this article [of the Creed] in such a way that it should be believed not only in general, that some people are forgiven, like David or Peter [had been forgiven], something also demons believe, but that it was God's commandment that we as individuals are to believe that our sins are forgiven. And he proved [to Luther] that this interpretation was confirmed by a saying of Bernard, and he showed him the *locus* in a speech [*concio*; i.e., sermon] on the Annunciation where these words are found.[40]

This passage demonstrates several things:

First of all, Luther was not a loner or a constantly depressed introvert. He always was in conversation with fellow friars. In this regard the biography of Richard Marius is mistaken, as mentioned above, by assuming that Luther in his "flight into the monastery" sought solitude in which then Luther's inner struggles were compounded by his monastic isolation.[41] Quite the contrary! Senior friars at Erfurt such as the anonymous *senex* were of decisive spiritual help to the young man, and so was Johann von Staupitz, his supportive superior (see Chapter 2. 5. 1.).

Secondly, the *senex's* help in advising Luther to read Bernard's sermon has far-reaching ramifications. Luther in the course of his career will quote or hint at Saint Bernard more than 500 times (see the

---

[40] . . . *Et hanc interpretationem confirmatam dicebat Bernardi dicto, monstratumque locum in concione de Annunciatione, ubi haec sunt verba;* CR 6, 159.

[41] Rightly, Jared Wicks criticized this kind of interpretation in his book review: "Facts and Fears in and Around Martin Luther," *Moreana* 37 (2000): 5–32; see LD 10 (2002): 230.

loci in WA). Quite in contrast, only one real quotation from Thomas Aquinas can be found, dated 1521 on receiving the Eucharist under both species.[42]

Thirdly, the *senex* had a print of Bernard's sermons at hand. The Erfurt monastic library catalogue shows that the Augustinians, indeed, had Bernard's *Sermones de tempore et de sanctis* (Basel: Nikolaus Kessler 1495) in their possession [43] which included Bernard's *Sermons on the Annunciation* with his theology of grace and penance.[44]

Melanchthon did not know about these editions of Bernardine sermons. He only reported that Luther was made aware of a certain passage in a certain sermon. Notable is the fact that since we do not have the book with the Bernard sermons (that the senior had shown him) Luther himself somehow tried to keep track of what he was reading about Bernard as Luther entered excerpts from Bernard into his desk copy of Anselm (1033–1109). Evidently, Luther looked up what the senior had told him, i.e., Bernard's "sermon on the Annunciation," but ended up reading Bernard's sermons about the gospel *Missus est angelus (In laudibus virginis matris)* [45] which are a different set of Bernardine *Sermons for the Feast of the Annunciation.* From the former he made his notes in Anselm's book. The homilies on *Missus est angelus* did not contain the decisive paragraph that the senior friar quoted to Luther about grace alone.

---

[42] See Denis R. Janz, *Luther on Thomas Aquinas. The Angelic Doctor in the Thought of the Reformer* (Stuttgart: Steiner, 1989), 83. With respect to Augustine, Luther quoted him more than one thousand times. However, quantity cannot be the only criterion for assessing influence; see Franz Posset, "Goldene Worte: Augustinus und Bernhard in der Sicht des alten Luther (1531–1546)," *Catholica* 54 (2000): 220–239.

[43] See Jun Matsuura, "Restbestände aus der Bibliothek des Erfurter Augustinerklosters zu Luthers Zeit und bisher unbekannte eigenhändige Notizen Luthers," *Lutheriana: Zum 500. Geburtstag Martin Luthers von den Mitarbeitern der Weimarer Ausgabe* (Cologne: Böhlau, 1984), 318, 324, 326; Franz Posset. "Bernard of Clairvaux as Luther's Source. Reading Bernard with Luther's 'Spectacles'," CTQ 54 (1990): 281–304, here 289; appeared in LD 1 (1993): 124–125; idem, "Bernhard von Clairvauxs Sermone zur Weihnachts-, Fasten- und Osterzeit als Quelle Martin Luthers" in LuJ 61 (1994): 93–116, here 114; English digest in LD 4 (1996): 215–218; Ulrich Köpf, "Zisterziensererbe im Protestantismus," *Cistercienser Chronik* 114 (2007): 311–327, here 313–314. English digest in LD 18 (2010): 23–25.

[44] The year 1495 saw at least two other editions of Bernard's *Sermones de tempore* coming off the presses, one from Johannes Emericus in Venice and one from Leonardus Pachel in Milan.

[45] See SBOp 4, 13–58.

Fourth, the source reference which the senior friar provided, according to Melanchthon, was precise, but not precise enough. Melanchthon faithfully reported the precise wording of the Bernardine quotation which the senior friar had pointed out to Luther, but not the exact source reference. The quotation is found verbatim in the *first* of the three sermons on the Annunciation (*Ann 1*).[46] The quotation was so important that Melanchthon cited it in full length. It is the longest direct quotation from any author in his biographical sketch of Luther.

Fifth, the Latin terminology (*locus, concio*) which Melanchthon used for the source reference is likely colored by the humanistic-rhetorical tradition.[47] When he reported that the friar "showed him the *locus* in the *concio* on the Annunciation where these words are found," he implied with respect to *locus* (Greek *topos*) that this passage contains the main idea of a larger text. The *locus* is lifted out of the context of the lengthy sermon (*Ann 1*) in order to mark a dogmatic point of Christian doctrine.

Sixth, what Luther reported to Melanchthon about the older friar's comments about the nature of "faith" has something to do with the two different concepts of "faith," a distinction which always was appealing to Melanchthon who contrasted "historical faith" (a "faith" that also demons would possess) and existential "trust" and justifying faith that brings certainty. Only the latter is meant by Paul's and by Bernard's concept of "faith": "The Spirit itself bears witness with our spirit that we are children of God" (Rom 8:16).[48]

---

[46] See SBOp 5, 13–15.

[47] On the rhetorical term *locus* which is central to Melanchthon's works, see Manfred Hoffmann, "Rhetoric and dialectic in Erasmus's and Melanchthon's interpretation of John's gospel" in *Festschrift Pesch 2007*, 140–170, here 159.

[48] Melanchthon maintained that "faith does not signify merely the knowledge of history, but 'trust' in the promised mercy because of Christ." In *Commentary on Romans,* trans. Fred Kramer (Saint Louis: Concordia, 1992; 2nd edition 2010), 18. Luther early on operated with the concept of faith as "trust." Denis Janz pointed out that by 1515 Luther regarded the scholastic understanding of it as "belief" as an impoverished, superficial distortion of what faith really means; see "What Did Luther Understand by 'Faith'?" in *Reforming the Reformation: Essays in Honour of Principal Peter Matheson*, ed. Ian Bernard (Melbourne: Australian Scholarly Publishing, 2004), 69–80. On Rom 8:16 see "Golden Words" in Chapter 3. 9.

3. 4. "For Me"—The Exact Quotation Is Taken from Bernard's *First Sermon on the Annunciation*. Melanchthon Quotes It, Most Theologians Ignore It

Luther apparently repeated to Melanchthon the exact wording which the senior friar had quoted to him. In the memoirs Melanchthon reported the Bernard quotation as follows:

> "But add to this that you also believe this: that through him [Christ] your sins are forgiven you [(*TIBI*). This is the testimony that the Holy Spirit gives in your heart [Rom 8:16], saying, 'Your sins are forgiven you' [1 Jn 2:12; Mt 9:5;]. For thus the Apostle [Paul] concludes that 'a person is justified freely [*gratis*] by faith' [contraction of Rom 3:24 and 28].'"[49]

In Melanchthon's account the Latin personal pronoun *tibi* is capitalized in order to emphasize the point of having to be personally concerned, whereas Bernard's original text did not have the capitalization. Here we have a case that the quotation is simultaneously also interpreted from a specific point of view, namely by the emphasis on personal concern. Melanchthon continued quoting Luther as follows:

> Luther said that he was not only strengthened by this voice [of the senior friar], but was also reminded of Paul's entire sentence [Rom 3:24–28] who so often inculcates this *dictum* that "by faith we are justified."[50]

Here, in the emphasis on "You," lie the origins of Luther's famous concept of "For Me": "Your sins are forgiven YOU" with the Latin capitalization of *TIBI* for emphasis. "Luther's Reformational theology" is constituted by this very formula "for me" (*pro me*)[51] which has its matrix in Bernard's *Ann 1.* One must not deny due

---

[49] *Ann 1.3* as translated by Franz Posset, *The Two-Fold Knowledge: Readings on the Knowledge of Self & the Knowledge of God Selected & Translated from the Works of Saint Bernard of Clairvaux* (Milwaukee: Marquette University Press, 2004), 119; for the Latin, see next note.

[50] *Hac se voce non solum confirmatum esse Lutherus dicebat, sed commonefactum etiam de tota Pauli sententia, qui toties inculcat hoc dictum: fide iustificamur;* CR 6, 159.

[51] See Bayer, "Das paulinische Erbe bei Luther," 175.

credit to the Pauline-Bernardine *dictum*. Therefore, one cannot act as if this were Luther's invention or own discovery. The least one must say is this: according to Melanchthon, Luther was made aware of it by the senior Augustinian friar who directed him to Saint Bernard.

Melanchthon reported that Luther told him that this quotation was Pauline teaching as it is incorporated within Saint Bernard's sermon: "For thus the Apostle concludes that 'a person is justified *gratis* by faith'." This is a contraction of Rom 3:24 and 28. Thus it was the young Luther at Erfurt who was told that this is Saint Bernard's teaching. And, as such this teaching would become Luther's center piece of his "reception of Paul" as it is the central locus of the Apostle's entire Letter to the Romans and as Luther would say later it is the central theological point of all of Scripture.[52] In Melanchthon's memoirs it is classified as a *dictum* which meant an authoritative statement or maxim.[53]

There is a direct line from the specific *locus* in Bernard's *Ann 1* which was mediated by the Erfurt friar to the consternated young Luther and from there to the mature Luther, the Bible translator. In his German Bible edition of 1545 he would enter (without the mention of Bernard) two words in capital letters from Rom 3:25: *SVNDE VERGIBT* ([he] FORGIVES SIN) and Luther would declare in a marginal (!) note what is most central (!) to all theology, namely the words of verse 25 from the immediate context of Paul's Rom 3:20–28,[54] which is the very passage that the senior Augustinian quoted to Luther from Bernard's *Ann 1*. When Luther referred to verse 25 he referred also to the entire passage of the Sacred Page, Rom 3:20–28, as we must remember Luther's style of quoting the Scriptures, text and context, namely that everything is "in the et

[52] See Bayer, "Das paulinische Erbe bei Luther," 176 (without any mention of Bernard).

[53] Melanchthon in his 1540 Commentary on Romans classified a statement by Augustine as a dictum: "I would not believe the Gospel if the authority of the church did not move me." In *Commentary on Romans*, 248–249.

[54] See Martin Schloemann, "Die zwei Wörter, Luthers Notabene zur 'Mitte der Schrift'," *Luther* 65 (1994) 110–123; referred to by Oswald Bayer, *Martin Luther's Theology. A Contemporary Interpretation*, trans. Thomas H. Trapp (Grand Rapids: Eerdmans, 2008) 6–7 (without mention of Bernard).

cetera."[55] The "etc" or "ec" in medieval folios is a gateway to the full meaning of a reference.[56]

3. 5. A Mistaken and Misinterpreted Opinion in Melanchthon's Memoirs

In his reporting Melanchthon inserted something that sounds like his own thesis about the young Luther reviewing the entire history of the interpretation of Paul's Letter to the Romans:

> Since he [Luther] had read the expositions of many [other interpreters of the Letter to the Romans], he saw the vanity in the interpretations that were en vogue then. [The insight into such vanity] was based both upon the words [of the senior friar] and upon the fact that Luther felt the consolation of mind after having noticed their faulty interpretations.[57]

Melanchthon's report, as it stands now, seems to be an invention rather than a historical insight from Luther. It does not fit with Luther's theological biography that, already at Erfurt, young Luther had recognized that the entire tradition of interpreting the Letter to the Romans was wrong.

Young Luther at that time could not possibly have studied the entire exegetical tradition on the Letter to the Romans! It looks like Melanchthon was quoting a subjective impression which he learned from Luther about the young Luther and his view of the popular understanding of the "justice of God." It was a hint at what was then en vogue, i.e., an impression about popular piety with which Luther had grown up and with which he had arrived at the Erfurt friary. Such popular belief was quickly corrected by the senior friar with his knowledge of Bernard's theology of grace as he set the young Luther straight. Therefore, Melanchthon in his memoirs is correct in saying that Luther "saw the vanity in the interpretations that were en vogue then" and "their faulty interpretations." The vanity in popular spirituality was exposed by the words of the senior friar and Luther

[55] Kenneth Hagen, "It Is All in the Et Cetera: Luther and the Elliptical Reference," LB 3 (1994): 57–67.

[56] See Skocir, "A Search for the Authentic Luther," 258.

[57] *De quo cum multorum expositiones legisset, tunc et ex huius sermonibus et sue mentis consolatione animadvertisse interpretationum, quae tunc in minibus errant, vanitatem*; CR 6, 159.

was comforted as having been liberated from such mistaken popular piety. However, Melanchthon confused the matter insofar as he seems to have proposed the idea that Luther was working against the entire exegetical tradition, i.e., that young Luther "had read the expositions of many" (i.e., of many other, earlier interpreters of the Letter to the Romans).

Melanchthon's thesis in this regard caused a lot of trouble for the Luther image among Catholics, as this thesis led to the accusation that Luther either had not read any of the earlier Christian teachers who correctly interpreted specifically Rom 1:17, or that Luther lied deliberately. This was the observation of the eminent Austrian Catholic scholar Heinrich Denifle who from his painstaking investigations into the history of the interpretation of the Letter to the Romans proved such a thesis wrong.[58] He showed that in the history of exegesis from Peter Lombard (ca. 1100–1160) up to Luther the notion *iustitia Dei* (the righteousness of God) is understood as "justification" and not as the punishing "justice of God" in terms of the "wrath of God" (as Melanchthon claimed that already the young Luther would hold this opinion about the entire exegetical tradition).

Why did the otherwise cautious and scrupulous Melanchthon write about this in his memoirs in the way he did? It would be wrong to suggest that it was Melanchthon's own speculation (or, invention). But the question remains: Did Melanchthon's report perhaps have a foundation in the historical Luther's own words? Indeed it does. Luther insinuated in his *Preface* of 1545 (which Melanchthon knew, of course) that he had felt like he was reborn into paradise after having recognized the true meaning of *iustitia Dei* ("justice of God"), namely that it has nothing to do with the wrath of God. Luther's statement makes sense, however, only if it pertained to his state of mind at the time prior to his becoming an Augustinian friar or during his early time in the Erfurt friary. He had grown up with the popular concept about the "justice of God" and was corrected by the senior

[58] Heinrich Denifle, *Luther und das Luthertum in der ersten Entwickung. Quellenmäßig dargestellt* (Mainz: F. Kirchheim, 1904–1909), revised edition 1906), vol. I,2. Idem, *Luther und das Luthertum. Ergänzungen*, vol. 1: *Quellenbelege; Die abendländischen Schriftausleger bis Luther über die Justitia Dei (Röm. 1,17) und Justificatio. Beitrag zur Geschichte der Exegese, der Literatur und des Dogmas im Mittelalter* (Mainz: F. Kirchheim, 1905). Marc Lienhard acknowledged that Denifle is right, in "Luther en perspective Catholique. Quelques Observations," *Revue d'histoire et de philosophie religieuses* 63 (1983): 167–177.

friar who persuaded him by quoting from Bernard's sermon. However, Luther in hindsight (rashly, superficiously) blamed the customary teaching of "all the teachers" who took "justice" in the philosophical sense as "active justice." [59] Melanchthon without questioning Luther's authority simply regurgitated what Luther had told him or what he read in Luther's *Preface*. "All the teachers" may not mean the entire exegetical tradition prior to Luther, but the majority of contemporary preachers and theologians who fostered the mistaken popular piety of work righteousness. The differentiation of contemporaries of Luther vis-à-vis the exegetical tradition is important in order to make sense of Luther's hyperbole.

If Denifle would have taken Melanchthon's and Luther's thesis about the understanding of *iustitia Dei* as a statement about their contemporary popular, misguided piety, and not as a scholarly statement concerning the entire, earlier exegetical tradition, he would not have come to the conclusion that Luther deliberately lied about his own scholarly research. Misunderstandings abound, one leading to another. One might wonder whether Luther's point would have been more welcome, if only he in hindsight had spoken less polemically and less enthusiastically (in his *Preface* of 1545) about his personal impressions about the "justice of God" with which he had grown up and from which he was freed.

Also, one might wonder how things would have turned out, if only Melanchthon (in his *Preface* of 1546, his memoirs) had not uncritically repeated Luther's remark, perhaps mistaking it as Luther's scholarly statement about the entire exegetical tradition (instead of a reference to misguided contemporaneous piety). And, if Denifle would have read more carefully Melanchthon's account about the young Luther being illuminated by Saint Bernard's sermon *Ann 1* on grace gratis, then his accusation that Luther was a liar could not have come into existence so easily. Luther was not a liar, if one understands his remarks as a reference to the misguided popular concept that he himself had internalized in growing up. However, as Luther worded his statement in 1545 as he did, about all the teachers, he opened himself up to the caviler's accusation of being a liar concerning the interpretation of the exegetical tradition. What all this

[59] *Oderam enim vocabulum istud 'Iustitia Dei', quod usu et consuetudine omnium doctorum eram philosophice intellegere de iustitia, ut vocant, formali seu active, qua Deus est iustus, et peccatores iniustosque punit*; WA 54, 185 (*Preface* of 1545).

proves, nevertheless, is this: Melanchthon faithfully reported everything that he was told by Luther or what he read in Luther's works, in particular the *Preface* to the First Volume. As the "theological secretary" of the Reformation movement Melanchthon never questioned what Luther had said about the "expositions of many." Notably, Melanchthon immediately added that Luther discovered such "vanity in the interpretations that were en vogue then" because of the senior friar's words about Bernard's sermon, which brought so much spiritual comfort to Luther. It looks like the "discovery" started at Erfurt with the fraternal advice Luther received. It is difficult to over-estimate the role the anonymous friar played for Luther's career.

Furthermore, with respect to the allegedely incompetent exegetical and theological teachers of old, Melanchthon would have contradicted himself in his memoirs (had he really meant the entire tradition, as Denifle assumed) because elsewhere in his memoirs Melanchthon was saying that there was a good tradition which saw "the light" which had been restored by Augustine, Prosper, Maximus, Hugo, "and others like them . . . up to the age of Bernard." (CR 6, 167).[60] His review of the patristic tradition (up to Bernard as the last of the fathers) evidently would have contradicted Luther's rash, but nevertheless explicit, statement that all the teachers had got it wrong. Therefore, one is compelled to interpret Melanchthon's statement about Luther reading "the expositions of many" (*multorum expositiones,* CR 6, 159) (a) as indeed a faithful citation of Luther's hyperbole; but (b) as Luther's reference to Luther's contemporary teachers, and not to the all the fathers of the exegetical tradition (as Denifle would have it). Ironically, Melanchthon's statement about Augustine, Prosper etc. up to Bernard, who all saw "the light" (CR 6, 167), basically is in agreement with Denifle's scholarly investgations about the history of exegesis of Rom 1:17 and its correct understanding.

---

[60] *Ac restituta lux Augustini scriptis posteritati profuit, Nam [sic] deinde Prosper Maximus* [sic, without a 'comma' between the two names], *Hugo, et aliqui similes, qui studia gubernarunt, usque ad Bernardi aetatem, propermodum Augustini normam sequuntur*; CR 6, 167.

3. 6. MELANCHTHON IN HIS *PREFACE* RETURNED A SECOND TIME TO THE SENIOR FRIAR'S ADVICE

The quotation from Bernard's *Ann 1* was so important to Melanchthon that he returned to this *senex* a bit later in his memoirs saying that the old man had remained a true teacher of the gospel and the pointer-out (*monstrator*) of the right teaching about the faith. Melanchthon thus wanted to make sure that he kept the memory of this particular, though anonymous, friar alive:

> I commemorate these things not only to defend Luther and his hearers, but also so that pious minds might ponder at this point in time and hereafter what the government of the true Church of God is and always was; how God through the word of the Gospel gathers the eternal Church for himself from that sinful mass, that is, from that great filthy collection of people, amongst whom the Gospel shines forth like a spark in the darkness. So it was in the times of the Pharisees when Zechariah, Elizabeth, Mary, and many others were guardians of the true doctrine; so it also was before these [our] times that many who called upon God in the right way maintained the doctrine of the Gospel, some more perspicuously than others. Such a man was also that senior [*ille senex*], i.e., the one of whom I have spoken before, the one who so often lifted Luther up when anxieties troubled him; the one who had become his [spiritual] advisor who pointed him to the right doctrine about the faith.[61]

It is generally agreed that Luther's understanding of "penance" was linked to his intention to reform popular piety.[62] According to Melanchthon it started at Erfurt with Luther's recognition of Bernard's theology of grace and penance. We must let go of the concept of a sudden breakthrough at Wittenberg ("The Discovery in

---

[61] . . . *Talis fuit et ille senex, de quo dixi, qui Lutherum conflict[t]antem pavoribus saepe erexit, eique aliquando modo monstrator fuit doctrinae de fide*; CR 6, 165.

[62] See Martin Brecht, "Luthers neues Verständnis der Buße und die reformatorische Entdeckung," *Zeitschrift für Theologie und Kirche* 101 (2004): 281–291. Does Brecht bring the Bernard factor into play? No; he examines the ways in which Luther was influenced (or not) by Staupitz, Erasmus, and Paul of Burgos.

the Tower,"[63] Tower Experience; see above, legend no. 2). Furthermore, Luther did not have to be skilled in Greek and Hebrew for recognizing the doctrine of justification by grace in faith.[64] To Luther, Bernard's Latin was clear enough.

The friars at Erfurt or at least the one anonymous senior friar had a strong preference for Bernard of Clairvaux.[65] And as such he made history through Luther. Luther may have realized that the "Bernard renaissance" was celebrating Saint Bernard as the "last of the church fathers."[66] Attending the Augustinian college of Erfurt Luther was fortunate to have had great teachers who knew the works of Bernard of Clairvaux. He found help with his "consternations."

Ann 1 is the one text from Bernard's biblical theology that led Luther to what we customarily call his Reformational insight of salvation by grace alone through faith alone.[67] Augustinian friars in reading Bernard's theology, not his mysticism, live off the matrix of the "Bernard renaissance" around 1500. The quotation from *Ann 1* turned out to be of central significance in Melanchthon's memoirs about Luther's life, since Melanchthon mentioned the senior Augustinian twice who had quoted it to the consternated Luther.

---

[63] This concept appears to have been invented by Grisar, 105–110. However, Grisar, 107, was mistaken when he accused Melanchthon of popularizing the idea that no other doctors of the Church understood Rom 1:17 correctly, as Grisar referred to CR 6, 159. Upon rereading the given passage such a popularization cannot be found.

[64] See Schwiebert 134

[65] See Posset, "Frater Augustinus," 30–47.

[66] *Ultimus inter Patres* (Mabillon's preface to the edition of Bernard's works), *Patrologia Latina* 182, 26; see Posset, *Pater Bernhardus,* 36–37.

[67] On this, see the comment of Weinacht, *Melanchthon und Luther* (2008), 63–64: "*Wir befinden uns mit dem Bernhard-Zitat also an einer der zentralen Stellen seiner Historia. Die Figur des alten Mönches, Johannes Greffenstein, spielt deshalb für Melanchthon im Leben Luthers eine beträchtliche Rolle. Er wird später ein zweites Mal erwähnt als derjenige, der Luther zur Erkenntnis des rechtfertigenden Glaubens geführt hat.*"

3. 7. Luther Increased His Knowledge of Bernard through Bonaventure

Fig. 9. Woodcut Illustration in Bonaventure's *Opuscula Parva* (Strasbourg 1495), a book read by Friar Luther in Erfurt.

Earlier Luther research had a hunch that reading Bonaventure (1221–1274) had pointed Luther to mysticism.[68] The hint is important, but not for its implication of mysticism. Until recently, Luther research had not known of any of Luther's marginalia on Bonaventure's *Opuscula parva.* From the meticulous research of Jun Matsuura (1949–) we know now that amongst Friar Luther's earliest extant marginalia made at Erfurt are those in the two volumes of Bonaventure's *Opuscula parva* (Strasbourg: Georg Husner, 1495) and those on Anselm's *Opuscula* (Basel: Johannes Amerbach, not after 1497).[69]

The two volumes with Bonaventure's works include several Pseudo-Bonaventure texts.[70] A few of Luther's notes are found in Part 1.[71] In Part 2 they increase; yet, young Luther did not discriminate authentic and spurious or Pseudo-Bonaventure texts.[72] May one

---

[68] See Grisar 59.

[69] Luther annotated the following works of Anselm and Pseudo-Anselm: *Cur deus homo, Liber seu epistola ad vrbanum papam de fide seu de incarnatione verbi contra iudęos, Liber de conceptu virginali et peccato originali, Declaratio cuiusdam super eodem libro, Monologion, Dialogus de casu diaboli, Liber pro insipiente, Liber de miseria hominis, Epistola siue Liber de diuersitate sacramentorum, Epistola siue Liber de fermentato et azymo, Liber de vestimentis, membris et actibus deo attributis, Liber de voluntate dei, Liber de concordia pręscientię et prędestinationis necnon gratię dei cum libero arbitrio, Dialogus de libero arbitrio, Dialogus de veritate, Liber de similitudinibus, Liber de mensuratione crucis, Liber meditationum, Liber de meditatione redemptionis humane, Homelia in euangelium secundum lucam, Liber de excellentia virginis marie, Liber epistolarum, De imagine mundi.* On Luther and Anselm, see Burnell F. Eckhardt, *Anselm and Luther On the Atonement: Was It "Necessary"?* (San Francisco: Mellen Research University Press, 1992). Eckhardt assumed that Luther annotated Anselm at Wittenberg during the first lectures on the psalms between 1513 and 1516 (in following Buchwald, WA 9, 104–105, 108, 17–33), whereas now one should concur with Matsuura (2009) that it was already at Erfurt, *Erfurter Annotationen 1509–1510/11,* 1–85.

[70] In the edition printed by Georg Husner in Strasbourg; see Matsuura, *Erfurter Annotationen 1509–1510/11,* 89–147.

[71] Content: *De reductione atrium ad theologiam, Breuiloquium, Confessionale, De septem donis spiritussancti* [sic], and *Epistola de eo quod christus et apostoli et discipuli eius incesserunt discalciati.*

[72] Content: *Canonisatio beati Bonauenture vel relation in eadem* (by Johannes Franciscus de Pavinis), *Speculum discipline seu de minimis ad nouitios* (by Bernardus a Bessa), *Speculum beate marie virginis* (by Conradus de Saxonia), *Tractatus de preparatione ad missam, Expositio misse* (spurious), *Soliloquium de quattuor mentalibus exercijs, Itinerarius mentis in deum, Paruum bonum, De septem itineribus eternitatis* (by Rudolf of Biberach), *De quattuor virtutibus cardinalibus, Fascicularius* (an excerpt from Gerard Zerbolt of Zutphen), *Tractatus de*

surmise that Luther studied texts like the authentic *Tractatus de preparatione ad missam* and the spurious *Expositio miss[a]e* as a follow-up after his ordination to the priesthood in 1507? (Luther had studied the *Canonis Missae Expositio* of Gabriel Biel [1410–1495] in preparation for ordination).

When Luther read Anselm he made cross-references to Bonaventure,[73] which presupposes his reading of this Franciscan. Luther's esteem for Bonaventure was likely based upon Bonaventure's esteem of Saint Bernard. Luther must have noticed Bonaventure's preference for Bernard whom the Franciscan author quoted 461 times.[74] Luther seemed to copy five Bernard-quotations while reading Pseudo-Bonaventure's *Meditationes vite domini nostri Iesu Christi* Chapter 17 as he entered them at spots where he found some empty space, namely on the inside of the book cover and on the title page of Anselm's *Opuscula*e (bound together with a work by Johannes Trithemius OSB [1462–1516]). Anselm's *Opuscula*e must have been in his possession as he used—without scruples—the space inside the book cover and on the title page for his lengthy entries.

In Bonaventure's *Meditationes vite domini nostri Iesu Christi* Luther found and then copied the following genuine Bernard texts:

(a) Bernard's Fourth Sermon about Luke's gospel text *Missus est angelus*. This Bernard-quotation comprises five printed lines about humility.[75]

(b) Bernard's Sermon 37 on the Canticle. This Bernard-quotation comprises ten printed lines and deals with the warning not to compare oneself to others, be they lower or higher in status, and to heed what is said in Lk 14:10, "Sit down in the lowest place."[76]

---

ecclesiastica hierarchia (spurious), *Meditationes vite domini nostri Iesu Christi* (by Johannes de Caulibus), *De vitiis et eorum remedies, Opusculum de perfectione vite ad sorores*.

[73] See Posset, "Frater Augustinus," 35–36.

[74] See Posset, "Frater Augustinus," 35.

[75] See the Latin quotation in Matsuura, *Erfurter Annotationen 1509–1510/11,* 8 (= SBOp 4, 54).

[76] See the Latin quotation in Matsuura, *Erfurter Annotationen 1509–1510/11,* 10–11 and 145 (= SBOp 2, 13).

(c) Bernard's First Sermon for the Feast of the Epiphany. This Bernard-quotation comprises more than four printed lines and contains Bernard's considerations about the humility of Christ.[77]

These quotations have the common theme "humility." Luther's early familiarity with Bernard and Bonaventure stayed with him for the years to come when he would praise both (and also Hugo of Saint Victor [died in 1141]) during his First Lectures on the Psalms, on Ps 41,[78] and toward the end of his life in the Lectures on Genesis: "Bernard loved the incarnation of Christ very much, so did Bonaventure."[79] With the knowledge of these sayings one may then trust a Table Talk according to which Luther compared Bernard and Bonaventure, saying that Bonaventure is closest to Bernard.[80]

Apparently Melanchthon was not told anything about Luther's early reading of Hugo, Bonaventure, Anselm, or Trithemius, as his *Preface* to Volume Two is silent on these authors. Luther in his own *Preface* to Volume One made no mention of them either. Luther's later, meager use of these other authors in comparison to the many later references to Saint Bernard by the young and the old Luther remains striking. He was less impressed by them.

From Melanchthon we may deduce that reading Augustine was not a top priority to the young Luther at Erfurt, at least not at first, which can be confirmed from Luther's annotations during his Erfurt years. Luther read Bonaventure and Anselm before he studied Augustine, and while he read (Pseudo) Bonaventure he kept a close eye on Bernard-quotations. This is not surprising because Luther was already sensitized about the great significance of Saint Bernard through the advice he had received from the senior friar about grace and forgiveness of sins.

---

[77] See the Latin quotation in Matsuura, *Erfurter Annotationen 1509–1510/11,* 11 (= SBOp 4, 299, 14–18); Posset, *Pater Bernhardus*, 219–220. I wish to correct my previous asumption since I no longer maintain the possibility that Luther copied the Bernard-quotation from the Sermon on the Epiphany in preparation for his first lectures on the Psalms (1513–1515) at Wittenberg. I now prefer the earlier time when Luther was still at Erfurt as his annotations prove.

[78] *Incredibile enim est, quantum reficiant animam lachryme deuotionis et spei, vt dicunt experti Bernhardus, Bonaventura, Hugo*; WA 55-I, 352, 1–2.

[79] *Bernardus valde dilexit incarnationem Christi, item Bonaventura*; WA 43, 581, 11.

[80] *Bernhardus pulcherrime praedicat neque sic disputat. Bonaventura proximus est post ipsum*; WA TR 3, 295, 1–2 (no. 3770a).

3. 8. LUTHER CONTRA-POSITIONED PETER LOMBARD AND BERNARD: "TO STAND STILL IS TO REGRESS"

What Peter Lombard in *Sentences II, Distinction 24* taught about human capabilities in paradise before the fall is commented with a *Contra* by Luther.[81] The issue is "standing still" (Latin: *stare*) and "making progress" (Latin: *proficere*). Lombard implied that Man could stand, but not make progress. Luther seized the opportunity to show off his knowledge of Bernard and to dissolve some seeming contradiction. For this purpose Luther quoted a well known Bernardine adage "On the road of life, not to progress means to regress" (*in via vitae non progredi regredi est*) and "To stand still is to regress" (*stare est retrogredi*), which Bernard articulated by paraphrasing Phil 3:13.[82] The quotation is known in the German rhyme of Johannes Tauler (ca. 1300–1361): *in dem wege Gotz ston, das ist hindrisch gon* (Standing still on the road to God is regressing) which is a nice translation of Bernard. Luther correctly understood it as a saying about Man after the Fall (*Sed b. Bern. loquitur de nostro statu*).

The Bernardine adage, *Stare est retrogredi,* is a paraphrase or the sum of numerous, authentic sayings of Bernard, but not a literal quotation from the Bernard opus.[83] The adage may be based though upon Bernard's authentic words which he usually connected to one of his favorite Pauline quotations, Phil 3:13. This verse is incorporated, for example, in his Second Sermon on the Purification of Mary:

> Anyone who does not care to advance in all the virtues needs to know that he is standing still and not moving on; yes he actually regresses, because on the road of life, not to progress means to regress, for presently nothing can yet be in the same [permanent] state . . . But rather we must extend ourselves to

[81] See Matsuura, *Erfurter Annotationen 1509–1510/1,* 458; Bell, *Divus Bernhardus*, 39–42.

[82] See the various sources in Farkasfalvy, "The Use of Paul by Saint Bernard as Illustrated by Saint Bernard's Interpretation of Philippians 3:13," 161–168; Posset, *The Two-Fold Knowledge*, 131–133 ("Know your direction and your spiritual progress"); Posset, *Pater Bernhardus*, 96–100.

[83] See Posset, *Pater Bernhardus*, 96.

> what is ahead and try unceasingly for the better [Phil 3:13], and leave our imperfection up to view of the divine mercy.[84]

Similar versions are found in Bernard's letters to Cluniac Abbots (Letter no. 91),[85] to Abbot Guerin of Aulpes (Letter no. 254),[86] or to the Monks of Saint Bertin (Letter no. 385).[87] Young Luther made use of the proverb that is shaped essentially from Bernard's spirituality. For example, Luther did so in his first lectures on the Psalms (*Dictata*, on Ps 4:2; Ps 16:5; Ps 119:122), in the lectures on Rom 3:11 and on Rom 12:2, also against Prierias in 1518. Then, for the last time in 1535 the elder Luther quoted Bernard, now as an ex-friar.[88]

For the proper understanding of the young Luther quoting Bernard against Lombard one also needs to call to mind what Bernard asked and taught in his *Ann 1* (i.e., the same sermon to which Luther was alerted by the esteemed friar). In that sermon one reads: "For if human nature was unable to stand while still in its integrity, how much less will it be able, corrupted as it now is, to rise [from the fall] on its own?"[89] This question is asked in the immediate context of Bernard's teaching that with the Spirit who is given us (Rom 8:16) we know that the forgiveness of sins cannot be had without God's indulgence (*Ann 1.1*) and that all human merits are the gift of God (*Ann 1.2*). In the same context is found the quotation which the *senex* had given Luther in order to comfort him in his spiritual troubles: "But add to this that you also believe this: that through him your sins are forgiven you" (*Ann 1.3*). Having received this insight from Bernard, Luther entered the following rhetorical *contra* in the margin for Lombard's *Dist 24* as follows:

> Contra: To stand still is to regress, says Blessed Bernard. Therefore, even if Man could stand (he could not), he could not remain innocent. Response: Standing still in the state of innocence was not a regressing. Just as in the blessed life [with God] there is no standing still [in terms of] regressing. Blessed

---

[84] SBOp 4, 340.
[85] See SBOp 7, 240.
[86] SBOp 8, 158.
[87] SBOp 8, 352.
[88] See Posset, *Pater Bernhardus*, 98–100.
[89] SBOp 5, 14; translation Posset, *The Two-Fold Knowledge*, 119.

> Bernard, however, speaks about our [fallen] status even if there would be a status that is not fluctuating.[90]

Luther, who was already fully convinced of Bernard's teaching about grace alone in every regard of human life, may quote here against Lombard the Bernardine saying which was well known to him and his contemporaries. In the years to come, time and again Luther would return to Saint Bernard who was quoted to him first by the anonymous friar at Erfurt. When he was transferred from Erfurt to Wittenberg he always seemed to have Bernard with him to be utilized in his biblical studies.

3. 9. "Golden Words": Rom 8:16 According to the Young Luther

After being appointed professor of biblical theology at Wittenberg, Luther sang the praises of Saint Bernard in the lecture hall, starting in his first lectures on the Psalms (*Dictata*, 1513–1515).[91] Luther utilized Bernard's *Ann 1* on Ps 31, but without an exact source reference. A seemingly joyful Luther exclaimed: "Bernard meditates beautifully in a certain sermon."[92] Unfortunately the recent WA edition (2000) of parts of the *Dictata* remains flawed concerning this particular Psalm lecture. The "critical edition" refers the reader to a Pseudo-Bernardine sermon *De duobus discipulis euntibus in Emmaus*, whereas the proper reference is to *Ann 1*,[93] the section which Luther had learned at Erfurt. It is hard to believe that the WA-editor disregarded Bernard's *Ann 1*, to which Luther would explicitly refer in the subsequent lecture on Romans.

In the spring of 1515, in his lectures on Saint Paul's Letter to the Romans, Luther showed his continued fascination for Bernard's *Ann 1*, with the Pauline verse which is so central to it, namely Rom 8:16

---

[90] *Contra: stare est retrogredi, dicit b. Bern. ergo si potuit tantum stare, (potuit non) non potuit manere innocens. Respondetur, Quod stare in statu innocentie non erat retrogredi. Sicut nec in beatitudine stare est retrogredi. Sed b. Bern. loquitur de nostro statu, si saltem status et non fluxus est*; Matsuura, *Erfurter Annotationen 1509–1510/1*, 458.

[91] See Bell, *Divus Bernhardus*, 42–81.

[92] See Posset, *Pater Bernhardus*, 168–169.

[93] See WA 55-II, 178; on this passage, see Posset, "Bernhard von Clairvauxs Meditation zu Psalm 31, 2 bei Martin Luther," LuJ 69 (2002): 71–78.

about the "testimony that the Holy Spirit gives in your heart."[94] Lecturing on this verse, Luther gave his students the longest quotation from Bernard's opus that he ever quoted, i.e., the same passage from *Ann 1* which the senior in Erfurt had pointed out to him. One must take Rom 8:16 with all of the "etc." and thus include at least the two preceding verses about being "children of God by adoption" who may call upon God as their "Abba, Father." Luther's exposition of Rom 8:16 may be a "culmination point" of the entire lecture series.[95] (In his lectures on Rom 15 he continued to make use of Bernard and his interpretation of the triple command to "feed," his concept of good pastoral care,[96] copied from Bernard; all this was dear to Luther's heart and mind).

In the WA edition of Luther's Lectures on Romans the quotation marks for the words from Bernard's *Ann 1* are entered incorrectly[97] and thus the quotation appears shorter than it is in reality. The WA editor did not recognize the phrase "But add this: That you also believe this" still belonging to the direct quotation from Bernard.[98] This editorial flaw corresponds with the carelessness of many Luther scholars in their neglect of Saint Bernard who as the theologian of grace was Luther's spiritual and theological mentor who guided him

[94] *"Das Bernhardzitat muß Luther maßlos gefesselt haben";* Bell, *Divus Bernhardus*, 98.

[95] Erich Kleineidam, "Ursprung und Gegenstand der Theologie bei Bernhard von Clairvaux und Martin Luther," in Wilhelm Ernst, K. Feiereis, and Fritz Hoffmann (eds.), *Dienst der Vermittlung: Festschrift zum 25-jährigen Bestehen des philosophisch-theologischen Studiums im Priesterseminar Erfurt*, (Leipzig: St. Benno Verlag, 1977), 221–247, here 235; Bell, *Divus Bernhardus*, 92.

[96] WA 56, 137, 26–27; see Posset, "Bernhard von Clairvauxs Sermone zur Weihnachts-, Fasten- und Osterzeit als Quellen Martin Luthers," 110–111.

[97] WA 56, 369, 28–370, 23 (on Rom 8:16), quoting Bernard's sermon, SBOp 5, 13, 9–15, 5; Posset, "Bernhard von Clairvauxs Meditation zu Psalm 31,2 bei Martin Luther," 75–77; idem, "Bernardus Redivivus: The *Wirkungsgeschichte* of a Medieval Sermon in the Reformation of the Sixteenth Century" *Cistercian Studies* 22 (1987): 239–249. Erich Kleineidam, "Ursprung und Gegenstand der Theologie bei Bernhard von Clairvaux und Martin Luther," in *Dienst der Vermittlung: Festschrift zum 25-jährigen Bestehen des philosophisch-theologischen Studiums im Priesterseminar Erfurt,* eds. Wilhelm Ernst, K. Feiereis, and Fritz Hoffmann (Leipzig: St. Benno Verlag, 1977), 221–247; Bell, *Divus Bernhardus*, 83–99.

[98] WA 56, 370, 8–9, given without quotation marks of what is taken verbatim from Bernard, SBOp 5, 14, 22.

across the centuries.[99] The same incorrect placement of the quotation marks for the same Bernardine passage of *Ann 1* was carried over into the translation of Melanchthon's *Commentary on Romans* of 1540 until very recently when it was ameliorated.[100]

Luther always took Bernard's *Ann 1* with him throughout his studies and lectures on the letters of Saint Paul,[101] and at other occasions. Luther returned to this Bernardine sermon in 1517 in his lectures on Hebrews (Heb 5:1): "Blessed Bernard in a certain sermon on the Annunciation."[102] In his commentary on Galatians of 1519 he alluded to *Ann 1*, but he did not mention it by name. He did, however, quote the Pauline passage, Rom 8:16.[103] Luther was so permeated by Bernard's message in *Ann 1* with its use of Rom 8:16 that it helped him also during the interrogation by Cardinal Cajetan at the meeting in Augsburg, on 14 October 1518. Luther did not hesitate to mention *divus Bernhardus* by name.[104] During the heated Leipzig Disputation of 1519 Luther countered his opponent with this protest: "I venerate Saint Bernard."[105] There is a direct connection from the young Luther's first becoming aware of Rom 8:14–16 at the Erfurt friary to Luther's lectures as just reviewed, and to Luther in mid-career. In his *Summer Postil* of 1526 he advised, speaking metaphorically, that the calling upon Abba by the children of God (in Rom 8:15–16) is worth

---

99 See Franz Posset, "Divus Bernhardus: Saint Bernard as Spiritual and Theological Mentor of the Reformer Martin Luther" in *Bernardus Magister*, 517–532 (see note above); appeared in LD 3 (1995): 65–67.

100 See the 2010 edition, 34.

101 See Bell, *Divus Bernhardus*, 104.

102 See Posset, *Pater Bernhardus*, 172–173; Bell, *Divus Bernhardus*, 99–106.

103 See Peter Manns, "Zum Gespräch zwischen M. Luther und der katholischen Theologie. Begegnung zwischen patristisch-monastischer und reformatorischer Theologie an der Scholastik vorbei" in *Thesaurus Lutheri: Auf der Suche nach neuen Paradigmen der Luther-Forschung. Referate des Luther-Symposiums in Finnland 11.–12. November 1986*, eds. Tuomo Mannermaa, Anja Ghiselli and Simo Peura (Helsinki: Luther-Agricola-Gesellschaft, 1987), 63–154, here 144–145; Bell, *Divus Bernhardus*, 107–109; Posset, *Pater Bernhardus*, 174.

104 *Et Bernhardus sermone de annunctiatione i*, WA 2, 15–35–16, 3 (*Acta Augustana*, 1518); Bell, *Divus Bernhardus*, 133–137; Posset, *Pater Bernhardus*, 173–174.

105 *Respondeo. Divum Bernardum veneror*; WA 59, 445, lines 411–412; Posset, *Pater Bernhardus*, 57.

being written "with golden letters" because they are so noble and comforting.[106]

The effect of Bernard's theology can be traced step by step during Luther's entire career.[107] The impact which the anonymous friar had with quoting Bernard to the young Luther was the starting point of a gradual process. "Remarks of this kind sank into Luther's mind, and took root there, though their fruit only ripened."[108] The American Luther scholar, Ernest G. Schwiebert (1895–2000) observed in 1950: "Philip Melanchthon also mentioned that, while in the monastery at Erfurt, Luther was not without aid . . . An old priest . . . consoled him by recalling . . . one of the sermons of St. Bernard."[109] This crucial element of Bernard's impact, although featured by a few scholars, is underexposed or deliberately left out from most recent Luther biographies, both Catholic and Protestant.

Luther, having heard the senior friar at Erfurt briefly quoting Rom 8:16 within the context of Bernard's *Ann 1* in order to comfort him in his consternations, apparently always kept the verses in high esteem. In 1527, around the time when Luther and some friends commemorated the controversy over the indulgences, the friends at Wittenberg had to "console" one another.[110] At that time Luther gave lectures on 1 Jn, declaring: "I myself have paid attention to no holier monk than Bernard; I rank him higher than Gregory [the Great] . . . " Luther then quoted the Bernardine sentence "My life is wasted and achieves nothing" and immediately added: "There is no better phrase in all of Bernard. Another one is in the Sermon on the

[106] *Und billich mit guldenen buchstaben zu schreiben*; WA 22, 136, 21–22. On other sayings for which Luther awarded the "gold medal" so-to-speak, see Posset, "Goldene Worte," 227.

[107] See Franz Posset, "The Elder Luther on Bernard: Part I: Martin Luther's Permanent Indebtedness to Bernard: Commemorating the 900th Birthday of Bernard of Clairvaux." Part II: "Last Exegetical Work," ABR 42 (1991): 22–52 and 179–201; appeared in LD 2 (1994): 118–126.

[108] Köstlin, *Life of Luther*, 42.

[109] Schwiebert 170.

[110] Letter to Amsdorf of 1 November 1527: "We drank in memory of them [indulgences] in this hour and consoled one another," WA Br 4, 275, 25–27 (no. 1164). Luther dates his letter with this hint: *Wittenbergae die Omnium Sanctorum, anno decimo Indulgentiarum conculcatarum, quarum memoria hac hora biblimus utrique consolati, 1527. T. Martinus Luther* (no. 1164); Junghans, *Der junge Luther,* 292.

Annunciation."[111] With "another one" Luther meant, of course, the passage he had learned from the anonymous Erfurt friar. Notably, the year 1527 is the year of the tenth anniversary of the "trampling of the indulgences." What Luther wrote to Nikolaus von Amsdorf (1488–1565) referred more likely to a small, private drinking party than to a formal, public celebration. It was not a "solemnity" (*Feierlichkeit*).[112] And, also notably, Luther's commemoration did not include any hint at a nailing of his theses to a door.

I advocate that Melanchthon's account about Luther and Bernard at Erfurt be rehabilitated. Melanchthon's view in his memoirs/*Preface* is easily corroborated from the study of Luther's own ample quotations of Bernard's theology and biography throughout his lectures, books, and sermons up to his old age. Melanchthon thus remained a trustworthy witness that Friar Martin was a theological disciple of Bernard of Clairvaux in following his monastic theology of salvation (not so much his "mysticism").[113] Insights from Bernard's monastic theology, mediated by the senior friar, remained important to Luther, the friar and the ex-friar.

As an aside, the contemporaneous controversialist and caviler, Johannes Cochlaeus, knew nothing about Luther becoming aware of Bernard's *Ann 1*, which can only mean that Cochlaeus was deprived of the intimate knowledge which Melanchthon was privileged to receive directly from Luther. Melanchthon was very specific about the fact that Luther received spiritual and theological advice in terms of Bernard's theology of grace, but Melanchthon was unspecific as to the date or year when such advice was given.

As another aside, the contemporaneous Johann Bugenhagen, a close friend of Luther, did not mention the Bernard factor either which Melanchthon so well demonstrated in his *Preface*. Bugenhagen conveyed the idea that Luther's insights about the "justice of God" occurred early on at Erfurt when Luther found confirmation (of what

[111] WA 20, 746, 13–18; Posset, *Luther's Catholic Christology*, 116–126, 201–221; Posset, *Pater Bernhardus*, 174–175.

[112] As Leppin assumed, "Geburtswehen und Geburt einer Legende," 149, note 13.

[113] It is problematic to consider Bernard of Clairvaux only in terms of so-called "mysticism," as Ulrich Köpf rightly pointed out: "Bernhard von Clairvaux—ein Mystiker?" in *Zisterziensische Spiritualität. Theologische Grundlagen, funktionale Voraussetzungen und bildhafte Ausprägungen im Mittelalter*, eds. Clemens Kasper and Klaus Schreiner (St. Ottilien: EOS Verlag, 1994), 15–32.

he knew from Bernard's *Ann 1*) in his somewhat later reading in 1509 of Augustine's *On the Trinity* and of Peter Lombard.[114]

In 1538 when the elder Luther compared Augustine and Bernard he concluded that Bernard alone is worthy of being called "Father Bernard" (*Pater Bernhardus*) because he was the "most righteous of all the monks"[115] who should be studied diligently. In his own original words:

> *Und [Bernhard] ist auch allein werd, das man ihnen Pater Bernhardus nenne und den man mit vleiss ansehe.*[116]

3. 10. No Need for Augustinianism

Apparently Melanchthon was not concerned about an exact date for the senior friar's advice to read Saint Bernard. To him the continuity from Bernard to Luther was important in terms of the understanding of justification by grace alone through faith alone, but not in the form of a sudden insight. Luther did not invent a new theology, but discovered the old Bernardine theology of justification by grace alone through faith alone.[117] This was the matrix of all of Luther's later theology and reform efforts of popular piety.

---

[114] On this see Martin Lohrmann, "A Newly Discovered Report of Luther's Reformation Breakthrough from Johannes Bugenhagen's 1550 Jonah Commentary," LQ 22 (2008): 324–330: "By pointing to the 1509 readings in Augustine and Lombard, Bugenhagen's account presents a new source in Luther research that describes how Luther may have been coming to significant evangelical discoveries about *iustitia Dei* and justification by faith already as a young teacher."

[115] . . . *den aller fromsten Munch*, WA 47, 109, 21; LW 22, 388. The Early New High German notion *from[m]/frum* is opalescent. Luther wanted the German notion *from/frum* to be the equivalent of Latin *iustus* (just, righteous); see Heide Wunder, "'iusticia, Teutonice fromkeyt.' Theologische Rechtfertigung und bürgerliche Rechtschaffenheit. Ein Beitrag zur Sozialgeschichte eines theologischen Konzepts" in Stephen E. Buckwalter and Bernd Moeller (eds.), *Die frühe Reformation in Deutschland als Umbruch* (Gütersloh: Gütersloher Verlagshaus, 1998), 307–332; Hugo Moser, "'Fromm' bei Luther und Melanchthon: Ein Beitrag zur Wortgeschichte in der Reformationszeit" in *Studien zu Raum- und Sozialformen der deutschen Sprache in Geschichte und Gegenwart* (Berlin: Schmidt-Verlag, 1979), 54–74; Posset, *Pater Bernhardus*, 59–60.

[116] WA 47, 109, 22–23; see Franz Posset, "Goldene Worte: Augustinus und Bernhard in der Sicht des alten Luther (1531–1546)," *Catholica* 54 (2000): 220–239.

[117] See Else Marie Wiberg Pedersen, "Justification and Grace. Did Luther Discover a New Theology or did He Discover Anew the Theology of Justification and Grace?" *Studia Theologica* 57 (2003): 143–161; idem, Pedersen, "The Significance of the Sola Fide and the Sola Gratia."

In Melanchthon's memoirs the historical Luther was presented *first* as a Bible reader ("Prophets and Apostles"), *then* as having been consoled and strengthened in his anxieties by Saint Bernard's words through the help of the *senex*, and only *after* all that did Luther become a reader also of Augustine and found him in support of what he already knew from Bernard about faith and consolation:

> Little by little, as he read and compared the sayings and lessons which are recorded in the Prophets and Apostles, and as he kindled his faith in daily prayer, he obtained more illumination. At that time he also began to read the works of Augustine, where he found many clear statements, in both the *Commentary on the Psalms* and *On the Spirit and the Letter*, which confirmed this doctrine concerning faith, and he found consolation, which had lit up in his own heart.[118]

According to Melanchthon's memoirs, Luther only after having been led via Saint Bernard to Paul's Letter to the Romans and to the reading of the Prophets began to pay attention also to Augustine. Melanchthon did not mention any lectures at Wittenberg. Melanchthon's recollection matches the statement which the historical Luther made about Augustine in a letter to Georg Spalatin on 19 October 1516 that, just because he was a friar in the Augustinian order, did not mean that he also would have to feel obligated to read him and to always stand up for him:

> Devotion to my order does not compel me to approve of the blessed Augustine. Before I had stumbled upon his books I had no regard for him in the least.[119]

Eventually, Melanchthon wrote, Luther read "all the works of Augustine."[120] Luther most likely in 1509 annotated the 1489 edition of *Aurelii Augustini opuscula plurima*, which was at the library since 1500.[121] This edition includes several texts that are Pseudo-

---

[118] CR 6, 159.

[119] *Non quod professionis meae studio ad b. Augustinum probandum traher qui apud me, antequam in libris eius incidissem, ne tantillum quidem favoris habuit*; Letter to Georg Spalatin, WA Br 1, 70, 19–21 (no. 27); see Balge 8–9.

[120] *Omnia Augustini monumenta*; CR 6, 159.

[121] See Matsuura, *Erfurter Annotationen 1509–1510/11,* 149, 153–249.

Augustinian.[122] The only authentic texts are the *Enchyridion* [sic] *ad Laurentium, Confessiones [Liber III-XII], De doctrina christiana [Liber I, III, IIII], Sermones duo de vita et moribus clericorum, Ex libro retractationem beati augustini in librum de vera religione eiusdem,* and *De decem chordis.*

This list of readings of the young Luther with his marginalia is usually disregarded and Luther's reading of the anti-Pelagian writings of Augustine is featured[123] in total neglect of what Melanchthon knew, namely the readings in this sequence: (1) The one locus from Bernard's *Ann 1,* (2) *Lectio divina* ("Prophets and Apostles"), (3) Augustinian works in the 1489 edition, and only then (4) Augustine's *Commentary on the Psalms* and the anti-Pelagian *On the Spirit and the Letter*. However, from Melanchthon's hint one cannot demonstrate that Luther at Erfurt was actually reading the anti-Pelagian writings, which come into his horizon only in Wittenberg in 1516, but which were included in the 1505/1506 edition of the collected works of Augustine, printed by Amerbach in Basel.[124] In the paragraph in which Melanchthon wrote that Luther "found many clear statements, in both the *Commentary on the Psalms* and *On the Spirit and the Letter*," Melanchthon made no distinction between what Luther was reading in Erfurt and in Wittenberg. No copies of Augustine's *Commentary on the Psalms* from Luther's desk are extant. Melanchthon only indicated that Luther found many clear statements in both of these. Most likely the message from Augustine's anti-Pelagian writings dawned on Luther only in Wittenberg in 1516, whereas he internalized Bernard's message of grace alone, early on at

[122] *De triplici habitaculo, Scala paradisi* (Guigo the Carthusian), *De duodecim abusionem gradibus, De assumptione beate virginis marie in corpore et anima, De honestate mulierum, De cura agenda pro mortuis ad Paulinum episcopum nolensem, De contemptu mundi ad clericos, De conuenientia decem preceptorum et decem plagarum egipti, De cognitione vere vite, De fide ad Petrum* (Fulgentius), *De vera et falsa poenitentia, De spiritu et anima, De vita christinaa ad sororem suam viduam, De diffinitionibus orthodoxe fidei et ecclesiae dogmatibus* (Gennadius), *Sermo de ebrietate* (Caesarius of Arles).

[123] Most recently, Oswald Bayer still held this position: "Das paulinische Erbe ist Luther besonders durch die Tradition des Augustinereremiten-Ordens, dem er angehörte, übermittelt worden." So far so good, but then follows the flawed view: "d. h. in der Hauptsache durch die Paulusinterpretation Augustins, wie sie sich vor allem in dessen antipelagianischen Schriften dokumentiert." In: "Das paulinische Erbe bei Luther," 171.

[124] See Matsuura, *Erfurter Annotationen 1509–1510/11,* XCI.

Erfurt, through the senior friar's hint. Melanchthon did not explicitly mention any other church fathers. However, this must not cause us to assume that Luther concentrated on Augustine exclusively.[125]

3. 11. WHAT ELSE?

Melanchthon, after mentioning Augustine, immediately added that Luther also read Cardinal *Cameracensis* (Petrus de Alliaco, Peter of Ailly, 1351–1420), Gabriel Biel, Johannes Gerson (Jean Gerson, 1363–1429), and William of Ockham (ca. 1285–1347):

> Nevertheless he did not completely abandon the *Sententiarii*. He was able to quote Gabriel Biel and Peter of Ailly by heart, almost word for word. He spent much time in thoroughly reading the writings of Ockham, whose acumen he preferred to Thomas [Aquinas] and [Johannes Duns] Scotus. He also had carefully read Gerson. He read all the works of Augustine, not only often, but he also remembered them the best. He began this most intense study at Erfurt, where he stayed for four years at the Augustinian College.[126]

As to Cardinal *Cameracensis*, Luther mentioned him in his first known Christmas sermon (1514/1515) on Jn 1,[127] which he delivered in Latin most likely to his confreres at the Wittenberg friary. His extraordinary philosophizing in this sermon[128] would not have been suitable for a Christmas sermon for the town folks. This sermon clearly demonstrates how deeply imbued Luther was in the philosophy of the academia of his time. Recognizing such deep involvement makes the liberation from it all the more striking, a liberation that was achieved decisively with the help of the senior at

[125] On this, see Junghans, *Der junge Luther*, 109: *"Aber diese Konzentration auf Augustin wird zu einer gefahrvollen Engführung, wenn es um die Genesis der Theologie Luthers geht."* How true!

[126] CR 6, 159. At this point in Melanchthon's memoirs one may expect a hint at Luther's ordination to the priesthood, but it is not there.

[127] See WA 1, 22, 7–21; see Walther von Loewenich, *Die Eigenart von Luthers Auslegung des Johannes-Prologes* (Munich: Verlag der Bayerischen Akademie der Wissenschaften. Philosophisch-Historische Klasse, 1960), 31–35; Theodor Dieter, *Der junge Luther und Aristoteles,* 346–377.

[128] Dieter comments on the nature of this sermon, saying that it is exceptional for its use of philosophy for the explanations of the theological issues of the Trinity, Christology and soteriology, in *Der junge Luther und Aristoteles,* 375–377.

Erfurt and his Pauline-Bernardine expertise and spirituality and pastoral skill.

Melanchthon reported that Luther preferred Ockham's *acumen* to Thomas Aquinas and to John Duns Scotus (ca. 1266–1308),[129] but Melanchthon did not indicate here that Luther actually read Thomas and Scotus. He merely said that Luther preferred Ockham.[130] Melanchthon's statement can be corroborated from examining Luther's annotations in extant copies of the Erfurt library from 1509 to 1510/11, in particular on the sacrament of the altar. Here one finds Luther's notes on Ockham's *On the Sacrament of the Altar* (*De sacramento altaris*), first printed in 1491,[131] on Gabriel Biel's Commentary on the Mass (*Canon Missae Expositio*),[132] and on the teachings of Cardinal *Cameracensis* (Peter of Ailly).[133] In his own notes during his time at Erfurt, Luther also hinted at the late medieval author Gerson—but only once, and then only within Luther's notes on Ockham.[134]

Luther's Erfurt notes show a reference to Thomas Aquinas, but only insofar as Thomas is quoted by Ockham concerning the doctrine of transubstantiation, in which Luther found logical flaws. This reference to Thomas does not prove Luther's direct knowledge of Thomas' commentary on the *Sentences*.[135] Luther's notes mirror a strong aversion against Scotus. In distancing himself from Scotus the young Luther simply seemed to follow Ockham, or perhaps Biel.[136]

Not everything Luther may have read in the Erfurt friary is to be mentioned here. We must leave aside much of Luther's study of Peter Lombard's *Sentences* during the period from the fall of 1509 to the fall of 1510,[137] except for one instance treated above (Chapter 3. 8).

---

[129] *Diu multumque legit scripta Occam, Huius acumen anteferebat Thomae et Scote*; CR 6, 159; see Junghans, *Der junge Luther*, 94.

[130] Luther's familiarity with, for instance, Thomas Aquinas is discussed by Dennis R. Janz, *Luther and Late Medieval Thomism: A Study in Theological Anthropology* (Waterloo: Wilfrid Laurier University Press, 1983).

[131] See Matsuura, *Erfurter Annotationen 1509–1510/11,* LXXVI-LXXVII, 647–709. The copy with Luther's notes is kept at Staatsbibliothek zu Berlin, vol. *Inc 2442,5.*

[132] See Matsuura, *Erfurter Annotationen 1509–1510/11,* CXXVII, 695–709.

[133] See Matsuura, *Erfurter Annotationen 1509–1510/11,* CXXIII, 699–701.

[134] See Matsuura, *Erfurter Annotationen 1509–1510/11,* CXXVII.

[135] See Matsuura, *Erfurter Annotationen 1509–1510/11,* CXXIV.

[136] See Matsuura, *Erfurter Annotationen 1509–1510/11,* CXXII.

[137] See Matsuura, *Erfurter Annotationen 1509–1510/11,* 251–560; Junghans, *Der junge Luther,* 96–108.

Brief mention should be made of Jun Matsuura's new discovery that Luther consulted the encyclopedia of Giorgio Valla (1447–1500), the humanist of Piacenza. The first Renaissance encyclopedia which is titled *De expetendis et fugiendis rebus* (Venice: Aldus Romanus, 1501) was available in two volumes. We also know that Luther's confrere Johann Lang entered notes in the sections on *Grammatica, Dialectica,* and *Rhetorica.*[138] Lang's are more numerous than Luther's who left only some underlining and several small geometrical drawings in the margin of the section on *Geometria* in Part 1[139] and some minor notes on *Dialectica* in Part 2.[140] Due to the lack of additional marginalia from Luther's pen we do not know whether he consulted Valla's opus for any other information (the encyclopedia had sections, for example, on Arithmetic, Music, Astrology, Medicine, and Moral Philosophy).[141] Be this as it may, the extant notes prove that Luther used it.

Luther browsed through *De statu et ruina monastici ordinis* by Johannes Trithemius.[142] However, as to the issues raised by Trithemius concerning monastic reforms the young Luther showed very little interest.[143] Evidently, church reform via the reforming of religious orders was not on the young friar's mind. With greater zeal Luther read in 1509 Hugo of Saint Victor, as his annotations demonstrate.[144] In 1509 Luther also read Augustine's *Sermones duo de vita et moribus clericorum* (Two sermons on the life and behavior of clerics) in Augustine's *Opuscula* as he entered this date (1509) on the title page of his desk copy.[145] His reading may have been preceded by heated discussions in the Erfurt friary, probably during the time span from summer 1506 to the fall of 1508, about the authenticity of some of the works attributed to Augustine and about Augustine not having been a "monk." This thesis had been proposed by the

---

[138] See Matsuura, *Erfurter Annotationen 1509–1510/11,* 716.
[139] See Matsuura, *Erfurter Annotationen 1509–1510/11,* 718–722 with Figs 6 to 9 which show Luther's added geometrical drawings in the margins.
[140] See Matsuura, *Erfurter Annotationen 1509–1510/11,* 724–727.
[141] See Matsuura, *Erfurter Annotationen 1509–1510/11,* 711–716.
[142] See Matsuura, *Erfurter Annotationen 1509–1510/11,* LII. There are no Bernard texts extant with Luther's notes and thus are not in Jun Matsuura's edition *Erfurter Annotationen 1509–1510/11,* except for the excerpts entered on the inside of the book cover of *Opuscula Anselmi*, 8. On this, see Posset, *Pater Bernhardus*, 98–99.
[143] See Posset, "Frater Augustinus," 44–46.
[144] See Matsuura, *Erfurter Annotationen 1509–1510/11,* CXXV.
[145] See Matsuura, *Erfurter Annotationen 1509–1510/11,* 153.

humanist priest Jacob Wimpfeling (1450–1528) in his book *De integritate* (Strasbourg, 1505).[146] Hugo's explanation of the Rule of Augustine (*Expositio in regulam Augustini*) was so important that it had to be available in every friary as the *Constitutions* of the Augustinian order stated,[147] and thus also to Luther. When Friar Luther was reading the two sermons on the life and behavior of clerics in Augustine's *Opuscula,* he was still quite incensed about Wimpfeling and entered some defensive, nasty marginalia against him:

> Hugo in like manner in his *Explanations of the Rule [of Augustine]* took the words as those of Augustine where Augustine had said: *Fateor de preciosa veste erubesco;* these are words found in the sermons [second sermon] that were given to the hermits. Why, you senile and deranged mask, do you find fault with Hugo? Why do you [Wimpfeling] correct the Church of God—what I mean is, why with your filthy lies do you say that these sermons are not by Augustine?[148]

Whatever else Luther may have read in his early years, one of the most lasting encounters with the theological tradition was with Bernard of Clairvaux to whom Luther had been directed by the senior advisor in the Erfurt friary.

3. 12. The New Vista on "Bernard and Luther"

When it comes to "Luther and Bernard," Melanchthon's view, based upon interviews with Luther, remains correct. The insight from Luther's statement of 1516 about his initial disregard for Augustine has opened up our new vista, which comes from the recognition of the great popularity of Saint Bernard of Clairvaux around 1500. In taking Bernard's theology (again, not his "mysticism") into serious

---

[146] See Junghans, *Der junge Luther*, 195, 213.

[147] See Matsuura, *Erfurter Annotationen 1509–1510/11,* CXXV, 218 with note 2.

[148] *. . . Hugo itidem in Expositionibus regule allegat verba augustini vbi dixerat Aug.: 'Fateor de preciosa veste erubesco' etc. que cum sint in sermonibus ad heremitas factis, Cur tu, senex et frenetica larua, Hugonem Incusas? Cur ecclesiam dei corrigis? id est cur tam Impurissime mentiris? Hos scil. non esse augustini*; Matsuura, *Erfurter Annotationen 1509–1510/11,* 217–218; see also WA 9, 12, 6–18. On this, see Manfred Schulze, "Martin Luther and the Church Fathers" in *The Reception of the Church Fathers in the West From the Carolingians to the Maurists*, ed. Iréna Backus (Leiden: Brill, 1997), vol. 2, 573–626, here 574.

consideration for the development of Luther's theology of penance and of grace, I have advocated since the end of the last century a "new paradigm of study" for the twenty-first century.[149]

It is a fallacy, perhaps an "intentional fallacy,"[150] or a derailment, by mostly German Lutheran scholars to interpret Bernard primarily in terms of so-called "mysticism"[151] whereas it is Bernard's *theology* of grace that is of utmost importance to Luther. They pay lip-service to supposedly mystical influences, and thus they avoid the challenge that recent Catholic Luther research presented that it is Bernard's biblical theology of grace.[152]

In light of all this, it seems insufficient that graduate course offerings in theology only include medieval "Augustinianism" (Augustine awakening) while completely neglecting the "Bernard renaissance." This goes also for the medieval monastic theology. One must recognize that monastic influence on Luther remained always very strong.[153] One must fully agree also with what another, well recognized, Lutheran Luther scholar, Reinhard Schwarz once said, namely, that Luther was bequeathed with an inalienable inheritance of monastic theology.[154] This insight is accepted by other recent Luther

---

[149]According to the perspective of Won Yong JI of St. Louis, MO, in his book review of my *Pater Bernhardus: Martin Luther and Bernard of Clairvaux* (1999) in *Concordia Journal* 28 (2002): 349.

[150] To this fallacy a Danish Lutheran theologian objected masterfully; see Wiberg Pedersen, "The Significance," 41. "It has been typical, particularly of German Lutheran scholarship to distinguish between theology and the so-called mysticism. In this vein, German Lutheran scholars from Ritschl over Harnack and Seeberg to the Oberman-school have tended to stress scholastic theology as a real theology comparable to Luther's in order to set the 'difference radicale', at the expense of monastic theology such as Bernard's . . . " (33, with note 38). The same strategy seems to be at work in the writings of the late Bernhard Lohse.

[151] Leppin unduly framed the intent of Theo Bell's *Divus Bernhardus* within "mysticism" by involving the Bernard factor solely within the issue of the *Bedeutung der Mystik für die Entwicklung der Reformation*; in: "Mystisches Erbe auf getrennten Wegen: Überlegungen zu Karlstadt und Luther " in *Luther und das monastische Erbe,* 154. A similar tendency emerges in Robert Kolb, *Martin Luther: confessor of the faith* (Oxford and New York: Oxford University Press, 2009), 27–29.

[152] See the studies by Theo Bell and my own.

[153] See Franz Posset, "Monastic Influence on Martin Luther," *Monastic Studies* 18 (Montreal: The Benedictine Priory of Montreal, 1988): 136–163; idem, "St Bernard's Influence on Two Reformers: John von Staupitz and Martin Luther," *Cistercian Studies* 25 (1990): 175–187; appeared in LD 1 (1993): 122–123.

[154] I was so impressed by Reinhard Schwarz who articulated this issue so that I translated his essay into English: Reinhard Schwarz, "Luthers unveräußerte Erbschaft

experts, namely that Luther inherited "essential elements of his thinking" from the monastic tradition.[155]

This means that Luther's monastic-theological inheritance would support to some degree the old conviction which connected the then conceived "Reformational Breakthrough" to the young Luther in Erfurt. This would have happened even prior to his *Dictata* on the psalms, delivered in Wittenberg. However, this does not mean that we must identify Luther's insight that he gained from reading Bernard with the so-called sudden "Reformational Breakthrough." It is a historical reality (which others, however, at times have disqualified as Melanchthon's unreliable cloister legend, *Klosterlegende*) that Luther's decisive theological insights originated at the Erfurt friary when he became familiar with one specific section of a sermon of Bernard (*Ann 1*).

With background information about Bernard's monastic theology of justification by grace gratis, and with his studies on the psalms and on Romans, Luther became convinced that he had to fight the error of one's own righteousness and cling to the trust in the righteousness of God (*iustitia Dei*) alone. This conviction was clearly expressed in Luther's letter to Friar Georg Spenlein (ca. 1485–1563) in Memmingen who should learn "to breathe and trust in the righteousness of Christ . . . . [Others] do not know the righteousness of God which is given to us in Christ abundantly and gratis."[156] This theological conviction sounds very much like Bernard, though he was not explicitly mentioned by name. However, Luther told Spenlein in no uncertain Pauline terms, by using 1 Cor 2:2, which is one of

---

an der monastischen Theologie" in *Kloster Amelungsborn 1135–1985,* 209–231; "Luther's Inalienable Inheritance of Monastic Theology," trans. Franz Posset, in ABR 39 (1988): 430–450.

[155] See Ulrich Köpf, "Monastische Traditionen bei Martin Luther," in *Luther—zwischen den Zeiten. Eine Jenaer Ringvorlesung*, ed. Christoph Markschies and Michael Trowitzsch (Tübingen: Mohr Siebeck, 1999), 17–35, here 22. On the continuity from Bernard to Luther, see also Pedersen, "Justification and Grace" (2003); "Ein furtrefflicher Munch. Luther and the Living out of Faith" in *Luther und das monastische Erbe*, 221–241; Pedersen, "The Significance of the Sola Fide and the Sola Gratia" (2009).

[156] *. . . in iustitia Christi respirare atque confidere . . . . ignorantes iustitiam Dei, quae in Christo est nobis, effusissime et gratis donata*; WA Br 1, 35, 16–19 (no. 11).

Bernard's most favorite verses:[157] "Therefore, my dear brother, know of 'Christ and him crucified' [1 Cor 2:2], learn to sing to him and in despairing about yourself learn to say to him: 'You, Lord Jesus, are my righteousness, but I am your sin . . . . Ruminate [Christ's] love and you will see his most sweet consolation."[158] Luther shared here what he had learned to believe from the senior at Erfurt during his earlier consternations, namely to trust in the freely given grace of God.

After such fraternal advice given in April 1516 Luther would soon venture to go public with his message on God's grace. In the spring of 1517 he would publish his German booklet on the Seven Penitential Psalms. Although in it Luther would not make explicit mention of Saint Bernard, he shared the theology which was permeated by what he had learned at Erfurt through the mediation of the anonymous friar: salvation is given by grace gratis. In this train of thought Luther concluded his first booklet in German, answering with a "yes" his own rhetorical question about the righteousness of man and of God:

> Is this all that you can say about human righteousness, wisdom, and power, and always expound the Scriptures only from the point of view of God's righteousness and grace? And can you only play on one string of the lyre and sing only this one song?[159]

When Luther preached on the feast of the Annunciation in 1539, he recommended "reading" Bernard because it is pure joy to do so because he loved Christ so much.[160] When comparing St. Francis, St. Dominic, and St. Bernard Luther favored Bernard: "Bernard has the

---

[157] On Bernard's favorite Pauline quotation (1 Cor 2:2), see excerpts in Posset, *The Two-Fold Knowledge. Readings on the Knowledge of Self & the Knowledge of God*, 103–108.

[158] *Igitur, mi dulcis Frater, disce Christum et hunc crucifixum* [1 Cor 2:2] *disce ei cantareet de te ipso desperans dicere ei: tu, Domine Ihesu, es iustitia mea, ego autem sum peccatum tuum . . . Istam charitatem eius rumina, et videbis dulcissimam consolationem eius;* WA Br 1: 35, 24–32 (no. 11).

[159] *Kanstu nit meer dann nur von menschen gerechtickeit, weyßheyt und stercke sagen, ymmer von gottis gerechtickeit und gnaden die schrifft außlegen, und alßo nit meer dan auff einer seyten lyren und nur ein lidleyn singen?* WA 1: 219, 21–24.

[160] *Is sic diligit Christum und redet und predigest susse von im, das ein lust ist, quando quis legit*; WA 47: 694, 5–6.

best knowledge of *religio*, as his writings show."[161] Luther displayed an enduring respect for *Pater Bernhardus*. This was so because Luther viewed Bernard "as one who truly understood the grace of God and lived in obedience to it."[162] This perspective was not always understood in Lutheranism or in Catholicism. Evidently, the Bernard factor in Luther's life and work was and is hard to accept for both sides.

As to the Roman side, a happy, early nineteenth-century exception to the general polarization was Saint Clement Mary Hofbauer (1751–1821). His positive opinion about Luther and the German Reformation almost cost him his canonization because it was offensive to Vatican ears.[163] Hofbauer as papal legate had arrived at the unconventional image of Luther and the Reformation:

> Ever since I have been in a position to compare, as papal legate, the religious situation of Catholics in Poland with that of Protestants in Germany, I have become certain that secession from the church has come about because the Germans both did and do feel the need of being religious. The Reformation has spread and taken root, not purely on account of men who were heretics and philosophers, but on account of men who genuinely sought after a religion of the heart. I have said this to the Pope and cardinals in Rome, but they did not believe me, maintaining rigidly that the cause of the Reformation was hostility to religion.[164]

CONCLUSION

We trusted Melanchthon's memoirs as guide. All in all, his account is reliable. One may have doubts about his hint at the posting of the *Propositiones* on indulgences at the castle church of Wittenberg since Luther himself nowhere mentions such an act. With his wording of *Propositiones* (for the text which was later known as the *Ninety-Five Theses*) Melanchthon closely followed Luther's own designations.

---

[161] *Ac antefero omnibus Bernhardum: habuit enim religionis optimum cognitionem: sicut ostendunt eius scripta*; WA 42: 453, 41–454, 1.

[162] Michael Casey, *Foreword* to Posset, *Pater Bernhardus*, 12.

[163] See Joachim Wanke (Catholic bishop of Erfurt), "War Luther ein Reformkatholik? Nach-Gedanken zu Werk und Wirkung Martin Luthers aus heutiger Perspektive" in *Luther zwischen den Kulturen*, 517–522, here 517.

[164] As quoted by Casey, *Foreword*, 7–8.

We found Melanchthon most reliable concerning the Bernard factor in Luther's spiritual and theological development; "most reliable" because one can easily demonstrate from Luther's authentic works (without relying on Table Talk) that Saint Bernard was his life-long, theological mentor from the early days in Erfurt to his old age at Wittenberg.

The historical Luther came to his insight of the forgiveness of sins by grace alone through Bernard's *Ann 1*. Luther did not develop his theology as a continuation of a medieval Augustinianism, Ockhamism or *German* mysticism.[165] Building on this well known older assessment, I say in positive terms that the historical Luther's theology is a rearticulating of Bernard's theology as Luther encountered it in *Ann 1* and as it was mediated by the fatherly advice of the older friar. Luther emerged as the *Bernardus Redivivus.*[166] Or more provocatively, the real Luther may not have been a "Lutheran" at all.[167]

It remains amazing that contemporary Luther biographies are still being written without ever mentioning the name and significance of Bernard of Clairvaux, or with just a hint at him in passing as if it were a *chose négligeable.* From now on, Luther biographies, if they want to present the authentic, historical Luther, can be convincing only if the Bernard factor is properly figured in, because the center piece of the historical Luther's doctrine of justification is identical with the one of Saint Bernard. From this perspective it appears that the doctrine of salvation no longer would need to separate the Christian denominations, and the mutual condemnations would become outmoded. The real Luther with the doctrine of justification has turned from the "Corruptor of the Faith" to the "Father in the Faith,"[168] a "Roman Catholic Prophet."[169] Already forty years ago, in

---

[165] See Junghans, "Luther's Development from Biblical Humanist to Reformer," 13; Markus Wriedt, "Produktives Mißverständnis. Zur Rezeption der Theologie des lateinischen Kirchenvaters Augustinus im Werk Martin Luthers (1483–1546)," in Norbert Fischer, ed., *Augustinus. Spuren und Spiegelungen seines Denkens Band 1: Von den Anfängen bis zur Reformation* (Hamburg: Meiner, 2009), 211–224.

[166] See Posset, "Bernardus Redivivus" (see note above).

[167] See Markus Wriedt, "What Makes Luther a Lutheran?" Paper of 2004 as posted on internet (accessed June 2010): www.mu.edu/theology/markuswriedtpresentations.shtml

[168] Rolf Decot, ed., *Vater im Glauben. Studien zur Theologie Martin Luthers. Festschrift Peter Manns* (Stuttgart: F. Steiner, 1988); Posset, "From the Corrupter of the Faith to the Father in the Faith" (see note above).

July 1970, Cardinal Jan Willebrands (1909–2006) as the President of the Vatican's Secretariat of Christian Unity declared Luther the ecumenical teacher to be shared as our "Common Teacher," *Gemeinsamer Lehrer—Doctor communis.* [170] Such intellectual, theological insight is great! Yet, it still needs to sink in after almost half a century from the head into the heart—which is evidently easier said than done—on both sides of the aisle.

Would it now not be about high time to take the real Luther's advice from his larger *Lectures on Galatians* (printed version, 1535)? Luther, in the credible self-awareness of being "by God's grace the evangelist of Wittenberg"[171] said:

> When the pope concedes to us that God alone out of pure grace justifies the sinner through Christ, then we wish not only to carry him on our hands, but also to kiss his feet.[172]

[169] Gregory Sobolewski, *Martin Luther Roman Catholic Prophet* (Milwaukee, Marquette University Press, 2001).

[170] The Latin title *Doctor communis* is the original honorific title of Saint Thomas Aquinas. Willebrands' speech is printed in J. Kardinal Willebrands, *Mandatum Unitatis. Beiträge zur Ökumene* (Paderborn: Bonifatius, 1989), 112–125; see also (Cardinal) Karl Lehmann, "Luther als Lehrer des Glaubens? Die ökumenische Bedeutung seiner Katechismen" in *Lutherische Kirche in der Welt* (Jahrbuch des Martin-Luther-Bundes 45) (Erlangen: Martin-Luther-Verlag, 1998), 131–146, with reference to Cardinal Jan Willebrands, 135–137. Lehmann's contribution is available in an English digest: LD 9 (2001): 148–149.

[171] *Martin Luther von gottes gnaden Euangelist zu Wittenberg*; Luther to Duke George of Saxony on 3 January 1523; WA Br 3, 5, 31–33 (no. 567); WA 10-II, 105, 17–18; see Kaufmann 21.

[172] *Hoc impetrato, scilicet quod solus ex mera gratia per Christum iustificet, non solum volumus Papam in minibus portare, imo ei osculari pedes;* WA 40-I, 181, 11–13. How to understand Luther's statement is open to interpretation. Can it be dismissed as a mere rhetorical exaggeration?

PART TWO

Luther Directed Melanchthon to Saint Bernard

1. THE YOUNG MELANCHTHON ON BERNARD[1]

The search for the historical Luther must include a few observations about Luther's impact on Melanchton in terms of the Bernard factor.[2] For this purpose we need to briefly recall the young Melanchthon's initial view of Saint Bernard and how he gradually came to appreciate the theology of this medieval saint.

The young Melanchthon, who did not grow up in a monastic milieu, was hardly familiar with Bernard's "monastic theology." He once admitted that he lacked those experiences which the monks and friars had when they daily prayed the psalms.[3] He had no experience of a life in a cloister and therefore cannot be expected to have read the works of a monastic author such as Saint Bernard even when his works were readily available in print at that time. They came off the presses in almost three hundred editions between 1464 and 1500.[4]

The self-conscious young humanist was interested in all branches of knowledge including philosophy, the natural sciences, ethics, history, the ancient languages, and classical literature.[5] At the age of twenty-three, he began to work on fundamental theological themes, the *Loci communes rerum theologicarum*. Melanchthon had kept

---

[1] The biography of Melanchthon by Heinz Scheible does not include any mention of Bernard of Clairvaux as being of significance to this reformer: *Melanchthon. Eine Biographie* (Munich: Beck, 1997). The same observation must be made regarding Scheible's *Melanchthon und die Reformation. Forschungsbeiträge*, eds. Gerhard May and Rolf Decot (Mainz: Philipp von Zabern, 1996). I am grateful to Timothy Wengert for providing me with additional hints on Melanchthon's use of Bernard.

[2] See Franz Posset, "A Humanist and Reformer Turns To Saint Bernard: Philip Melanchthon and Bernard of Clairvaux," *Analecta Cisterciensia* 55 (2005): 301–315.

[3] See Wilhelm Maurer, *Der junge Melanchthon zwischen Humanismus und Reformation*, (Göttingen: Vandenhoeck & Ruprecht, 1969), vol. 2, 251.

[4] See Posset, "Saint Bernard of Clairvaux in the Devotion," 309–15.

[5] See Sachiko Kusukawa, ed., *Philip Melanchthon: Orations on Philosophy and Education*, trans. Christine F. Salazar (Cambridge and New York: Cambridge University Press, 1999).

Luther informed about the progress of his work. Melanchthon in his lectures on Matthew and on Romans was dependent upon Luther. They may even have served him in preparing his *Loci* issued 1521.[6]

In the opening of his chapter on "The Power of Man, Especially Free Will," Melanchthon noted that Augustine and Bernard wrote on free will, and that the former revised his ideas extensively in the books that he later wrote against the Pelagians, while Bernard appeared "not consistent."[7] In the summary of this chapter he simplistically "lumped"[8] together this monastic theologian, Bernard, and the Scholastics, in a sweeping statement: "You see, dear reader, with how much more certainty we have written about free will (*arbitrium*) than Bernard or any of the Scholastics."[9]

Melanchthon sooner or later must have backed away from his negative view of Bernard because in the later editions of his *Loci* he dropped his earlier comments. Why did Melanchthon change his mind on Bernard? In order to provide a full explanation, Melanchthon's entire opus would have to be investigated as to all of his statements on Bernard, which may be a task for the future that cannot be done here. Only one aspect shall be pursued: Melanchthon's reception of a small section from Bernard's *Ann 1*, namely only the first three paragraphs (*Ann 1.1–3*) from this rather lengthy sermon.[10]

We know that the Pauline verses of Rom 8:16 are part of the Bernardine sermon *Ann 1* which the senior friar had quoted to Luther at Erfurt. In this connection it is worthwhile to take a look at a text of

[6] See Wilhelm H. Neuser, "Luther und Melanchthon—Ein Herr, verschiedene Gaben," in Wolf-Dieter Hauschild, Wilhelm H. Neuser, and Christian Peters, eds., *Luthers Wirkung: Festschrift für Martin Brecht zum 60. Geburtstag* (Stuttgart: Calwer Verlag, 1992), 47–62; English digest in LD 3 (1995): 60–64.

[7] Editor Wilhelm Pauck's introduction in *Melanchthon and Bucer* (Philadelphia: The Westminster Press, 1969), 22.

[8] "St. Bernard is lumped together with the Scholastics," Peter Fraenkel, *Testimonia Patrum. The function of the patristic argument in the theology of Philip Melanchthon* (Geneva: E. Droz, 1961), 30, note 101.

[9] The original reads as follows: *Vides, lector, quanto certius de libero arbitrio scripserimus quam vel Bernardus vel ulli scholastici*, 1,70; Horst Georg Pöhlmann, *Loci communes 1521: Lateinisch-Deutsch*, translated and annotated (Gütersloh: G. Mohn, 1993), 47; see also Pauck, 30; Bell, *Divus Bernhardus*, 348; Posset, "Saint Bernard of Clairvaux in the Devotion," 336–37.

[10] See SBOp 5, 13–15. One must note, however, that Melanchthon hardly ever specifies that this quotation is taken from the first of Bernard's three sermons on the Annunciation.

1522 which Melanchthon wrote in German on the distinction of secular and spiritual righteousness. In this text the young Melanchthon made use of Rom 8:16 in such a way that one is reminded of what Luther was told by the senior Augustinian confrere (according to Melanchthon's own memoirs in the *Preface* to Volume Two). What Melanchthon wrote there is essentially the same what he had heard Luther telling him about the Erfurt friar who helped him so decisively in his spiritual consternations. The passage concerns spiritual righteousness:

> Human reason and work is useless for salvation. The Holy Spirit is needed for the proper knowledge of God. It is the divine righteousness in us which Christ works in us through the Holy Spirit. Our heart is moved by the Holy Spirit and grasps grace and pardon of sin through Christ. The heart receives consolation and gains a happy certainty. Such a heart comes to the right conclusion about God only when the Holy Spirit is present because it is the Holy Spirit who gives testimony to our heart about it according to Romans 8 (and Jn 16).[11]

Melanchthon here in 1522 gave no credit to either Luther or Bernard for the theological insights he offered. It sounds like a summary of Bernard's *Ann 1* as Melanchthon would present it in his *Preface* of 1546. It is open for speculation how the young man of 25 years of age came to those deliberations that he penned down in 1522.

---

[11] See Melanchthon, *Unterschidt zwischen weltlicher und Christlicher Fromkeyt*, in *Melanchthons Werke in Auswahl*, ed. Robert Stupperich (Gütersloh: C. Bertelsmann, 1951–1975), vol. 1, 171–175. Noteworthy, Helmar Junghans translates Early New High German *fromkeyt* with contemporary German *Gerechtigkeit*. The notion *fromkeyt* (*frumkeyt* and similar spellings) is complex. Luther wants this German notion to be the equivalent of Latin *iustitia* (justice, righteousness); see Wunder, "iusticia, Teutonice fromkeyt" and Moser, "'Fromm' bei Luther und Melanchthon" (see above p. 116, n. 115). Martin Brecht, "Rechtfertigung oder Gerechtigkeit? Überraschungen auf den Spuren von Luthers Bibelübersetzung," LuJ 77 (2011): 81–105.

2. MELANCHTHON IN MID-CAREER ON BERNARD (1531)

One observes an increase of references to Bernard in Melanchthon's correspondence of 1530.[1] In that year the Diet of Augsburg was in session when on 25 June the *Augsburg Confession* was read to the Emperor and to the international congress (called "diet"). By 3 August 1530, the Emperor accepted the Roman party's *Confutation*. Melanchthon, however, continued to prepare the *Apology of the Augsburg Confession*, especially on its Article 4 on "justification."

By May 1531 when the first edition of the *Apology*[2] was printed with the *Augsburg Confession* (called the quarto edition) Melanchthon appears to have integrated into the text of Article 12, on repentance, the quotation from Bernard's *Ann 1.*[3] The positive reception of Bernard by Melanchthon at that time may have something to do with his "everyday interaction in Wittenberg"[4] and with the intense intellectual exchange and sharing of life experiences between him and Luther (and others), especially during the time span

---

[1] *Melanchthons Briefwechsel: Kritische und kommentierte Gesamtausgabe*, ed. Heinz Scheible (Stuttgart: Frommann-Holzboog, 1977–), nos. 991, 994, 1008 (all of 1530); (hereafter quoted as MBW).

[2] The translations of the quotations of Bernard's *Ann 1* in the *Apology of the Augsburg Confession* within both *The Book of Concord* editions of 1959 and of 2000 are not consistent. The latest translations, based on the revised, octavo Latin version of September 1531, are found in *The Book of Concord: The Confessions of the Evangelical Lutheran Church*, ed. by Robert Kolb and Timothy J. Wengert, trans. by Charles Arand, Eric Gritsch, Robert Kolb, William Russell, James Schaaf +, Jane Strohl, Timothy J. Wengert (Minneapolis: Fortress Press, 2000). I use the given new translations verbatim except for the quotations from Bernard's *Ann 1*, which are my own translation.

[3] "Neu eingefügt," according to Christian Peters, *Apologia Confessionis Augustanae. Untersuchungen zur Textgeschichte einer lutherischen Bekenntnisschrift (1530–1584)* (Stuttgart: Calwer Verlag, 1997), 386.

[4] See Timothy Wengert, "Melanchthon and Luther / Luther and Melanchthon," LuJ 66 (1999): 56.

from 1530 to 1533.[5] In his Article 12 he no longer stated that Bernard is uncertain, but that Bernard is "correct,"[6] as Melanchthon contracted two different quotations from the same *Ann 1* (from paragraphs 1 and 3) which he made to look like one quotation (Bernard's words are bold printed):

> Therefore let pious consciences know that God commands them to believe that they are forgiven freely on account of Christ and not on account of our works. Let them sustain themselves with this command of God against despair and against the terrors of sin and death. Let them know that this position has been extant among the saints in the church since the beginning of the world. For Peter clearly cites the consensus of the prophets, and the writings of the apostles bear witness that they hold the same position. Nor do we lack testimonies from the Fathers. For Bernard says the same thing in words that are not at all obscure: **"For it is necessary first to believe that you cannot have forgiveness of sins except through God's indulgence; second, that you cannot claim any good work whatever unless He himself grants it to you; finally, that you cannot merit eternal life by any works of yours, unless it too is given to you gratis** [*Ann 1.1*]; **but add to this that you also believe that through him [Christ] your sins are forgiven you [*tibi*]. This is the testimony that the Holy Spirit gives in your heart [Rom 8:16], saying, 'your sins are forgiven you' [Mt 9:5]. For in this way the Apostle concludes that 'a person is gratis justified through faith' [Rom 3:24, 28]"** [*Ann 1.3*]. Bernard's words wonderfully shed light on our position, because he not only requires that we believe in a general way that sins are remitted through mercy, but he urges that we add personal faith by which we believe that our own sins have been forgiven. Moreover, he teaches us how we may be certain about the forgiveness of sins, namely, when by faith our hearts are uplifted and find rest through the Holy Spirit. What more do our opponents need? Do they still

[5] On Luther and Melanchthon, see also Junghans, "Philipp Melanchthon als theologischer Sekretär," in Günter Frank, ed., *Der Theologe Melanchthon* (Sigmaringen : Jan Thorbecke, 2000), 129–152. Martin Brecht, "Melanchthon und Luther oder: Samsons Kinnbacke," ibid., 83–102.

[6] *Et Bernardus recte dicit.* CR 27, 521.

> dare to deny that we receive the forgiveness of sins by faith or that faith is a part of repentance?[7]

The fact that Melanchthon in the same Article 12 in the octavo edition of the *Apology* (September 1531) explicitly added a quotation from Bernard's *Third Sermon on the Annunciation*[8] may be an indication that perhaps by that time, over the summer of 1531, Melanchthon had read all three sermons of Bernard on the Annunciation.

With the May 1531 quarto edition Melanchthon in Article 27, on monastic vows, quotes also from *Ann* 1.2:

> In addition, they dishonor Christ when they say that human beings merit eternal life through a monastic life. . . . As Bernard also says very powerfully, **"For it is necessary first to believe that you cannot have forgiveness of sins except through God's indulgence; second, that you cannot claim any good work whatever unless He himself grants it to you; finally, that you cannot merit eternal life by any works of yours, unless it too is given to you gratis"** [*Ann 1.1*]. We cited this and what follows earlier,[9] but at the end of it[10] Bernard adds: **"Let nobody be deceived' [1 Cor 3:18], for with careful consideration, a person will undoubtedly discover that not even 'with ten thousand soldiers could an individual stand up against the one who comes at such a**

---

[7] Bernard's words in the original Latin read as follows: *Necesse est primo omnium credere, quod remissionem peccatorum habere non possis, nisi per indulgentiam Dei, [Ann 1.1] sed adde, ut credas et hoc, quod per ipsum peccata tibi donantur. Hoc est testimonium, quod perhibet Spiritus sanctus in corde tuo dicens: Dimissa sunt tibi peccata tua. Sic enim arbitratur Apostolus, gratis iustificari hominem per fidem* [*Ann* 1.3], SBO 5:13, 10–11 and 14, 22–15, 2. CR 27: 521 and 546. *The Book of Concord*, 199–200. Only at this point does the new edition of *The Book of Concord* refer to a Bernard-edition, namely to the outdated PL; it only refers to the "Sermon on the Feast of the Blessed Virgin Mary I,i" instead of *Ann* 1, 1 and 3. For a Dutch translation of *Ann 1*, see Theo Bell in his *Honing uit de rots: Teksten van Bernard van Clairvaux* (Zoetermeer: Uitgeverij Meinema, 2001), 100–115.

[8] See *The Book of Concord*, 196 (italic section).

[9] Melanchthon referred here to his own reference to Bernard in Article 12 (quarto and octavo editions) where he quoted *Ann* 1.1 more fully by including the phrase "but add further that you also believe that through him your sins are forgiven. This is the testimony that the Holy Spirit gives in your heart [cf. Rom. 8:16], saying, 'your sins are forgiven you'." *The Book of Concord*, 199.

[10] "At the end of it" can only mean the end of the paragraph of *Ann* 1.2, where the words of Luke 14:31 are quoted which Melanchthon repeated here.

> **one with twenty thousand' [Lk 14:31]"** [*Ann 1*]. Since we do not merit the forgiveness of sins or eternal life even by the works of the divine law but must seek the mercy promised in Christ, so much less do monastic observances, which are mere human traditions, deserve the credit for meriting the forgiveness of sins or eternal life.[11]

We note that Melanchthon did not indicate the exact source references when he quoted from *Ann* 1. Only when he quoted from the *Third Sermon* (*Ann* 3) in his Article 12, on repentance, in the second, octavo edition of the *Apology* of September 1531, did he give this source reference.[12] In Article 4, on justification, of that same octavo edition, Melanchthon kept the familiar quotations from *Ann* 1.1 and 2 that he had used already in Article 27 of the earlier (quarto) edition. He did this in the following context:

> Bernard also says correctly: **"For it is necessary first to believe that you cannot have forgiveness of sins except through God's indulgence; second, that you cannot claim any good work whatever unless He himself grants it to you; finally, that you cannot merit eternal life by any works of yours, unless it too is given to you gratis"** [*Ann* 1.1]. And a little later, **"'Let nobody be deceived' [1 Cor 3:18], for with careful consideration, a person will undoubtedly discover that not even 'with ten thousand soldiers could an individual stand up against the one who comes at such a one with twenty thousand' [Lk 14:31]"** [*Ann* 1.2].[13]

---

[11] *The Book of Concord*, 282–83.

[12] "In his third sermon on the annunciation," *The Book of Concord*, 196. See SBO 5, 36, 10–26. However, Bernard in his sermon quotes the Vulgate Psalm 146:11 (*Beneplacitum est Domino super timentes eum, et in eis qui sperant super misericordia eius*) and not Psalm 32/33:18 (*ecce oculi Domini super metuentes eum qui sperant super misericordia eius*) which Melanchthon or the editors of *The Book of Concord* assume is being quoted here.

[13] Bernard's words in the original Latin read as follows: *Necesse est primo omnium credere, quod remissionem peccatorum habere non possis, nisi per indulgentiam Dei; deinde quod nihil prorsus habere queas operas boni, nisi et hoc dederit ipse; postremo quod vitam aeternam nullis potes operibus promereri, nisi gratis tibi detur et illa* [*Ann* 1.1]. *Nemo itaque se seducat, quia si bene cogitare voluerit, inveniet procul dubio, quod nec 'cum decem millibus posit occurrere ei, qui cum viginti millibus venit ad se'* [Luke 14:31] [*Ann* 1.2], SBO 5, 13, 10–13; *The Book of Concord*, 168 (italic section).

The negative view of Bernard in the 1521 *Loci communes* of the young humanist was no longer carried over, when a revised German version of the *Loci* (by Justus Jonas)[14] was in the making in 1533, which was published in 1535. Here, a complete turn-around surfaced, as Melanchthon's work now reads on the topic of free will that after the apostolic times, time and again, holy men recognized and preached the truth, some more clearly that others, such as Basil, Ambrose, Augustine, Prosper, Maximus, Hugo, Bernard, Tauler, Wessel, and Luther.[15] Now Bernard was listed among the witnesses of the evangelical faith. This was the case also in his *Preface* of 1545 to Augustine's *De spiritu et litera*, where Bernard and Tauler were named as true believers.[16]

In his *Commentarii in Epistolam Pauli ad Romanos* of 1540 Melanchthon again referred to Bernard's *Ann 1* (as always, he preferred the humanistic expression *concio*, "speech") and he repeated the entire quotation (composed of *Ann* 1.1 and 1.3) which he had incorporated already into his *Apology*. However, he did not indicate the exact locus, i.e., the first of the three sermons on the Annunciation. He introduced the quotations by saying only that it was worthwhile to listen to the celebrated voice of Bernard.[17] He concluded, after this quotation, that similar statements are to be found elsewhere in Bernard even though he is one of the more recent authors. Melanchthon carried on by interpreting Bernard's concept of faith (*fides*) as trust (*fiducia*) in the way he and his friends understood it.[18]

---

[14] On Jonas and his work of translating Luther's and Melanchthon's Latin texts into German, see Martin Lehmann, *Justus Jonas Loyal Reformer* (Minneapolis: Augsburg Publishing House, 1963), 183–186.

[15] *Und sind nach der Aposteln zeit für und für heilige Menner [Männer] gewesen, die diese wahrheit erkannt und gepredigет haben, doch etliche klerer und reiner, etliche tunckeler, als Basilius, Ambrosius, Augustinus, Propser, Maximus, Hugo, Bernhardus, Taulerus, Wesselus und Lutherus etc*, CR 22, 166; see Johannes Schilling, "Melanchthons deutsche Dogmatik," in Günter Frank, ed., *Der Theologe Melanchthon,* 243–257, here 253. Wessel is Johannes Gansfort (1419–1489).

[16] See MBW, no. 3973; CR 5, 805 (no. 3235).

[17] *Digna et Bernhardi vox est quae celebritur, cuius haec sunt verba in concione de Annuntiatione: Necesse est primo credere* [*Ann* 1.1] . . . *Sed adde adhuc ut credas, et hoc, quod per ipsum peccata T i b i donantur* . . . .*Sic enim arbitrator Apostolus gratis iustificari hominem per fidem* [*Ann* 1.3]. CR 15, 520. The CR edition has the explicit emphasis on "you" (*Tibi*).

[18] *Extant et similes sententiae aliquot apud hunc, quanquam recenten scriptorem, sed tamen non rudem spiritualium exercitiorum: in quibus didicit acquiescere*

In his *Enarratio* on Romans of 1556, Melanchthon in commenting on Rom 5:9 again reminded his readers of Bernard's saying (*dictum*), as he paraphrased the sermon text (but again, without the exact source reference, *Ann 1*).[19] Melanchthon added further deliberations on Augustine whom he saw as torturing himself with this issue.[20] It is noteworthy, that Luther in his lectures on Romans (1515/16)[21] had already quoted Bernard's *Ann 1*, and quite extensively at that. One may wonder whether Melanchthon with his quoting of Bernard's *Ann 1* depends on Luther's early lectures that were known to him.

In 1541 Melanchthon worked on his *Enarratio Epistolae ad Timotheum*. In the section on the notion "faith" (*fides*) he presented Bernard as an example of one of the good writers after the apostles, and he again quoted Bernard's *dictum* about the priority of trust in the remission of sins by the mercy of God—before anything else—and about the importance of the personal conviction of being forgiven. He called Bernard's statement a "perspicuous testimony" that is helpful to make one strong. Here, for the first and only time, Melanchthon concludes his quotation with the precise source reference that "these words are extant in the first speech on the Annunciation."[22] Perhaps it was at this time (1541) that Melanchthon felt compelled to actually look up (again?) the quotation which in previous years he had used several times by simply referring to the "speech of Bernard on the Annunciation." The Wittenberg library catalogue of that time (1536) shows that indeed the library possessed two editions of Bernard's

conscientiam non posse, nisi fide statuat gratis remitti peccata propter Christum. Intelligit igitur fidem, ut nos, de fiducia; CR 15, 520. See Fred Kramer's English translation, *Commentary on Romans,* 34.

[19] *Ac utile est meminisse dictum Bernardi, qui inquit: Necesse est credere, quod tantum per gratiam, non propter merita tua habeas remissionem peccatorum, et credere te necesse est, t i b i remitti. Sic etiam necesse est credere, quod gratis donetur vita aeterna propter Christum, non propter tua merita*; CR 15, 935.

[20] *Augustinus torquet se;* CR 15, 935.

[21] See WA 56, 79, 15–370, 23.

[22] *Etsi autem scriptores post Apostolos fuerunt negligentiores, tamen interdum quid senserint ostendunt. Etsi dictum Bernardi tenendum, quia testimonium perspicuum est, et ad confirmandos aliquos prodest. Necesse est primo omnium credere, quod remissionem peccatorum habere non possis, nisi per indulgentiam Dei, sed adde . . . Sic enim arbitrator Apostolus Gratis [sic] iustificari hominem per fidem. Haec verba extant in prima concione de annunciatione;* CR 15, 1312.

works: *Bernardi opera* (Lyon: Jean Clein, 1515) and the *Floretus*, that is *Bernhardinj Floretum* (Lyon: S. Vincent, 1510).[23]

In his explanation of the Letter to Timothy, Melanchthon continued with his "definition of faith." To him "faith" meant agreement or assent (*assensus*) by which we embrace the entire teaching handed down to us by God, and in this faith we also embrace the promise of grace, and this is the trust (*fiducia*) that rests on the mediator and on God; in this trust we call upon Abba, the Father, [24] an explicit reference to Rom 8:16 (which is the reference used by the novice master in counseling Luther). With his mention of "Abba" in connection with a Bernard text, he here (and only here) takes up Bernard's Pauline reference to Rom 8:16 on the testimony in one's heart according to *Ann 1*, which he must have come across when he was looking up the entire sermon text. Perhaps here he tacitly also took up Luther's scholium on Rom 8:16 in which Luther himself had used Bernard's *Ann 1* so extensively and where he had provided the exact source reference.[25]

When in April/May 1542 Melanchthon wrote to the Saxon chancellor Gregor Brück (ca. 1485–1557), he indicated that "even Bernard" (*im[m]o Bernardus*) clearly votes in favor of their doctrine of justification, and that similar good statements may be found also in Bonaventure.[26] In his *Tertia Aetas Locorum Theologicorum ab ipso Melanthone editorum* of 1543–1559 he again quoted *Ann 1* in the same words that he had quoted in his *Apology of the Augsburg Confession* of 1531.[27]

---

[23] See *A Wittenberg University library catalogue of 1536*, ed. Sachiko Kusukawa (Binghamton, N.Y.: LP Publications, 1995), nos. 191 and 199. On Luther and Melanchthon as users of the library, see C. G. Brandis, "Luther und Melanchthon als Benützer der Wittenberger Bibliothek," *Theologische Studien und Kritiken* 90 (1917): 206–21.

[24] *Sic igitur definition fidei. Fides est assensus, quo amplectimur totam doctrinam a Deo nobis traditam, et in hac promissionem Gratiae quoque, et est fiducia acquiescens in mediatore et in Deo iuxta promissionem, et clamas: Abba Pater*; CR 15, 1312–13.

[25] See WA 56, 369, 25–370, 22: *preclarissime ostendit B. Bernardus, plenus eodem spiritu, sermone de annunciatione 1* (line 29).

[26] See MBW, no. 2950; CR 5, 234 (to Brück); *Imo Bernhardus clarissime suffragatur nobis de iustificatione. Sunt et Bonaventurae quaedem satis bonae sententiae.* See also in 1543 to Gregorius Pontanus, CR 5, 234, MBW, no. 2803.

[27] *Addam et Bernhardi testimonium, quod extat in concione [I.] de Annuntiatione [Mariae]. "Necesse est . . .* [*Ann 1.1*] *sed adde . . .* [*Ann 1.3*]. *In hoc dicto perspicue*

For the feast day of the Annunciation (*Die annunciationis Mariae*), 25 March 1544, Melanchthon offered a sermon. In the second paragraph he spoke of Mary's concern and he explained that the scriptural examples show that when God speaks to human beings there is terror at first, but consolation always follows afterwards. The same thing happens in one's conversion, as we see with David and Paul. At this point Melanchthon declared that Bernard was discussing this matter "in his sermons for this feast day" (*in concionibus huius festi*). Bernard, he said, hands down memorable statements about the faith.[28] This text is one of the few if not perhaps the only locus where Melanchthon demonstrated his awareness that there is not only one sermon on the Annunciation, but several, as he used the plural (*in concionibus*) here. Melanchthon then summarized the central statement of Bernard's text that one not only has to believe in the forgiveness of sins, but also that one must believe that it is "gratis given," and that it is personally given "to you because of Christ." "By such faith, the Apostle says, a person is justified."[29]

In the doctoral disputation texts for Maximilian Maurus (Moerlin), 1516–1584), of 12 March 1546, that is, shortly after Luther's death on 16 February 1546,[30] Melanchthon paid tribute to the Bernard factor by letting the disputation of that day be centered on Bernard's *Ann* 1.3 (without however specifying in this academic disputation that it is the first of the three sermons). Melanchthon apparently wanted to inculcate the significance of Bernard's Pauline concept of faith for Luther, who had died recently.

In thesis 4, the insufficient concept of a "general faith" (*generalem fidem*) was being introduced which is without any personal concern. In thesis 5 the position was expressed that the Gospel promise is the annunciation of the forgiveness of sins. But this is no good to you

---

et proprie recitatur sententia Ecclesiarum nostrarum, et extant similia testimonia apud hunc auctorem; CR 21, 748.

[28] *Exempla sunt passim abvia in scriptures, quae ostendunt hunc esse ordinem, quoties Deus loquitur, ut praecedant terrors, sequatur consolation: hic ordo etiam in conversione cernitur. David, Paulus, arguuntur, et expavescunt, posterea eriguntur. Et in concionibus huius festi Bernardus de hac re disserit, et memorabilem sententiam tradit de fide*; CR 14, 462. It appears that here for the first time Melanchthon spoke of several sermons of Bernard on the Annunciation.

[29] *Non solum hoc credas, remitti peccata, sed gratis remitti, et tibi remitti credas propter Christum. Hac fide Apostolus ait, Iustificari hominem*; CR 14, 462.

[30] *Themata, quae post mortem reverendi viri D. Martini Lutheri, in Academia Witebergensi sunt disputata*; CR 12, 543–544.

either, if you believe that this happens only to others in general, and not to you. Thesis 6 then declared that those who teach only this "general faith" destroy the Gospel, and with it any true and salutary comfort to the consciences. Thesis 7 stated Paul's concept of faith by which one does penance (*qua agens poenitentiam*) and by which one believes in one's forgiveness of sins, as Paul says: "Justified by faith we have peace." Thesis 8 continued with rejecting this "general faith" as not being helpful to an anxious mind. Such faith would know the Son of God only as the judge (Judas and the devils have this kind of faith). Having built the disputation up to this point, Melanchthon articulated in thesis 9 the "correct" teaching of Bernard:

> Rightly therefore Bernard said: **"But add to this that you also believe that through him [Christ] your sins are forgiven you [*tibi*]. This is the testimony that the Holy Spirit gives**[31] **in your heart [Rom 8:16], saying, 'your sins are forgiven you' [Mt 9:5]. For in this way the Apostle concludes that 'a person is gratis justified through faith' [Rom 3:24, 28]"** (*Ann* 1.3).[32]

Thesis 10 then claimed that this is precisely what "our churches teach, when they [publicly] tell [*enarrant*] of Paul's saying: we are justified by faith."[33]

Melanchthon's turn to Bernard (following Luther's lead) is mirrored also in Melanchthon's oration on the occasion of the funeral of Luther on 22 February 1546. Melanchthon included Saint Bernard in a list of God's witnesses that ends with Luther:

> After the Apostles there follows a multitude which, although it was weaker, is nevertheless honoured with God's testimonies: Polycarp, Irenaeus, Gregory of Nyssa, Basil, Augustine, Prosper, Maximus, Hugo, Bernard, Tauler and some others. Although this last dotage of the world is more obscure, God nevertheless always preserved some remnants. And it is clear

---

[31] The text edition has the spelling mistake, *prohibit*, instead of the correct wording, *perhibet*.

[32] *Recte igitur Bernhardus dixit: Sed adde ut credas et hoc, quod per ipsum peccata t i b i donantur. Hoc est testimonium quod prohibit [sic] Spiritus sanctus in corde tuo dicens: Dimissa sunt tibi peccata tua. Sic enim arbitrator Apostolus, gratis iustificari hominem per fidem*; CR 12, 545.

[33] *Idem nostrae Ecclesiae docent, cum enarrant dictum Pauli: Fide iustificamur*; CR 12, 545.

that a more brilliant light of the Gospel was lit by the voice of Luther.[34]

Equipped with Bernardine insights, Melanchthon apparently meant to participate in the deliberations of the Council of Trent. For this purpose he prepared the *Confessio Saxonica* in 1551, published in 1552. Its full title reveals that this *Confession* was meant as a repetition of the *Augsburg Confession* according to the teaching of the Saxon churches; it too contained the article on justification.[35] In this context Melanchthon mentioned first Augustine's anti-Pelagian work *De spiritu et litera* that on the basis of the law we fear God, but in faith we take refuge in God's mercy. Then Melanchthon quoted Bernard's *Ann* 1.1 and *Ann* 1.3, which, as always with him, are contracted into what looks like one continuous quotation.[36] Melanchthon concluded that "the statement of our churches is clearly and properly supported (*citatur*) by this saying (*in hoc dicto*)" of Bernard.[37]

One may wonder whether Melanchthon had knowledge of the speeches that were delivered at Trent five years earlier, in 1546, on the issue of "justification." At that time several speakers at Trent made use of Bernard's same sermon.[38] If this is so, one may surmise that perhaps for this additional reason Melanchthon kept quoting Bernard's *Ann* 1 for the rest of his life in support of his position, as we observe this, for example, in his letter to Johann Sebastian Pfauser (1520–1569) of the year 1556. In this letter Melanchthon repeated

[34] *Philip Melanchthon: Orations on Philosophy and Education*, 257. In his *Loci* of 1535 a similar list of names appeared; see above.

[35] *Repetitio Confessionis Augustanae sive Confessio doctrinae saxonicarum ecclesiarum*. CR 28, 370ff.

[36] *Bernhardus in concione de Annunciatione, Necesse est . . . per fidem*; CR 28, 288–289.

[37] *In hoc dicto perspicue et proprie citatur sententia Ecclesiarum nostrarum;* CR 28, 389.

[38] On 23 July 1546, Cardinal Seripando quoted *Ann* 1.2, *Concilium Tridentinum*, ed. Societas Goerresiana (Freiburg MCMXI), vol. 5, 374, 3–18; from here on quoted as CT; CT 12, 634, 20–26. On 1 October 1546, Aloysius Lippomanus of Verona quoted *Ann* 1.3, CT 5, 460, 6–11. The same passage is quoted again in CT 12, 702, 12–28. On 15 October, 1546, Franciscus Visdominus quoted *Ann 1.1–4*, CT 5, 533, 46–534, 5. On 15 October also Ricardus Cenomanus quoted *Ann 1.3*, CT 5, 539, 32–36. On 19 October 1546, Andreas Navarra quoted *Ann 1.3*, CT 5, 559, 20–24. On 26 October 1546, Iacobus Laynez quoted *Ann 1.2*, CT 5, 620, 18–24.

that "Bernard in his sermon on the Annunciation said that you must believe that you are forgiven."[39]

In his 1559 *Loci communes* Melanchthon included now the additional statement which is taken from Bernard's *Sermon on the Canticle* 68.6: "It is enough for merit to know that merit is not enough."[40] This same quotation was used already in 1546 by council fathers at the Council of Trent.[41] All in all, demonstrably since 1531, Melanchthon was always concerned with calling upon Bernard with his *Ann 1* as a supporter of the Lutheran doctrine of justification by faith and grace alone. He wanted to show Bernard as a witness to the evangelical truth.[42]

---

[39] *Bernhardi in sermone de annunciatione: oportet te credere, tibi remitti*; CR 8, 711 (no. 5953).

[40] *Bernhardus: . . . sufficit ad meritum scire, quod not sufficiat meritum* (sermon on the Canticle 68.6), CR 21, 798.

[41] See Cardinal Seripando on 25 June 1546, CT 12, 634, 28–29, and the Prior General of the Carmelite Friars on 23 July 1546, CT 5, 377, 8. Melanchthon had used the same quotation already in 1544 in his *Annotationes in Evangelia*, on Mt 20: *Ideo erumpit Bernhardus in hanc vocem, sufficit ad meritum scire, quod non sufficit meritum*, CR 14, 217.

[42] See E. P. Meijering, *Melanchthon and Patristic Thought: The Doctrines of Christ and Grace, the Trinity and the Creation* (Leiden: Brill, 1983), 95–97.

3. Melanchthon's Change of Mind

The disputation of 12 March 1546 (shortly after Luther's death) and Melanchthon's other texts that were quoted here and that include quotations from this sermon (*Ann 1*) do indeed exactly mirror the story which Melanchthon reported he heard from Luther personally concerning Bernard's sermon. Melanchthon had learned these decisive Bernardine insights from Luther himself. Thus Luther was the one who changed Melanchthon's view of Bernard. Melanchthon published his information, gained from interviews with Luther probably in 1530/31, in his *Preface* to the Second Volume of the Latin edition of Luther's works (1546), which he edited after Luther's death.

In his *Preface* of 1546, with its sketch of Luther's life, Melanchthon indirectly provided the answer to the question: Why did he change his mind on Bernard since 1530/31, i.e., some time prior to September 1531, when the quotations from Bernard's *Ann 1* emerged for the first time in Melanchthon's works? The answer is: Melanchthon "must often have talked to Luther about this period of his life"[1] in the friary at Erfurt in 1508. And based on such interviews with Luther in Wittenberg, Melanchthon pointed out that Luther was enlightened and strengthened by Bernard's *Ann 1* which had been quoted to him by a senior Erfurt friar (whose name we assume was Johann von Greffenstein). Bernard's text had reminded Luther of the meaning of "the just shall live by faith" in Paul's teaching. Melanchthon even included the direct quotation from Bernard's *Sermon* without, however, giving the precise source reference to the first of the three sermons.

[1] See Schwiebert, *Luther and His Times,* 170.

PART THREE

MELANCHTHON'S MEMOIRS: THE PREFACE TO THE SECOND VOLUME OF LUTHER'S WORKS (1546)

MELANCHTHON'S MEMOIRS[1]

<155> Reverend Martin Luther gave us hope that he would relate his *curriculum vitae* and the occasions of his struggles, and he would have done so if he had not been called from this mortal life into the everlasting community of God and the heavenly Church. Both a lucidly written reflection of his private life would have been useful, full of examples, which would have been useful in strengthening the piety in good minds, <156> as well as a recitation of the events which could have been made known to posterity about many things. Such an account also would have refuted the slanders of those who spread the fiction that he, incited by political leaders or others, destroyed the dignity of the bishops, or that he himself, inflamed by private lust, broke the bonds of monastic servitude. He himself would have exposed these things, wholly and copiously set forth and commemorated. For even if evil wishers were to reproach with that common saying, "he blows his own trumpet,"[2] we know nevertheless that there was so much seriousness in him that he would have related the account with the utmost fidelity. And many good wise men are still living, to whom it would have been ridiculous for another account to be mixed in, as sometimes happens in poems, since he knew they were aware of the order of these events. But because his day of death turned aside the edition of such an account, we shall recite in good faith about the same matters those things which partly we heard from the man himself, partly those which we ourselves saw.

His is an old family, with many descendants in the middle class by the name Luther, in the district of the distinguished counts of Mansfeld. Indeed, the parents of Martin Luther first made their home in the town of Eisleben, where he was born, and then they moved to the town of Mansfeld, where his father, Hans Luther, belonged to the magistrate and because of his integrity was one of the most liked of

---

[1] Translated from CR 6, 155–170. The page numbers in <> refer to this edition.

[2] Diogenianus 3.16. Melanchthon may have taken it from Erasmus' *Adages*; another version in English would be: "He toots his own horn."

all the good people. In his mother Margaret, the wife of Hans Luther, all the virtues of an honest matron were seen coming together—especially her modesty, fear of God,[3] and prayer—so that the other honest women looked to her as an example of virtues. She answered me as I kept asking several times about the time of her son's birth that she remembered the day and hour exactly, but she was uncertain of the year. However, she affirmed that he was born the night of 10 November after eleven o'clock, and the name Martin was given to the infant, because the next day, on which the infant was brought into the Church of God through baptism, had been St. Martin's Day. His brother Jacob, an honest and upright man, said that the family believed that the year of his birth was A.D. 1483.

After he reached the age of being able to learn doctrine, his parents diligently accustomed their son Martin, by instructing him at home, to the knowledge and fear of God and to the duties of the other virtues; and, as is the custom of respectable people, they saw to it that he learned to read and write; <157> and since he was still a little boy the father of Georg Aemilius carried him to school. This man[4] can testify to the truth of this story because he is still living. At that time grammar schools in Saxon towns were fairly average. Therefore, when Martin reached his fourteenth year, he was sent to Magdeburg together with Johannes Reineck, whose virtue was later so outstanding that he was a highly esteemed authority in these regions. There was always exceptional mutual kindness between Luther and Reineck, be it by natural sympathies or rising from that boyhood companionship during their studies. Nevertheless, Luther did not remain in Magdeburg longer than a year. In the school at Eisenach he studied for four years with an educator who taught grammar more correctly and skillfully than others elsewhere. I remember Luther praising his intelligence. He was sent to that city because his mother had been born there of a respectable and old family. Here he completed his grammar study. Since he was highly intelligent and showed a special talent for eloquent speech, he quickly passed ahead of his peers. He easily surpassed the rest of the young people, who at that same time were learning the art of speaking, both in his wording

---

[3] *Timor Dei* ("fear of God," reverence of God, a virtue) is mentioned several times; see below on Luther's "fear and faith" (*timor et fides*).

[4] Nicholas Aemilius (Oemler).

and in the richness of his expressions, and also in speech-writing and verse.

After having tasted the sweetness of literature, by nature burning with the desire for learning, he sought out the academy, as the source of all learning. With such great a power of intelligence he would have been able to grasp all the arts in proper order, if only he had found suitable professors. And, the gentler studies of true philosophy and the care for oral communication would perhaps have benefited him in softening the vehemence of his nature. However, at Erfurt he encountered a rather prickly—for his own age—teaching of dialectics. He quickly seized it, since with his mental acuteness he grasped the causes and sources of the precepts better than the rest of the students. Since now his mind was eager to learn, seeking more and better things, he read on his own [*ipse*] most of the writings of the ancient Latin writers, Cicero, Virgil, Livy, and others. He read them, not as boys do, picking out the words only, but, as lessons for human life. Therefore, he took a closer look at the advice and the sayings of these writers, and because he had a reliable and good memory he could keep them always before his eyes even if he had read and heard them only once. <158> Thus, young man Luther stood out and his intelligence was admired by the entire academic community. Decorated then with the degree of Master of Philosophy, at the age of twenty, on the advice of his relatives, who thought that so great a power of intelligence and eloquence should be brought forth into the light and into public service, he began the study of law. However, a short time later, when he was twenty-one, suddenly he went to a *colloquium* with the Augustinian friars at Erfurt and petitioned for admission, against the opinion of his parents and relatives. Once he was admitted, he soon not only eagerly learned the doctrine of the Church, but also gained self-mastery by the strongest severity of the [monastic] discipline, and he by far surpassed the others in all the exercises of reading, disputing, fasting, and praying. He who by nature was neither small nor feeble did not need much food and drink, something about which I often wondered. I saw him, even though he was completely healthy, on four consecutive days not taking any food or drink. I often saw at many other times that he was content with a tiny bit of bread and a herring per day.

The reason for entering this kind of life [in a friary] which he deemed more suitable for piety and for the studies of the teachings about God, was the following, as he himself told [us] and as many do know: Often, when he thought more intently about the wrath of God or the awesome examples of punishments, great terrors so suddenly overcame him that he almost died. When he was overcome by tension in a certain disputation about doctrine, I myself saw him going into the nearby room to lay down on the bed, where he repeatedly called upon God and mixed the following verse into his prayer: "For God delivered all to disobedience, that he might have mercy upon all" [Rom 11:32]. He felt those terrors either for the first time or most sharply in that year when he lost a companion—I do not know the circumstances. Therefore, not poverty but eagerness for piety led him into this mode of monastic life. Although he daily learned what was the customary learning in the schools and also read the commentators on the Sentences [of Peter Lombard], and although in public disputations he eloquently explained to amazed crowds the labyrinths which are inexplicable to others, he nevertheless did not seek to make a name for himself in that kind of life, but instead sought nutriments for piety. He actually treated these studies as if they were some side interest, as it was easy for him to appropriate those scholastic methods. Meanwhile he himself avidly read the sources of the heavenly doctrine, i.e., the writings of the Prophets and the Apostles, in order to have an erudite mind about the will of God <159> and in order to support his fear[5] and faith from the firm testimonies [i.e., the Scriptures]. His continued striving after the study [of the heavenly doctrine] was motivated by his sorrows and fears.[6] And he narrated that he was often strengthened by the words of a senior [friar] in the Augustinian College at Erfurt to whom he exposed his confused fears.[7] He heard him discuss much about the faith, and he said that he was led to the Creed, in which is said, "I believe in the forgiveness of sins." [The senior friar] had interpreted this article [of the Creed] in such a way that it should be believed not only in general, that some people are forgiven, like David or Peter had been forgiven, something also demons believe, but that it was God's commandment that we as

[5] *Timor* [reverence]. Notably, one of Luther's first sermons has the theme "Fear of God" (1514); WA 4, 659–666. On this term, see Thorsten Dietz, *Der Begriff der Furcht bei Luther* (Tübingen: Mohr Siebeck, 2009).

[6] The Latin here has *dolor* and *pavor* (not *timor* or *consternatio*).

[7] The senior is most likely Friar Johannes von Greffenstein, novice master at Erfurt (died 1520).

individuals are to believe that our sins are forgiven. And he proved [to Luther] that this interpretation is confirmed by a saying of Bernard, and he showed him the *locus* in a sermon on the Annunciation where these words are found: "But add to this that you also believe that through Him [Christ] your sins are forgiven you [*TIBI*]. This is the testimony that the Holy Spirit gives in your heart [Rom 8:16], saying, 'your sins are forgiven you' [1 Jn 2:12; Mt 9:5]. For thus the Apostle concludes that 'a person is justified freely by faith' [contraction of Rom 3:24 and 28].' "[8]

Luther said that he was not only strengthened by this voice [of the senior friar], but that he was also reminded of Paul's entire sentence [Rom 3:24–28] who so often inculcates this *dictum*: "by faith we are justified." Since he read many expositions on this he saw the vanity in their interpretations that were en vogue then. [The insight into such vanity] was based both upon the words [of the senior friar] and upon the fact that Luther felt the consolation of mind after having noticed their faulty interpretations. Little by little, as he read and compared the sayings and lessons which are recorded in the Prophets and Apostles, and as he kindled his faith in daily prayer, more of the light came to him. At that time he also began to read the works of Augustine, where he found many clear statements, in both the *Commentary on the Psalms* and the *On the Spirit and the Letter*, which confirmed this doctrine concerning faith and concerning the consolation which had entered his own heart. He did not completely abandon, however, the commentators on the *Sentences*. He was able to quote Gabriel [Biel] and Cameracensis [Peter of Ailly] by heart, almost word for word. He spent much time in thoroughly reading the writings of Ockham whose acumen he preferred over Thomas and Scotus. He also had carefully read Gerson.[9] But he not only read all the works of Augustine but also remembered them the best. He began this most intense study at Erfurt, where he stayed for four years at the Augustinian College.

---

[8] For the English translation of Bernard's passage and its immediate context, see Franz Posset, *The Two-Fold Knowledge: Readings on the Knowledge of Self & the Knowledge of God Selected & Translated from the Works of Saint Bernard of Clairvaux* (Milwaukee: Marquette University Press, 2004), 119.

[9] Ockham, d'Ailly, Gerson, and Biel may be grouped together as "Nominalists" (*via moderna*).

<160> At this time Reverend Staupitz who had helped getting the Academy of Wittenberg started was eager to promote the study of theology in the new academy. He had confidence in Luther's intelligence and learning and for this reason he transferred him to Wittenberg, in 1508, when Luther was just twenty-six years old. Here, amidst the daily exercises of the school and of preaching, his genius began to shine even more. And since wise men, such as Doctor Martin [Pollich] and others, would listen to him attentively, Mellerstadt often said that there was so great an intellectual power in that man that he clearly foresaw that he would change the traditional form of learning, which was the only one being employed in the schools at that time.

Here he first lectured on Aristotle's dialectics and physics,[10] yet all the while he did not abstain from eagerly reading theological writings.[11] After three years he set out for Rome, on account of controversies among the friars. When he returned that same year [1512], Duke Frederick, Elector of Saxony, offered to cover the fees for receiving his doctoral degree,[12] as we call it, in the usual manner of scholars. He had heard Luther preach and had marveled at the intellectual power, the vigor of his speech, and the excellence of his explications in preaching. And so that you [my reader] may see that the doctor's degree was assigned to him for his maturity of judgment so to speak, you should know that this was in the thirtieth year of Luther's life. He himself told us that he was ordered by Staupitz, even though he was quite opposed to the idea, to allow [himself] to be decorated with this [graduate] degree. Staupitz jokingly said that God had a great deal of tasks ahead to be done in the Church, for which he would use his [Luther's] works. This statement, even as it was uttered jokingly at that time, was fulfilled in the way in which many premonitions would precede the coming changes.

---

[10] *Hic* is a reference to Wittenberg. The note on the subjects that he taught is imprecise since Luther lectured on Aristotle's Dialectics and Ethics (not Physics). However, Luther did work on Aristotle's Physics (Book 1) in early 1517 as he wrote in his letter of 8 February 1517 to Johann Lang; WA Br 1, 88, 19–20 (no. 34).

[11] Melanchthon's observation can be solidified from Luther's letter to Johann Braun of 17 March 1509, sent from Wittenberg; WA Br 1, 17, 41–43 (no. 5).

[12] The doctoral degree was conferred on 18/19 October 1512; see Luther's invitation to this event in WA Br 1, 18–19 (no. 6). The duke is Frederick the Wise.

Afterwards he began to lecture on the Epistle to the Romans, next on the Psalms.[13] He explained these writings in such a way that, as light after a long, dark night—by the judgment of all pious and prudent men—new light was shed on doctrine. Here he pointed out the essential difference of Law and Gospel;[14] here he refuted the error which reigned at that time in the schools and in the pulpits, and which taught that men merited forgiveness of sins by their own works, and that men were justified before God by [external] disciplining as the Pharisees have taught. Luther thus called the people's minds back to the Son of God, <161> and, like the Baptist, he pointed to the Lamb of God, who takes away our sins [Jn 1:29]. He said that sins are forgiven without our actions on account of the Son of God, and that this favor must be accepted by faith. He also clarified other parts of the ecclesiastical doctrine. These beginnings with the most important themes made him a great authority, especially since his morals matched up with what he was saying, and what he said came not just over his lips, but came forth from being born in his heart. Admiration for his life produced great inclination toward him in the minds of his audience, just as the ancient authors have said: "A blameless way of life is the strongest proof."[15] Because of it, respectable men who knew him were less vehemently opposed [to him] when he later on changed certain accepted religious ceremonies. And, concerning the statements in which they saw with great sadness, the world being torn apart, they

---

[13] *Postea enarrare epistolam ad Romanos coepit, deinde Psalmos.* On *enarratio / enarrare* see Kenneth Hagen, "Commentary as 'Enarratio'," in *Luther's Approach to Scripture as seen in his 'Commentaries' on Galatians 1519–1538* (Tübingen: Mohr Siebeck, 1993), 49–66. Melanchthon simply followed Luther's *Preface* to Volume 1 where Luther neglected to mention his first lectures on the Psalms. Luther later indicated that "meanwhile in that same year [1519], I had begun interpreting the Psalms once again;" WA 54, 185, 12. Important to Melanchthon was the fact that Luther worked at that time with the proper distinction of Law and Gospel on which Melanchthon elaborated. Melanchthon's mention of the Psalm lectures that are delivered after the one on Romans may have been inspired by the praise which Luther's second lectures (*Operationes in Psalmos*, published on 27 March 1519) received from Erasmus in his letter to Luther of 30 May 1519; WA Br 1, 413, 50–51 (no. 183).

[14] On Melanchthon's view of Law and Gospel, see Heinz Scheible, "Die Bedeutung der Unterscheidung von Gesetz und Evangelium für theologische Ethik und Praktische Theologie am Beispiel Melanchthons" in *Aufsätze zu Melanchthon* (Tübingen: Mohr Siebeck, 2010), 241–252.

[15] Aristotle's *Art of Rhetoric,* 1356a. The 1554 German translation has this rendering: *ein züchtig leben behalt gemeinglich am meisten glauben.*

agreed with him on account of his authority, which he had previously acquired on account of his illumination of important things and on account of the sanctity of his morals.

Back then Luther, however, did not change anything yet in the religious ceremonies. Rather, he himself was a strict guardian of the discipline among his peers, and he did not mess with any shocking opinions, but more and more he clarified the universal doctrine which is absolutely necessary to all, [i.e.,] about penance, the remission of sins, faith, and the true consolations [that are found] in the cross. By the sweetness of this doctrine all pious people were captivated. The learned, too, were pleased that Christ, the Prophets, and the Apostles were led so-to-speak out of the darkness, jail, and squalor; that the essential difference between Law and Gospel, between the promises of the Law and the promise of the Gospel, between Philosophy and the Gospel[16] was recognized—all of this was certainly not found in Thomas, Scotus and others like them—the difference between spiritual righteousness and [righteousness in] political matters.[17] In addition to all that, with his writings Erasmus had invited young people to the study of Latin and Greek. Many of them who were endowed with good and free minds and having been shown the sweeter kind of doctrine began to abhor the barbaric and fallacious doctrine of the monastic authors. Luther began to dedicate himself to the study of Greek and Hebrew, so that having learned the peculiar quality of a language and its diction, and the doctrine drawn from its sources he might all the more be able to make better judgments.

When Luther was in this course of studies, indulgences were on sale and were circulated in these regions by Tetzel the Dominican, a most shameless deceiver. Luther, angered by Tetzel's impious and execrable sermons and, burning with the eagerness for piety, issued

[16] Melanchthon may have Luther's contra-positioning of Gospel and Aristotelian philosophy (scholasticism) in mind. According to Luther's recollection in 1534 the theology professor at Erfurt and auxiliary bishop of Mainz, Johannes Bonemilch (died 1510; i.e., the bishop who ordained Luther to the priesthood) told them that that one could not be a real theologian without knowing Aristotle; Luther, Afterword to *Epistola Theologorum Parisiensium* (1534), WA 60, 125, 38–44; Luther, Disputation Against Scholastic Theology (September 1517), WA 1, 226, 14–16.

[17] This topic is important to Melanchthon who wrote a pamphlet on it: *Unterschidt zwischen weltlicher und Christlicher Fromkeyt* (1522).

propositions[18] <162> concerning indulgences which are extant in the first volume of his [Latin] writings. And he publicly attached these [propositions] at the [to the] Temple adjacent to Wittenberg Castle, on the eve of All Saints Day, in the year 1517.[19] This Tetzel, true to his character and also hoping he would obtain favor with the Roman Pontiff, summoned his own council, i.e., a few friars and theologians who were lightly imbued in some way or other with his sophistry, and he ordered them to compose something against Luther. Meanwhile, Tetzel himself, not wanting to be a silent bystander,[20] brandishes not just sermons, but thunderbolts against Luther. He cries aloud everywhere that this heretic must be condemned and burned. He even publicly hurls Luther's propositions and the sermon concerning indulgences into the flames.[21] These ravings of Tetzel and of his escort forced Luther to a more expansive discussion of these matters and to protect the truth.

These were the beginnings of this controversy when Luther, as yet not suspecting anything, would not even dream of making changes in [religious] customs, as he was not at all trying to get rid of indulgences completely, but only urging moderation! Therefore, they

---

[18] The 1554 German translation has *Artickel* (articles) for Latin *propositiones*. The 19th century German translator has here the careful rendering: "Luther issued some sentences on indulgences" (*Luther ließ etliche Sätze vom Ablaß ausgehen*). Latin *edere* may or may not imply that they were issued in printed form.

[19] No mention of a door. Luther in his *Preface* to Volume 1 reported about this time period in a less detailed way. Luther actually wrote that he first had written two letters, one to Archbishop Albrecht of Mainz, the other to Bishop Jerome of Brandenburg (the ordinary of the place), asking them to put an end to the shameful dealings with indulgences. However, the bishops disregarded him. Because Luther felt detested (as he wrote), he issued a "slip of paper for discussion" (*Disputationis scedulam* = the so-called *Ninety-Five Theses* of 1517) and "simultaneously" a sermon in German about indulgences (*edidi simul et germanicam concionem*), and "shortly afterwards the Resolutions" (*paulo post etiam Resolutiones*) in which, as he wrote, he did not condemn indulgences altogether, but would prefer charitable works (*ut indulgentiae non damnarentur quidem, sed bona opera caritatis illis praeferrentur*). Luther "edited" the German speech (*concio*, sermon) mentioned here shortly before his *Resolutiones* of 30 May 1518. One must assume that Luther's *simul* is not to be taken literally, as there cannot be a literal simultaneity of *Disputationis scedula* (with presumed date of 31 October 1517) and the time shortly before 30 May 1518 as the given time for the German sermon.

[20] "A silent mask" or a "mask without a voice," a technical term in ancient Greek theater; see Cicero, *Letter to Atticus* 13, 29.

[21] This report is not easily confirmed by historical sources from the early sixteenth century.

falsely accuse him who say that he began under false pretenses, so that afterwards he could change the [affairs of the] state and seek power either for himself or for others. And it is far from the truth that he was secretly instigated and incited by people at the court, as the Duke of Braunschweig wrote.[22] Rather, Duke Frederick [the Wise] was deeply concerned that struggles would be set in motion, although the beginning was from a plausible matter, but that little by little the flame would grow higher, as is said in Homer about a quarrel: "Small at first, soon it [a quarrel] lifts itself into the open air."[23] Frederick was the one prince of our era who was most fond of public tranquility and the least looking out for his own advantage; and he was especially accustomed to set forth plans for the common well-being of the world, which may be seen from many matters. He did not instigate nor applaud Luther, and he often made his concerns known which he continually expressed as he feared greater dissensions. The wise man that he was did not only follow worldly judgments, which bid that the even gentle beginnings of any changes should most quickly be suppressed, but also used divine norm in decision making, which bids the Gospel to be heard, and which forbids any opposition to the known truth, and which calls the stubborn resistance to the truth a blasphemy which is horribly damned by God. This man did what many other pious and wise men did: he yielded to God <165> and he carefully read what was written, and what he judged to be true he did not want to do away with.[24] I happen to know that he [Frederick] often requested the opinions of erudite and learned people about these matters. At the assembly which Emperor Charles V [1500–1558] held in Cologne after his coronation he kindly asked Erasmus of Rotterdam to tell him frankly if he reckoned that Luther erred in these controversies about which he had discoursed.[25] At that occasion Erasmus clearly said that he thought Luther was correct, but that he wished his style were smoother. Duke Frederick afterwards wrote to Luther about this most serious matter and strongly admonished him to

[22] Heinrich von Braunschweig-Wolfenbüttel (Henry II, the Younger, 1489–1568).
[23] Homer, *Ilias* 4, 442–443 (about Eris, the goddess of quarrel). Eris provoked a quarrel among the goddesses which led to the Judgment of Paris and so to the Trojan War (according to later embellishments). Melanchthon's Latin quotation is actually from Virgil's *Aeneid*, Book 4, 176 (about "rumors" [*fama*]).
[24] Melanchthon's description of Frederick the Wise appears to have been copied from Luther's *Preface* to Volume 1.
[25] They met most likely on 5 November 1520.

tone down his harshness.[26] It is a known fact that Luther promised Cardinal Cajetan to remain silent, if he [Cajetan] would also enjoin silence on his opponents. From this it can clearly be seen that, indeed, at that time he was not yet determined to set other struggles in motion, but that he wanted tranquility. Little by little, however, he was dragged into other subjects as uneducated authors challenged him from all sides.

Disputations then followed concerning the distinction of divine and human laws, concerning the abominable profanation of the Lord's Supper in its sale and application for others [i.e., offering Masses for other people]. Here the entire reasoning about the sacrifice [of the Mass] was set forth and the [proper] use of the sacraments was to be shown. And when pious men in the monasteries heard that such idolatry must be fled, they began to depart from their impious servitude. Therefore, Luther added to the explanation of the doctrine on penance, remission of sins, faith, and indulgences also the following issues: the distinction of divine and human laws, the doctrine on the [proper] use of the Lord's Supper and the other sacraments, and [monastic] vows. These were the principal points of contention. But Eck pushed the question about the power of the Roman Bishop[27] for no other reason than to fire up the animosity of the pontiff and of the kings against him [Luther]. He retained the Apostolic, Nicene, and Athanasian Creeds in all their purity. Next he fully explained in many writings what and why something should be changed in religious customs and human traditions. And whatever he wanted to be retained and what form of doctrine and of administration of the sacraments he approved of may be seen from the confessional statement which Duke John, Elector of Saxony,[28] and Philip Landgrave of Hessen[29] and others presented to Emperor Charles V in 1530 at the Diet of Augsburg. <164> The same is clear also from the way in which the rites of the Church are handled in this same city[30] and from the doctrine which sounds forth in our Church, the sum of which is publicly expressed in the *[Augsburg] Confession*. I make

---

[26] Such a letter is lost.

[27] Melanchthon has the Leipzig Disputation of the summer of 1519 in mind.

[28] I.e., John the Constant, also known as the Steadfast (1468–1532).

[29] See Jean-Yves Mariotte, *Philippe de Hesse (1504–1567): Le Premier Prince Protestant* (Paris: Honoré Champion, 2009).

[30] Augsburg.

mention of this so that pious people not only see which errors Luther reproached and which idolatry he removed, but also that they know that he embraced the Church's universal and necessary teaching, and that he not only restored purity to the rites, but also showed the pious people examples of renewal of the Churches. And it is useful for posterity to know what Luther had approved.

At this point I do not want to recollect who first publicly offered the Lord's Supper under both species, or who first stopped private Masses, or where monasteries were first abandoned. Luther did not discuss much about these matters prior to the diet which was held in the city of Worms in 1521. He himself did not change the rite [of the Mass]; it was Karlstadt and others who in his absence changed the rite. And since Karlstadt had done certain things tumultuously, Luther returned and declared what he would approve or disapprove by giving out clear testimonies of his opinion.[31]

We know that politicians vehemently detest all changes, and it must be admitted that even when upheavals are set into motion by the most just causes, something evil gets mixed into this sad disorder of human life. Nevertheless it is necessary that in the Church God's command is preferred to all things human. The eternal Father said this about his Son: "This is my beloved Son, listen to him" [Mk 9:5]. And he threatens everlasting wrath against blasphemers, that is, against those who endeavor to obliterate the known truth. It was thus Luther's pious and necessary duty, especially since he was teaching the Church of God, to reproach destructive errors which Epicureans were heaping up with new shamelessness. And, his hearers had to agree to what he correctly taught. If, however, change is truly despised, if there are many discomforts in upheavals, as we see with great sadness that there are, then those who first spread the errors are to be blamed, and then also those who now protect those errors with diabolic hatred. I commemorate these things not only in order to defend Luther and his hearers, but also so that pious minds ponder at this point in time and hereafter what the government of the true Church of God is and always was; how God through the word of the Gospel gathers the eternal Church <165> to himself from that sinful mass, that is, from that big mess [*colluvies*] of people, amongst whom the Gospel shines forth like a spark in the dark. As it was in the times of the Pharisees

[31] As documented in his *Invocavit* Sermons of March 1522.

with Zechariah, Elizabeth, Mary, and many others who were guardians of the true doctrine, so it also was before our own times that many, who called upon God in the right way, maintained the doctrine of the Gospel, some more perspicuously than others. Such a man was also that senior [friar], i.e., the one of whom I have spoken before, the one who so often lifted Luther up when anxieties [*pavoribus*] troubled him; the one who had become somewhat of a trailblazer [*monstrator*] toward the [right] doctrine about the faith. Let us pray with fervent voices that God may preserve the light of the Gospel in many people just as Isaiah prays for his listeners: "Seal the law in my disciples" [Is 8:16].[32] This commemoration then shows that counterfeited superstitions do not last, but are rooted out by divine action. Since this is the reason for any changes, care must be taken that no errors are taught in the Church.

But I return to Luther. Just as from the start he entered upon this cause without self-serving motivation so he, who by nature was fiery and irascible, nevertheless was always mindful of his task and battled only by teaching and vetoed taking up arms; and he wisely distinguished between the totally diverse offices of a bishop who is teaching the Church of God and of a [secular] magistrate who is supposed to restrain the multitude of a given location by the sword. Therefore, when at times the devil, who is eager to disperse the Church through scandals and to insult God, and in his deceitful *schadenfreude* takes pleasure from the errors and downfall of pitiable people, has inflamed seditious minds toward disturbances, like [Thomas] Müntzer and his kind, he [Luther] most sharply condemned such raging. He not only honored but also firmed up the dignity and all bonds of the political order. When I ponder how often many great men in the Church have been hallucinating in this matter, I come to the conviction that his heart was governed not only by human diligence but also by divine light in order to remain so strictly within the boundaries of his task. Consequently, he cursed not only the seditious teachers of his time, Müntzer and the Anabaptists, but also those bishops of the city of Rome who most boldly and shamelessly claimed with their decrees that [Saint] Peter was given not only the task of proclaiming the Gospel but also political power. In short, he exhorted everybody to give to God the things of God; to Caesar the

[32] Vulgate: *Obsigna legem in discipulis suis.*

things of Caesar [Mt 22:21], that is, to serve God with true penance, with the recognition and propagation of the true doctrine, with true invocation, and with the obligations of a good conscience. <166> Let each man respectfully obey his government in all civic duties for God's sake. And Luther himself was such a man who gave to God the things of God; he taught properly, he called on God properly. He possessed also the other virtues necessary in a person who is pleasing to God. Finally, in political matters he most firmly avoided any seditious plans. I judge these virtues to be so precious that there are no greater ones to be wished for in this life.

The virtue of this man, who reverently used the gifts of God, surely is praiseworthy. We nevertheless must give thanks especially to God that through him He restored the light of the Gospel to us. And, we must keep the memory of his teaching and propagate it. I am not disturbed by the shouts of Epicureans or hypocrites who either laugh at or curse the evident truth. I hold that there is uninterrupted consensus between the Catholic Church of God[33] and the teaching that is heard in our churches, and that the recognition of this teaching necessarily is to shape invocation and life. In short, this is the same doctrine of which the Son of God says: "Whoever loves me will keep my word, and my Father will love him, and we will come to him and make our dwelling with him" [Jn 14:23]. I am speaking of the sum of the doctrine as it is understood and explained by the pious and learned in our churches. For even though some people at times explain something more properly and elegantly than others, or someone speaks less sophisticated than another, there is nevertheless a consensus among the pious and learned about matters that are of the greatest importance.

As I often think hard about the doctrine throughout all the ages, there appeared—since the age of the Apostles—four distinguishable mutations in doctrine which came up after the original purity. Even though there were some people who had the right thinking such as Methodius[34] who condemned Origen's nonsense, the age of Origen turned the hearts of the multitude away from the Gospel toward philosophy, that is, he [Origen] spread the conviction that moderate, reasonable disciplining would merit the remission of sins; and that

---

[33] Latin: *catholica Ecclesia Dei.* The 1554 translation into German has *All gemeyne Kirche Gottes*; Walch translated with *ganze, allgemeine Kirche Gottes.*

[34] Teacher and author, third century.

this would be the righteousness of which is said [in Rom 1:17]: "The one who is righteous will live by faith." This age [of Origen] almost completely lost the essential distinction of Law and Gospel and gave up the apostolic word. For it did not keep the original meaning of the words "letter," "spirit," "justice" [righteousness], "faith." And once the proper meaning of a word is lost <167>—words are designations for things—something else must necessarily be configured. From those seeds Pelagius' error arose which spread widely. Whereas the apostles had given to the Church the pure doctrine or clear and most salutary sources, Origen poured much filth into them.

God raised up Augustine so that the errors of that age would be corrected, at least in part. This man cleaned up the sources somewhat, and I have no doubt, that if this man were the judge over the controversies of this [our] age, he would side with us. He certainly agrees with us explicitly concerning the gratuitous remission of sins, justification by faith, the use of the sacraments, and the indifferent things [*adiaphora*]. Even if here and there he explained more or less eloquently or properly what he wanted, a reader, who with candor and skill would approach him for evaluation, would recognize that he thinks as we do. For when our adversaries sometimes cite Augustine against us, after having picked out sayings from him and making an appeal to the Fathers with great noise, they do not do this out of concern for the truth and antiquity. They deceitfully manufacture their idols from the authority of the ancients who had not known those idols that came into existence at a more recent age. It is apparent, however, that seeds of superstition existed already during the age of the Fathers. On that account Augustine decided certain things about vows, although he spoke less uncouthly about them than others did. The pollutions of a given time always sprinkle some of the follies also onto individuals who are good persons, because we are as disposed to our homeland as we are to the contemporary rites with which we grew up. How so very true is Euripides' saying: "Everything familiar is pleasant."[35] Would that all those who boast that they follow

[35] *Tragicorum Graecorum Fragmenta,* ed. Bruno Snell (Göttingen: Vandenhoeck & Ruprecht, 1971), *Incertorum fabularum fragmenta*, no. 1046, 3–4. Melanchthon seems to want to clarify or complement Luther's reference to a proverb on the same subject which Luther mentioned in his *Preface* to Volume 1: "How true the proverb is: 'It's hard to abandon customs' and 'Custom is a second nature'," WA 54, 183, 23–24.

Augustine actually return to the entire context, and, if I may put it this way, see [the motivation in] the heart of Augustine, and not merely twist some mutilated sayings to fit their own opinions.

And the light that has been restored by the writings of Augustine benefited posterity as thereafter Prosper, Maximus, Hugo,[36] and others like them who governed the studies, were virtually following the norm of Augustine—up to the age of Bernard. Meanwhile, however, the realms and the wealth of the bishops grew as if it were the age of the Titans. Worldly and uneducated men reigned in the Church, some of whom had refined training [only] in the arts of the Roman court or in the teaching of law.

<168> Therefore, Dominicans and Franciscans arose, who, as they saw the luxury and wealth of the bishops, detested their worldly morals and set up a more modest way of life. They shut themselves up as if in jails of [monastic] discipline. However, their lack of knowledge, first of all, increased the superstitions. Secondly, when they saw that the studies of the men in the schools were turned solely toward legalistic doctrine, because litigations at Rome increased the power and wealth of many, they themselves tried to call the people back to the theological studies; but they lacked good counsel. Albert [the Great] and those like him who had given themselves over to the doctrine of Aristotle began to transform the doctrine of the Church into a philosophy. And this, the fourth age poured into the evangelical sources not only filth but also poison, i.e., opinions that allow for idolatry. There are so many great labyrinths and false opinions in Thomas, Scotus, and in people like them, that the more sane theologians always longed for another kind of teaching, plainer and purer.

Only with remarkable shamelessness may one maintain that there was no need for a change of this teaching, since it is evident that not even they who grew old in this kind of teaching understood the larger parts of the sophisms in those disputations. Besides that, idol mania is openly confirmed when they teach the efficaciousness of the sacrifice [of the Mass] *opere operato* ["from the work done"], when they excuse invocations of statues [of the saints], when they deny that sins are gratuitously forgiven by faith, when from some human ceremonies they make a torture of consciences. In short, there are still

[36] Prosper of Aquitaine (ca. 390–ca.455), an Anti-Pelagian author; Maximus the Confessor (ca. 580–662); Hugo of Saint Victor (died 1141).

many other things more hideous and blasphemous which make my whole body shudder, when I think about them.

Therefore, let us give thanks to God, the eternal Father of our Lord Jesus Christ, that He wanted the filth and poisons to be removed from the evangelical sources by the ministry of Martin Luther, in order to restore the pure doctrine of the Church. When they think about all this, all pious people in the whole world rightly join their voices and sighs and beg with burning hearts that God may strengthen that which He has worked within us, for the sake of His holy temple [the Church]: O living and true God, eternal Father of our Lord Jesus Christ, Creator of all things and of the Church, this is Your word and promise: 'For the sake of my name I shall pity you, for my sake I shall not be blasphemed' [Is 48:11]. I pray You with my whole heart, on account of Your glory and of Your Son, that by the word of Your Gospel You always gather to You the eternal Church from among us; <169> and on account of Your Son our Lord Jesus Christ crucified for us and resurrected, the mediator and intercessor,[37] that You rule our hearts through the Holy Spirit, so that we may truly call upon You and fulfill the duties which are pleasing to You. May You rule also the studies of the doctrine and may you govern and preserve the political orders and their disciplining; they are the hospices for your Church and its teachings. Since You created the human race for the reason that You be known and invoked by the people, wherefore You also made Yourself known by splendid testimonies, you will not allow that the troops are destroyed among whom Your doctrine is sounding forth. And since Your Son our Lord Jesus Christ, as he was about to undergo his agony, prayed for us, "Father, sanctify them in the truth, Your word is truth" [Jn 17:17], we join our prayers to the plea of this our Priest and together with Him we beg that Your doctrine may always shine out in the human race and govern us.

We heard Luther daily pray for this and during these prayers his soul was calmly called from his mortal body, at a time when he had already completed his sixty-third year.

Posterity has many documents of the man's doctrine and piety. He issued teachings in which he embraced the doctrine that is salutary and necessary for all, instructing good minds about penance, faith, the true fruits of faith, the use of the sacraments, the distinction of Law

---

[37] Melanchthon alludes to Rom 8:34: "It is Christ who died, rather, was raised, . . . who intercedes for us."

and Gospel, the distinction of Gospel and philosophy, the dignity of the political order, in short, the principal articles of doctrine which must of necessity be held up in the Church. Next he added polemical treatises in which he refuted many errors that are detrimental to the people. He also issued exegetical writings, that is, many commentaries on the prophetic and apostolic writings. As to the latter, even his enemies generally do admit that he surpasses all the extant commentaries. All pious minds understand that these merits are great. Indeed, these works are equal in usefulness and labor to the translation of the Old and New Testament, in which there is such great clarity that the German reading as such can take the place of a commentary. [The translation] is not just the naked text, but includes the most learned annotations and the summary-arguments of the individual sections which teach the most important parts of the heavenly doctrine. They educate the reader also about literary genre so that any good mind would be able to ladle solid testimonies of doctrine from the very sources themselves. <170> For Luther did not want people to stick to his writings, but wanted to lead the people's minds to the sources [*ad fontes*]. He wanted us to hear the [original] voice of God itself, and through it he wanted true faith and prayer to be kindled in many, so that God would be truly worshipped and that many would be made inheritors of eternal life. It is fitting to praise with thankful heart this purpose and these so great labors, and to remember them as an example, so that we, too, each of us in our own ways, will be eager to be an adornment to the Church. The whole of life and all the studies and plans of life must be referred to these two ends: first, that we make known the glory of God; secondly, that we are of use to the Church. About the first, Paul says: "Do everything for the glory of God" [1 Cor 10:31]. About the other, [we read in] Psalm 122 [verse 6]: "Pray for the peace of Jerusalem." In the same verse the most sweet promise is added that those who love the Church will be happy and blessed.[38] May these heavenly commands and these promises invite everybody to learn the doctrine of the Church correctly, to love the ministers of the Gospel and the teachers of salvation, and to direct their eagerness and works to the propagation of the true doctrine and to the protection of the concord of the true Church.

---

[38] Jerusalem is an image for "Church." Melanchthon paraphrased Vulgate Ps 121:6: *Rogate pacem Hierusalem sit bene his qui diligunt te.*

Fare well, dear reader. Wittenberg, on the first day of June, in the year of the Lord, 1546.

Appendix

The Young Luther: Chronology from 1501–1517

Erfurt:

1501–1505	Study at the University of Erfurt (grammar, rhetoric, logic, ethics, and metaphysics); *Magister artium*
17 July 1505	Admitted to the Augustinian friary at Erfurt
Late summer 1506	Final vows
Spring 1507	Studying Biel's commentary on the Mass in preparation for the ordination to the priesthood
2 April 1507	Ordination at Erfurt cathedral
2 May 1507	First Mass
18 April 1508–Fall	Lecturing on Aristotelian Philosophy at Erfurt

Wittenberg:

October 1508	Immatriculation at Wittenberg
November or December 1508	Lecturing on Aristotle's Dialectics and Ethics
9 March 1509	Degree of *Baccalaureus biblicus*
17 March 1509	Letter to Braun, from Wittenberg, in which Luther expresses preference for studying theology over lecturing on philosophy (WA Br 1, no. 5)

Erfurt:

October 1509	First (a recent discovery) sources from Luther's pen: annotations on

	Bonaventure, Anselm, Trithemius; first group of notes on *Augustini opuscula* (with Luther's entry of the date '1509')
Fall 1509–Spring 1510	First annotations on the *Sentences* I and III, also IV; notes on *De Trinitate*; Degree of *Baccalaureus sententiarius,* substitute teacher (for the deceased Friar Leonard Heutleb); commenting on the *Sentences*
Summer 1510	Annotations on the *Sentences* II, and on the second group of *Augustini opuscula;* while reading Augustine's *De civitate Dei*
Fall/Winter 1510	Annotations on *Sentences* III
Winter 1510–Summer 1511	Annotations on *Ockham*, *Giorgio Valla* (a recent discovery), and again on *Sentences* III
Wittenberg:	
16 September 1511	Staupitz summons a "synod" at Wittenberg; decision is made to send a delegation to Rome
After 4 October 1511	Delegation (Johann von Mecheln as *litis procurator* and Luther as his associate) departs from Wittenberg for Rome; during the winter semester 1511/1512
Rome:	
Christmas 1511–Early January 1512	
January 1512	Departing from Rome
Erfurt, Cologne:	
2 May 1512	Luther attends Chapter Meeting in Cologne as a delegate of the Wittenberg friary. He report about his trip to Rome. He is appointed subprior

	and director of studies at the friary at Wittenberg starting in summer or fall
Pentecost Monday 1512	Luther delivers his first known sermon, on Jn 3:16, at Erfurt: *Serm. Ex autographo* [in Greek letters] *quod inveniebatur in Monasterio Augustinen. Erffurdiae* (WA 4, 595–604); it includes a reference to the comet seen in the sky in March and April of 1512 (WA 4, 597, 33).
Wittenberg:	
June 1512	Luther as ghostwriter for Georg Mascov composes a sermon on 1 Jn 5:4. Mascov is the prior of the Premonstratensian monastery of Leitzkau (Litzka, northwest of Wittenberg) who delivers the sermon at the diocesan assembly at the bishop's residence, the castle of Ziesar, on 22 June 1512; the reform synod was summoned by Bishop Jerome Schulze (WA 1, 10–17)
1512?–1517	Luther working on a tractate on asylum in church, published in 1517(?)
22 September 1512	Letter to the Augustinians of Erfurt about his doctoral promotion
18 October 1512	Doctor's degree of Wittenberg University
6 October 1513	Egidio da Viterbo (the general of the order) appoints Luther officially as a lector at the Wittenberg friary
Fall 1513	Beginning of Luther's *Dictata super Psalterium*; Luther begins to read Johann Reuchlin's Hebrew/Latin book on the Seven Penitential Psalms (published in 1512)

1513 or 1514	City council of Wittenberg calls Luther to become preacher at the city church, a position he keeps until his death
5 August 1514	Letter to Spalatin about Reuchlin (oldest extant original letter by Luther; WA Br 1, no. 9)
Christmas 1514	First known Christmas sermon (WA 1, 20–29)
26 December 1514	Sermon on St. Stephen's Day, on Mt 23–24 (WA 1, 30–37)
27 December 1514	Sermon on St. John's Day, *De timore Dei* (WA 1, 37–43 = WA 4, 659–666)
4 December 1515	Sermon on St. Barbara's Day, *De diva Barbara*, on Ps 45:5 (WA 4, 639–644)
1514–1516	Luther comes upon a tract from ca. 1350 (known as the *Frankfurter* or as *Theologia deutsch*, which he edits in parts in 1516, and in full in 1518; Preface of 1516 (WA 1, 153)
1515–1516	Lectures on Romans
8 April 1516	Letter to Friar Spenlein in Memmingen about trusting in the righteousness of God *(iustitia Dei)* instead of one's own (WA Br 1, 35–36, no. 11)
31 October/1 November 1516	*In die dedicationis temple sermo*; Luther's sermon with critical comments on the indulgences (WA 1, 94–99 = WA 4, 670–674)
1516–1517	Lectures on Galatians
1516 (–1520?)	Annotations on Hebrew texts of the Psalms, *INSTITVTIVNCVLA* || *in Hebræam linguam* || *Autore Volphan* || *go Fabro Pro* || *fessore Theo* || *logi* (WA 9, 115–116); Annotations on Jerome's works (edition 1516)

Summer 1516– End of February 1517	Series of Sermons on Decalogue (published in 1518)
December 1516	Luther's annotations on Tauler's sermons in the 1508 edition
7 December 1516 (or 6 December 1517?)	Sermon for Second Advent (WA 1, 104–106)
24 February 1517	Luther's sermon on Mt 11:25–30, with critical remarks on indulgences (WA 1, 141)
March/April 1517	Luther's German publication on the *Seven Penitential Psalms*
4 September 1517	"Positions against Scholastic theology" (Franz Günther's 99 "Theses")
15 August 1517	Sermon on the Assumption of the Blessed Virgin Mary (WA 4, 645–650) *Tractatulus de indulgentiis ex sermone habito Dominica X. post Trinitatis* (WA Br 12, 5–10)
31 October 1517	Luther sends letters to two ecclesiastical authorities concerning the indulgence business; one to Albrecht of Brandenburg (WA Br 1, 39–41, no. 48), archbishop of Magdeburg and Mainz and *primas* of German speaking lands; the other to Bishop Jerome Schulze of Brandenburg to whose jurisdiction Wittenberg is subject. The letter to Bishop Schulze is not extant. According to Melanchthon, Luther posts *Propositiones* at the "church adjacent to Wittenberg Castle, on the eve of All Saints Day, in the year 1517" (CR 6, 162).

Select Bibliography

Primary Sources

Corpus Reformatorum. Vols 1–28 [Melanchthon]. Carolus Gottlieb Bretschneider and H. E. Bindseil, eds. Halle: C. A. Schwetschke, 1834–1860.

D. Martin Luthers Werke. Kritische Gesamtausgabe. Weimar: Hermann Böhlaus Nachfolger; Graz: Akademische Druck und Verlagsanstalt, 1883–.

Dokumente zur Causa Lutheri (1517–1521). Fabisch, Peter and Iserloh, Erwin, eds., Münster: Aschendorff, 1988.

Dr. Martin Luthers Sämmtliche Schriften. Vol. 14. Johann Georg Walch, ed. St. Louis: Concordia, 1898.

"Historia D. Martini Lutheri Text." Pages 15–47 in Harald Weinacht. *Melanchthon und Luther. Merkmale einer Kirchenreform. Martin Luthers Lebensbeschreibung durch Philipp Melanchthon. Deutsch–Lateinisch.* Zurich: Theologischer Verlag, 2008.

Johann von Staupitz: Gutachten und Satzungen. Sämtliche Schriften vol. 5. Wolfgang Günter, ed. Berlin and New York: Walter de Gruyter, 2001, 144–319.

Martin Luther Studienausgabe. Berlin: Evangelische Verlagsanstalt, 1979–1999.

Melanchthons Briefwechsel: Kritische und kommentierte Gesamtausgabe. Heinz Scheible, ed. Stuttgart: Frommann–Holzboog, 1977–.

Melanchthon, Philipp and Ritter, Mathias. *Beschreibung des Lebens und handlungen des Ehrwürdigen Herrn D. Martini Lutheri.* Frankfurt a. M.: 1554.

Philipp Melanchthon's *Erzählung vom Leben D. Martin Luthers, in Dr. Martin Luthers Sämmtliche Schriften*. Johann Georg Walch, ed. St. Louis: Concordia, 1880–1910.

Sancti Bernardi Opera. Jean Leclercq, Henri Rochais, and Charles H. Halbot, eds., 8 vols. Rome: Editiones Cistercienses, 1957–1977.

English Translations

Luther's Works. American Edition of Martin Luther's Works. General editors Helmut T. Lehmann, Jaroslav Pelikan, and Christopher Boyd Brown. Vols. 1–75. St. Louis: Concordia; Philadelphia and Minneapolis: Fortress, 1955–.

Luther's Lives: Two Contemporary Accounts of Martin Luther. Elizabeth Vandiver, Ralph Keen, and Thomas D. Frazel, eds. Manchester and New York: Manchester University Press, 2004.

The Book of Concord: The Confessions of the Evangelical Lutheran Church. Robert Kolb and Timothy J. Wengert, eds., trans. by Charles Arand, Eric Gritsch, Robert Kolb, William Russell, James Schaaf +, Jane Strohl, Timothy J. Wengert. Minneapolis: Fortress Press, 2000.

Secondary Literature

Backus, Irena. "Luther: Instrument of God or Satan's Brood. Main Developments in Luther Biography, 1546–81." Pages 1–46 in *Life Writing in Reformation Europe: Lives of Reformers by Friends, Disciples and Foes.* Aldershot: Ashgate, 2008.

Balge, Richard D. "Martin Luther, Augustinian." Pages 7–20 in *Luther Lives. Essays in Commemoration of the 500th Anniversary of Martin Luther's Birth.* Edited by Edward C. Friedrich, Siegbert W. Becker, David P. Kuske. Milwaukee: Northwestern Publishing House, 1983.

Beer, Theobald and von Stockhausen, Alma, eds. *Vigilius von Thapsus, "Die Disputation zwischen Arius und Athanasius." Luthers erste Klosterlektüre. Ein Beitrag zur Lutherforschung.* Weilheim-Bierbronnen: Gustav-Siewert-Akademie, 1999.

Bell, Theo. Divus Bernhardus. *Bernhard von Clairvaux in Martin Luthers Schriften*. Mainz: Philipp von Zabern, 1993.

Beutel, Albrecht, ed. *Luther Handbuch.* Tübingen: Mohr Siebeck, 2005.

Bornkamm, Heinrich. *Thesen und Thesenanschlag Luthers. Geschehen und Bedeutung*. Berlin: Töpelmann, 1967.

Braaten, Carl E. and Jenson, Robert W., eds. *The Catholicity of the Reformation.* Grand Rapids, MI: W. B. Eerdmans, 1996.

Brecht, Martin. "Rechtfertigung oder Gerechtigkeit? Überraschungen auf den Spuren von Luthers Bibelübersetzung." LuJ 77 (2011): 81–105.

Brosseder, Johannes and Wriedt, Markus, eds. "Kein Anlass zur Verwerfung." *Studien zur Hermeneutik des ökumenischen*

Gesprächs. Festschrift für Otto Hermann Pesch. Frankfurt: Verlag Otto Lembeck, 2007.

Brückner, Wolfgang. "Luther, heiliger Mann oder falscher Prophet? Legende und Antilegende zwischen 1517 und 1630." Pages 37–57 in *Mythen Europas: Schlüsselfiguren der Imagination,* vol. 4 of *Renaissance*. Edited by Christine Strobl. Regensburg: Pustet, 2006.

Bulisch, Jens. "Wie alt ist Martin Luther geworden? Zum Geburtsjahr 1482 oder 1484." LuJ 77 (2010): 29–39.

Bultmann, Christoph, Leppin, Volker and Lindner, Andreas, eds. *Luther und das monastische Erbe.* Tübingen: Mohr, Siebeck, 2007.

Burger, Christoph. "Der Augustinereremit Martin Luther in Kloster und Universität bis zum Jahre 1512." Pages 161–186 in *Kloster Amelungsborn 1135–1985.* Edited by Gerhard Ruhbach and Kurt Schmidt-Clausen Hannover: Missionshandlung Hermannsburg, 1985.

———. "Nieuw onderzoek naar Luthers wijsgerige en theologische vorming en haar doorwerking," LB 12 (2003): 61–71.

Constable, Giles. "The Popularity of Twelfth-Century Spiritual Writers in the Late Middle Ages." Pages 5–28 in *Renaissance Studies in Honor of Hans Baron.* Edited by Anthony Molho and John A. Tedeschi DeKalb: Northern Illinois University Press, 1971.

Cummings, Brian. "Luther and the Book: The Iconography of the Ninety-Five Theses." Pages 222–232 in *Papers Read at the 2000 Summer Meeting and the 2000 Winter Meeting of the Ecclesiastical History Society*. Edited by R. N. Swanson. Rochester NY: Boydel Press, 2004.

Denifle, Heinrich Suso. *Luther und das Luthertum in der ersten Entwickung. Quellenmäßig dargestellt.* Vol. I,2. Mainz: F. Kirchheim, 1904–1909, revised edition 1906.

———. *Luther und das Luthertum. Ergänzungen*, vol. 1. *Quellenbelege; Die abendländischen Schriftausleger bis Luther über die Justitia Dei Röm. 1,17 und Justificatio. Beitrag zur Geschichte der Exegese, der Literatur und des Dogmas im Mittelalter*. Mainz: F. Kirchheim, 1905.

Dienst, Karl. "Geistliches und Weltliches. Martin Luther im Spiegel seiner Tischreden." *Blätter für pfälzische Kirchengeschichte und religiöse Volkskunde* 63 (1996): 327–341.

———. "Martin Luther als Tischredner. Eine Tischrede." *Luther* 70 (1999): 145–150.

Dieter, Theodor. *Der junge Luther und Aristoteles. Eine historisch-systematische Untersuchung zum Verhältnis von Theologie und Philosophie*. Berlin and New York: Walter de Gruyter, 2001.

Dietz, Thorsten. *Der Begriff der Furcht bei Luther*. Tübingen: Mohr Siebeck, 2009.

Dörfler-Dierken, Angelika. "Luther und die heilige Anna. Zum Gelübde von Stotternheim." LuJ 64 (1997): 19–46.

Ebeling, Gerhard. *The Word of God and Tradition: Historical Studies Interpreting the Divisions of Christianity*. Translated by S. H. Hooke. Philadelphia: Fortress Press, 1964.

———. *Umgang mit Luther*. Tübingen: Mohr Siebeck, 1983.

Endermann, Heinz. "Martin Luther in Erfurt: Student, Mönch und Wissenschaftler." *Luther* 72 (2001): 83–95.

Farkasfalvy, Denis. "The Use of Paul by Saint Bernard as Illustrated by Saint Bernard's Interpretation of Philippians 3:13." Pages 161–168 in *Bernardus Magister: Papers Presented at the Nonacentenary Celebration of the Birth of Saint Bernard of Clairvaux*. Sponsored by the Institute of Cistercian Studies Western Michigan University 10–13 May 1990. Edited by John R. Sommerfeldt. Kalamazoo, Michigan: Cistercian Publications and Cîteaux: Commentarii Cistercienses, 1992.

France, James. *Medieval Images of Saint Bernard of Clairvaux* Kalamazoo: Cistercian Publications, 2007 (with compact disk).

Frank, Günter, ed. *Der Theologe Melanchthon*. Stuttgart: Thorbecke, 2000.

Gesamtkatalog der Wiegendrucke. Leipzig: Hiersemann, 1925–.

Grisar, Hartmann. *Martin Luther. His Life and Work*. Westminster, MD: The Newman Press, 1930; reprinted in 1953.

Grislis, Egil. "Piety, Faith, and Spirituality in the Quest for the Historical Luther." *Consensus* 19 (1993): 29–51.

Grosse, Sven. "Heilsgewissheit des Glaubens. Die Entwicklung der Auffassungen des jungen Luther von Gewissheit und Ungewissheit des Heils." LuJ 77 (2010): 41–63.

Grüneberg, Theodor. "Martin Pollich von Mellerstadt, der erste Rektor der Wittenberger Universität." Vol. 1, pages 87–91 in *450 Jahre Martin-Luther-Universität Halle-Wittenberg*. Halle: Universität Halle-Wittenberg, 1952.

Hagen, Kenneth. "Martin Luther (1483–1546)." Pages 212–220 in *Historical Handbook of Major Biblical Interpreters*. Edited by Donald K. McKim. Downers Grove, IL: Inter-Varsity Press, 1998.

———. *Foundations of Theology in the Continental Reformation Questions of Authority*. Milwaukee, 1974; copyright Kenneth Hagen.

———. "It Is All in the Et Cetera. Luther and the Elliptical Reference" LB 3 (1994): 57–67.

———. *Luther's Approach to Scripture as seen in his 'Commentaries' on Galatians 1519–1538*. Tübingen: Mohr Siebeck, 1993.

———. "So You Think Luther Was a Monk? Stop It." *Logia* 19 (2010): 35–37.

Haile, Harry G. *Luther: An Experiment in Biography.* Garden City, N.Y.: Doubleday, 1980; Princeton University Press, 1983.

Hamm, Berndt. *Frömmigkeitstheologie am Anfang des 16. Jahrhunderts. Studien zu Johannes Paltz und seinem Umkreis.* Tübingen: Mohr Siebeck, 1982.

Hausrath, Adolf. *Luthers Leben.* Berlin: G. Grote'sche Verlagsbuchhandlung, 1904.

Hillerbrand, Hans J. "The Spread of the Protestant Reformation of the Sixteenth Century: A Historical Case Study in the Transfer of Ideas." *The South Atlantic Quarterly* 67 (1968): 265–286.

Immenkötter, Herbert. "Von Engeln und Teufeln: Über Luther-Biographien des 16. Jahrhunderts." Pages 91–102 in *Biographie und Autobiographie in der Renaissance. Arbeitsgespräch in der Herzog August Bibliothek Wolfenbuttel vom 1. bis 3. November 1982: Vorträge*. Edited by August Buck. Wiesbaden: Harrassowitz, 1983.

Iserloh, Erwin. *The theses were not posted: Luther between Reform and Reformation.* Toronto: Saunders of Toronto, Ltd., 1966; Boston: Beacon, 1968.

Isewijn, Jozef. "Die humanistische Biographie." Pages 1–19 in *Biographie und Autobiographie in der Renaissance. Arbeitsgespräch in der Herzog August Bibliothek Wolfenbüttel vom 1. bis 3. November 1982: Vorträge*. Edited by August Buck. Wiesbaden: Harrassowitz, 1983.

Janz, Denis. "What Did Luther Understand by 'Faith'?" Pages 69–80 in *Reforming the Reformation: Essays in Honour of Principal*

Peter Matheson. Edited by Ian Bernard. Melbourne: Australian Scholarly Publishing, 2004.
Junghans, Helmar. "Bibelhumanistische Anstöße in Luthers Entwicklung zum Reformator." *Revue d'Histoire et de Philosophie Religieuses* 85 (2005): 17–42.
———. *Der junge Luther und die Humanisten.* Weimar: Hermann Böhlaus Nachfolger, 1984; Göttingen: Vandenhoeck & Ruprecht, 1985.
———. "Die Tischreden Martin Luthers." Pages 155–176 in *Spätmittelalter, Luthers Reformation, Kirche in Sachsen. Ausgewählte Aufsätze*. Edited by Michael Beyer and Günter Wartenberg. Leipzig: Evangelische Verlagsanstalt, 2001.
———. "The History, Use and Significance of the Weimar Luther Edition." *Theology and Life* 25 (2002): 43–71; reprinted in LQ 17 (2003): 267–287.
Kaufmann, Thomas. *Martin Luther.* Munich: Beck, 2006; 2nd edition 2010.
Kleineidam, Erich. "Ursprung und Gegenstand der Theologie bei Bernhard von Clairvaux und Martin Luther." Papes 221–247 in *Dienst der Vermittlung: Festschrift zum 25 jährigen Bestehen des philosophisch-theologischen Studiums im Priesterseminar Erfurt.* Edited by Wilhelm Ernst, K. Feiereis, and Fritz Hoffmann. Leipzig: St. Benno Verlag, 1977.
Köpf, Ulrich. "Bernhard von Clairvaux im Werk Martin Luthers. Bemerkungen zur neueren Forschung." *Rottenburger Jahrbuch für Kirchengeschichte* 18 (1999) 225–233.
———. "Martin Luthers Lebensgang als Mönch." Pages 187–208 in *Kloster Amelungsborn 1135–1985.* Edited by Gerhard Ruhbach and Kurt Schmidt-Clausen. Hannover: Missionshandlung Hermannsburg, 1985.
———. "Monastische Traditionen bei Martin Luther." Pages 17–35 in *Luther—zwischen den Zeiten. Eine Jenaer Ringvorlesung.* Edited by Christoph Markschies and Michael Trowitzsch. Tübingen: Mohr Siebeck, 1999.
———. "Zisterziensererbe im Protestantismus." *Cistercienser Chronik* 11 (2007): 311–327.
Köstlin, Julius. *Life of Luther.* New York: Scribner's, 1913.
Kolb, Robert. *Martin Luther as Prophet, Teacher, and Hero. Images of the Reformer, 1520–1620*. Grand Rapids: Baker Books; Paternoster Press, 1999.

———. "Umgestaltung und theologische Bedeutung des Lutherbildes im späten 16. Jahrhundert." Pages 202–231 in *Die lutherische Konfessionalisierung in Deutschland.* Edited by Hans-Christoph Rublack. Gütersloh: Gütersloher Verlagshaus, 1992.

Kusukawa, Sachiko, ed. *A Wittenberg University Library Catalogue of 1536*, Binghamton, N.Y.: LP Publications, 1995.

Leppin, Volker. "Geburtswehen und Geburt einer Legende." *Luther* 78 (2007): 145–150.

———. *Martin Luther*. Darmstadt: Wissenschaftliche Buchgesellschaft, 2006; revised edition 2010.

———. "Martin Luther, Reconsidered for 2017." LQ 22 (2008): 376–377.

Lexutt, Athina, Mantey, Volker and Ortmann, Volkmar, eds. *Reformation und Mönchtum. Aspekte eines Verhältnisses über Luther hinaus.* Tübingen: Mohr Siebeck, 2008.

Lienhard, Marc. "Luther en perspective Catholique. Quelques Observations." *Revue d'histoire et de philosophie religieuses* 63 (1983): 167–177.

Lohrmann, Martin. "A Newly Discovered Report of Luther's Reformation Breakthrough from Johannes Bugenhagen's 1550 Jonah Commentary." LQ 22 (2008): 324–330.

Lohse, Bernhard. "Albrecht von Brandenburg und Luther." Pages 73–83 in *Erzbischof Albrecht von Brandenburg 1490–1545. Ein Kirchen- und Reichsfürst der Frühen Neuzeit.* Edited by Friedhelm Jürgensmeier. Frankfurt: Knecht, 1990.

———. *Evangelium in der Geschichte.* 2 vols. Göttingen: Vandenhoeck & Ruprecht, 1988 and 1998.

———. "Luther und Athanasius." Pages 97–115 in *Auctoritas Patrum. Zur Rezeption der Kirchenväter im 15. und 16. Jahrhundert.* Edited by Leif Grane, Alfred Schindler and Markus Wriedt. Mainz: Philipp von Zabern, 1993; reprinted in *Evangelium in der Geschichte*, vol. 2: 191–212.

———. *Martin Luther. Eine Einführung in sein Leben und sein Werk.* Munich: Beck, 1981; 3rd completely revised edition, 1997.

Maron, Gottfried. *Das katholische Lutherbild der Gegenwart. Anmerkungen und Anfragen, Bensheimer Hefte* 58 (1982).

Maschke, Timothy, Posset, Franz and Skocir, Joan, eds. *Ad fontes Lutheri: Toward the Recovery of the Real Luther. Essays in Honor of Kenneth Hagen's Sixty-Fifth Birthday.* Milwaukee: Marquette University Press, 2001.

Matsuura, Jun. *Erfurter Annotationen 1509–1510/11*. Archiv zur Weimarer Ausgabe der Werke Martin Luther. Böhlau, 2009.

———. "Luther als Dozent an der Erfurter Universität. Auf den Spuren Seiner Anfänge. Erfurter Universitätslesungen 1991–1992, 47–67.

———. "Restbestände aus der Bibliothek des Erfurter Augustinerklosters zu Luthers Zeit und bisher unbekannte eigenhändige Notizen Luthers." *Lutheriana: Zum 500. Geburtstag Martin Luthers von den Mitarbeitern der Weimarer Ausgabe* Cologne: Böhlau, 1984.

———. "Zu 'Fromm' bei Luther." *Die deutsche Literatur. Herausgegeben von der Japanischen Gesellschaft für Germanistik* 73 (1984): 124–137. Edited by Doitsu Bungaku.

Maurer, Wilhelm. *Der junge Melanchthon zwischen Humanismus und Reformation*. Göttingen: Vandenhoeck & Ruprecht, 1969.

Medick, Hans and Schmidt, Peer, eds. *Luther zwischen den Kulturen. Zeitgenossenschaft—Weltwirkung*. Göttingen: Vandenhoeck & Ruprecht, 2004.

Moeller, Bernd. *Luther-Rezeption. Kirchenhistorische Aufsätze zur Reformationsgeschichte*. Edited by Johannes Schilling. Göttingen: Vandenhoeck & Ruprecht, 2001.

Moeller, Bernd and Stackmann, Karl. *Luder—Luther—Eleutherius. Erwägungen zu Luthers Namen*. Göttingen: Vandenhoeck & Ruprecht, 1981.

Moser, Hugo. "'Fromm' bei Luther und Melanchthon: Ein Beitrag zur Wortgeschichte in der Reformationszeit." Pages 54–74 in *Studien zu Raum- und Sozialformen der deutschen Sprache in Geschichte und Gegenwart*. Berlin: Schmidt-Verlag, 1979.

Mullett, Michael A. *Martin Luther*. London and New York: Routledge, 2004.

Murphy, Lawrence. "Martin Luther, the Erfurt Cloister, and Gabriel Biel: The Relation of Philosophy to Theology." ARG 70 (1979): 5–24.

Oberman, Heiko A. "'Tuus sum, salvum me fac.' Augustinreveil zwischen Renaissance und Reformation." Pages 349–394 in *Scientia Augustiniana. Studien über Augustinus, den Augustinismus und den Augustinerorden. Festschrift P. Dr. theol. Dr. phil. Adolar Zumkeller OSA zum 60. Geburtstag*. Edited by Cornelius Petrus Mayer and Willigis Eckermann. Würzburg: Augustinus-Verlag, 1975.

Ott, Joachim and Treu, Martin, eds. *Luthers Thesenanschlag—Faktum oder Fiktion.* Schriften der Stiftung Luthergedenkstätten in Sachsen-Anhalt 9. Leipzig: Evangelische Verlagsanstalt, 2008.

Pedersen, Else Marie Wiberg. "Justification and Grace. Did Luther Discover a New Theology or Did He Discover Anew the Theology of Justification and Grace?" *Studia Theologica* 57 (2003): 143–161.

———. "The Significance of the Sola Fide and the Sola Gratia in the Theology of Bernard of Clairvaux 1090–1153 and Martin Luther 1483–1546." LB 18 (2009): 20–43.

Pesch, Otto Hermann. "Wat heeft Luther de katholieken nog te zeggen?—Enn soort 'in memoriam.'" LB 6 (1997): 4–22.

———. "Wo steht die katholische Lutherforschung?" LB 13 (2004): 85–106.

Petri, Franz. "Herzog Heinrich der Jüngere von Braunschweig-Wolfenbüttel." ARG 72 (1981): 122–158.

Pilvousek, Josef. "Martin Luther und Erfurt." Pages 13–27 in *Luther in Erfurt und die katholische Theologie.* Edited by Josef Freitag. Leipzig: St. Benno Verlag, 2001.

Posset, Franz. "A Humanist and Reformer Turns To Saint Bernard: Philip Melanchthon and Bernard of Clairvaux." *Analecta Cisterciensia* 55 (2005): 301–315.

———. "Amplexus Bernardi: The Dissemination of a Cistercian Motif in the Late Middle Ages and the Reformation Time." *Cîteaux* 54 (2003): 251–400.

———. "Bernard of Clairvaux as Luther's Source. Reading Bernard with Luther's 'Spectacles.'" CTQ 54 (1990): 281–304.

———. "Bernardus Redivivus. The *Wirkungsgeschichte* of a Medieval Sermon in the Reformation of the Sixteenth Century." *Cistercian Studies [Quarterly]* 22 (1987): 239–249.

———. "Bernhard von Clairvauxs Meditation zu Psalm 31, 2 bei Martin Luther." LuJ 69 (2002): 71–78.

———. "Bernhard von Clairvauxs Sermone zur Weihnachts-, Fasten- und Osterzeit als Quelle Martin Luthers." LuJ 61 (1994): 93–116.

———. "Bible Reading 'With Closed Eyes' in the Monastic Tradition: An Overlooked Aspect of Martin Luther's Hermeneutics." ABR 38 (1987): 293–306.

———. "Frater Augustinus Martin Luther in Erfurt und seine Lektüre geistlicher Autoren, insbesondere Bernhards. Zum Gedächtnis des

850. Todestags des heiligen Bernhard von Clairvaux im Jahr 2003." LB 11 (2002): 30–47.

———. "From the Corrupter of the Faith to the Father in the Faith: 100 Years of Catholic Luther Research." Pages 79–141 in *Luther Study* 14 (2000) of the Luther Study Institute, Luther Theological University, Korea.

———. "Goldene Worte: Augustinus und Bernhard in der Sicht des alten Luther 1531–1546." *Catholica. Vierteljahresschrift für ökumenische Theologie* 54 (2000): 220–239.

———. "'Heaven is on Sale.' The Influence of the Italian Humanist and Carmelite Friar Baptist Mantuanus on Martin Luther." *Carmelus* 36 (1989): 134–144.

———. "Lehrer der Seelsorge. Das ökumenische Potential der Seelsorge-Konzeption des alten Luther." *Luther* 72 (2001): 3–17.

———. *Luther's Catholic Christology According to his Johannine Lectures of 1527*. Milwaukee: Northwestern Publishing House, 1988.

———. "Luthers Predigt von 1515 gegen das Laster der Verleumdung und seine mittelalterliche Quelle." *Luther* 75 (2004): 142–149.

———. "Martin Luther Biographies." *Biography: An Interdisciplinary Quarterly* 8 (1985): 356–365.

———. "Martin Luther OSA and Markus von Weida OP: Auseinandersetzung um das Rosenkranzbeten." LB 13 (2004): 45–62.

———. "Monastic Influence on Martin Luther." *Monastic Studies* (Montreal: The Benedictine Priory of Montreal) 18 (1988): 136–163.

———. *Pater Bernhardus: Martin Luther and Bernard of Clairvaux*. Kalamazoo: Cistercian Publications, 1999.

———. "Pater et Doctor Meus Est, Immo Sanctae Ecclesiae, Intellectu Profundissimus." Pages 513–543 in *Collectanea Augustiniana: Augustine: Mystic and Mystagogue*. Edited by Frederick Van Fleteren, Joseph C. Schnaubelt, and Joseph Reino. New York etc: Peter Lang, 1994.

———. "Polyglot Humanism in Germany circa 1520 as Luther's Milieu and Matrix: The Evidence of the 'Rectorate Page' of Crotus Rubeanus." *Renaissance and Reformation* 27 (2003, issued in 2004): 5–33.

———. "Preaching the Passion of Christ on the Eve of the Reformation." CTQ 59 (1995): 279–300.

———. "'Recommendations by Martin Luther of St Bernard's On Consideration," *Cistercian Studies [Quarterly]* 25 (1990): 25–36.

———. "Saint Bernard of Clairvaux in the Devotion, Theology, and Art of the Sixteenth Century." LQ 11 (1997): 306–352.

———. "Sola Scriptura—Martin Luther's Invention? Commemorating the 500th Anniversary of the Printed Edition of the Constitutions of the Order of St. Augustine in Nuremberg in 1504–1506." *Augustiniana* 56 (2006): 123–127.

———. "St Bernard's Influence on Two Reformers: John von Staupitz and Martin Luther." *Cistercian Studies [Quarterly]* 25 (1990): 175–187.

———. "The 'Double Right to Heaven': Saint Bernard's Impact in the Sixteenth Century," *Cistercian Studies Quarterly* 38 (2003): 263–273.

———. *The Two-Fold Knowledge: Readings on the Knowledge of Self & the Knowledge of God Selected & Translated from the Works of Saint Bernard of Clairvaux.* Milwaukee: Marquette University Press, 2004.

Rusch, William G. ed. *Justification and the Future of the Ecumenical Movement. The Joint Declaration on the Doctrine of Justification.* Collegeville: Liturgical Press, 2003.

Schneider, Hans. "Contentio Staupitii. Der 'Staupitz-Streit' in der Observanz der deutschen Augustinereremiten 1507–1512." ZKG 118 (2007): 1–44.

———. "Neue Quellen zum Konflikt in der deutschen Reformkongregation der Augustinereremiten zu Beginn des 16. Jahrhunderts." *Analecta Augustiniana* 71 (2008): 7–37.

Schuessler, Hermann. "Sacred Doctrine and the Authority of Scripture in Canonistic Thought on the Eve of the Reformation." Pages 55–68 in *Reform and Authority in the Medieval and Reformation Church.* Edited by Guy Fitch Lytle and Uta-Renate Blumenthal. Washington DC: The Catholic University of America Press, 1981.

Schuster, Peter-Klaus. "Individuelle Ewigkeit: Hoffnungen und Ansprüche im Bildnis der Lutherzeit." Pages 121–173 in *Biographie und Autobiographie in der Renaissance. Arbeitsgespräch in der Herzog August Bibliothek Wolfenbüttel vom 1. bis 3. November 1982: Vorträge*. Edited by August Buck. Wiesbaden: Harrassowitz, 1983.

Schwarz, Reinhard. *Luther*. Göttingen: Vandenhoeck & Ruprecht, 1986; 3rd edition, 2004.

———. "Luther's Inalienable Inheritance of Monastic Theology." trans. Franz Posset. ABR 39 (1988): 430–450.

———. "Luthers unveräußerte Erbschaft an der monastischen Theologie." Pages 209–231 in *Kloster Amelungsborn 1135–1985*. Edited by Gerhard Ruhbach and Kurt Schmidt-Clausen. Hannover: Missionshandlung Hermannsburg, 1985.

Schwiebert, E[rnest] G. *Luther and His Times. The Reformation from a New Perspective.* Saint Louis: Concordia, 1950.

Scribner, Robert W. *Popular Culture and Popular Movements in Reformation Germany.* London and Ronceverte, WV: Hambledon Press, 1987.

Seebaß, Gottfried. "Ein Luther ohne Goldgrund—Stand und Aufgaben der Lutherforschung am Ende eines Jubiläumsjahres." Pages 49–85 in *Lehren aus dem Lutherjahr. Sein Ertrag für die Ökumene.* Edited by Otto Hermann Pesch. Freiburg: Katholische Akademie, 1984.

Smith, Thurman L. "Luther and the Iserloh Thesis from a Numismatic Perspective." SCJ 20 (1989): 183–201.

Sonntag, Franz Peter. "Luther in katholischer Sicht." *Die Zeichen der Zeit* 39 (1985): 195–204.

Stange, Carl. *Bernhard von Clairvaux: Studien der Luther-Akademie.* Berlin: Alfred Töpelmann, 1954.

Treu, Martin. "Der Thesenanschlag fand wirklich statt," *Luther* 78 (2007): 140–144.

———. "Die Leucorea zwischen Tradition und Erneuerung. Erwägungen zur frühen Geschichte der Universität Wittenberg." Pages 31–51 in *Martin Luther und seine Universität. Vorträge anläßlich des 450. Todestages des Reformators.* Edited by Heiner Lück. Cologne, Weimar, Vienna: Böhlau, 1998.

Urban, Wolfgang. "Die 'via moderna' an der Universität Erfurt am Vorabend der Reformation." Pages 311–330 in *Gregor von Rimini: Werk und Wirkung bis zur Reformation.* Edited by Heiko A. Oberman. Berlin and New York, de Gruyter, 1981.

Vercruysse, Joseph E. "Luther in der römisch-katholischen Theologie und Kirche," LuJ 63 (1996): 103–128.

———. "The Catholic View of Luther Five Hundred Years After His Birth." *Pro Mundi Vita. Europe. North American Dossier* 21 (1983): 2–22.

Vogel, Lothar. "Zwischen Universität und Seelsorge: Martin Luthers Beweggründe im Ablasstreit." ZKG 118 (2007): 187–212.

Watanabe, Morimichi. "Martin Luther's Relations with Italian Humanists: With Special Reference to Ioannes Baptista Mantuanus." LuJ 54 (1987): 23–47.

Weiss, James Michael. "Erasmus at Luther's Funeral: Melanchthon's Commemorations of Luther in 1546." SCJ 16 (1985): 91–114.

Wengert, Timothy J. "Beyond Stereotypes: The Real Philip Melanchthon." Pages 9–32 in *Philip Melanchthon: Then and Now 1497–1997. Essays Celebrating the 500th Anniversary of the Birth of Philip Melanchthon, Theologian, Teacher and Reformer.* Edited by Scott H. Hendrix and Timothy J. Wengert. Columbia, SC: Lutheran Southern Seminary, 1997.

———. "Melanchthon and Luther / Luther and Melanchthon." LuJ 66 (1999): 55–88.

Wicks, Jared. "Brother Martin, Augustinian Friar." *Lutheran Forum* 42 (2008): 33–36.

Wiedenhofer, Siegfried. "Zum katholischen Melanchthon-Bild im 19. und 20. Jahrhundert." *Zeitschrift für Katholische Theologie* 102 (1980): 425–454.

Winterhager, Wilhelm-Ernst. "Ablasskritik als Indikator historischen Wandels vor 1517: Ein Beitrag zu Voraussetzungen und Einordnung der Reformation." ARG 90 (1999): 6–71.

Wolgast, Eike. "Biographie als Autoritätsstiftung: Die ersten evangelischen Lutherbiographien." Pages 41–71 in *Biographie zwischen Renaissance und Barock: Zwölf Studien.* Edited by Walter Berschin. Heidelberg: Mattes, 1993.

Wriedt, Markus. *Gnade und Erwählung: Eine Untersuchung zu Johann von Staupitz und Martin Luther.* Mainz: Philipp von Zabern, 1991.

———. "Theologische Innovation und konservatives Beharren bei Martin Luther und Philipp Melanchthon." Pages 59–80 in *Luther und die Freiheit*. Edited by Werner Zager. Darmstadt: Wissenschaftliche Buchgesellschaft, 2010.

———. "Zwischen Angst und Zuversicht: Melanchthon als Mensch des 16. Jahrhunderts." Pages 9–32 in "*Man weiß so wenig über ihn." Philipp Melanchthon, ein Mensch zwischen Angst und*

Zuversicht. Edited by Predigerseminar der Lutherstadt Wittenberg. Wittenberg: Drei-Kastanien-Verlag, 2004; 2nd edition. In English translation: "Between Angst and Confidence: Melanchthon as a Man of the Sixteenth Century." *Concordia Journal* 23 (1997): 277–294.

Wunder, Heide. "'iusticia, Teutonice fromkeyt.' Theologische Rechtfertigung und bürgerliche Rechtschaffenheit. Ein Beitrag zur Sozialgeschichte eines theologischen Konzepts." Pages 307–332 in *Die frühe Reformation in Deutschland als Umbruch*. Edited by Stephen E. Buckwalter and Bernd Moeller. Gütersloh: Gütersloher Verlagshaus, 1998.

Zeeden, Ernst Walter. *The Legacy of Luther. Martin Luther and the Reformation in the Estimation of the German Lutherans from Luther's Death to the Beginning of the Age of Goethe*, trans. by Ruth Mary Bethell. Westminster, MD.: Newman Press, 1954.

Zumkeller, Adolar. "Martin Luther und sein Orden." *Analecta Augustiniana* 25 (1962): 254–290.

———. "The Augustinian School of the Middle Ages." in *Theology and History of the Augustinian School in the Middle Ages*. Edited by John E. Rotelle. Villanove: Augustinian Press, 1996.

Index